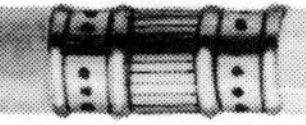

MAGAZINE

BIG BOOK of GAMES II

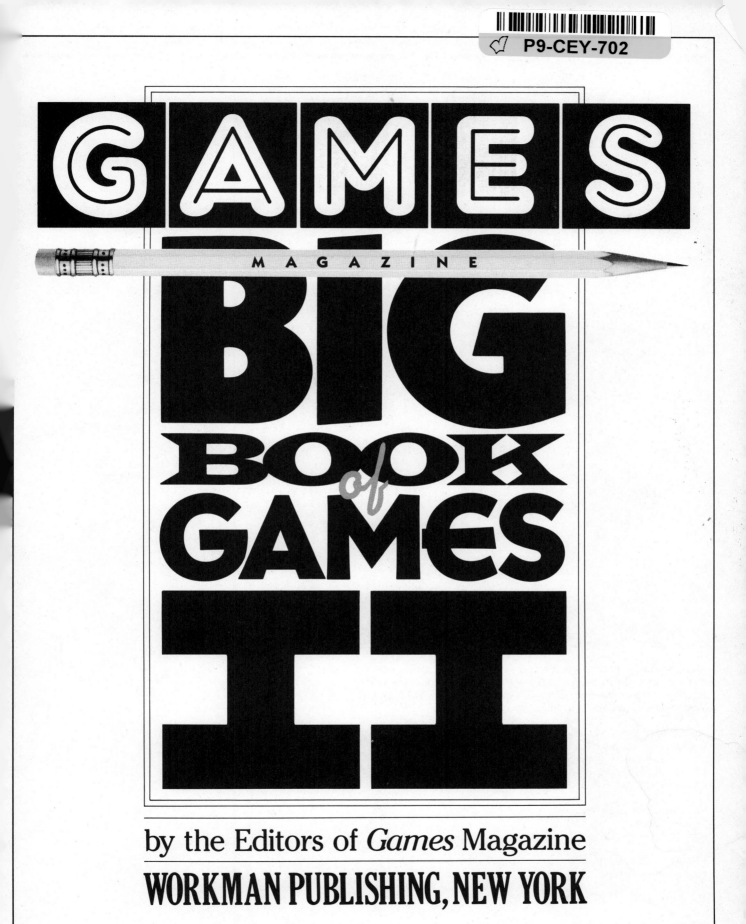

by the Editors of *Games* Magazine

WORKMAN PUBLISHING, NEW YORK

 Published simultaneously in Canada by Saunders of Toronto Ltd.

Library of Congress Cataloging-in-Publication Data
Games magazine big book of games II.
1. Indoor games. 2. Puzzles. I. Games.
II. Title: Big book of games II.
GV1229.G186 1988 793 88-40256 ISBN 0-89480-632-7 (pbk.)

Workman Publishing Company, Inc.
708 Broadway
New York, New York 10003

Manufactured in the United States of America
First printing, October 1988

10 9 8 7 6 5 4 3 2 1

Ten Puzzling Years . . . and Counting

For more than a decade, *Games* magazine has amused and confused readers with its unique brand of verbal and visual high jinks. This collection, like the first *Big Book of Games,* published in 1984, showcases the variety and originality that set *Games* apart from ordinary puzzle magazines—and that have helped *Games*'s readership continue to grow to what is now an all-time high.

Games readers are demanding puzzle connoisseurs who expect to see fresh ideas in each issue. But they are also an enthusiastic and appreciative group; not only do they spend many hours per issue solving puzzles, working on contests, and writing to offer suggestions, but they also reward the *Games* staff's creative efforts with nearly fanatical loyalty.

The challenges in this book are, in a sense, the fruits of the extraordinary interaction between *Games* magazine and its readers. Here you'll find puzzles to satisfy your every taste and interest, from unusual word games and quizzes on subjects ranging from hairdos to holidays, to picture mysteries and logic problems. Some puzzles give an offbeat twist to familiar objects like baby pictures and the yellow pages, while others explore concepts as unfamiliar as Egyptian hieroglyphics. Among the many unusual kinds of crosswords you'll find are strange hybrids that incorporate comic strips or trivia quizzes. A special sixteen-page full-color section offers games like The Egg Hunt that are almost as much fun to look at as they are to play.

The final puzzle in this book—the Puzzle Decathlon—deserves special mention. Designed to celebrate *Games* magazine's tenth anniversary, it originally appeared as a contest. More than 12,000 *Games* readers entered the Decathlon contest, and many others wrote that working on it had given them hours of puzzling pleasure. The Decathlon consists of a few puzzles that are relatively easy, others that look easy but contain hidden tricks, and still others that look hard and *are*. This mix reflects the range of game type and difficulty found throughout the book, making the Decathlon an especially fitting final challenge.

Happy solving!

R. Wayne Schmittberger

R. Wayne Schmittberger
Editor
Games Magazine

Contents

1

TEASERS TO GET YOUR MIND IN GEAR 7

Where in the Whorl? 7
Quote Boxes 8
Compound Interest 8
Directory Assistance 9
Initial Reactions 10
Strip Tease 12
Character Study 14
Family Pictures 15
Cartoonerisms 16
Address Correction Requested 18
Sketchwords 19
Scrambled Comics 20
Picture Dominoes 22
Signs of Trouble 23
Bon Appetit! 24
What's So Funny? 26
The Beadless Abacus 28

2

SEE-WORTHY OBSERVATION PUZZLES 29

Terror Incognitus 29
Eye Exam 30
Match Play 32
Out of This World 33
A Better Mousetrap 34
The Buck Starts Here 36
A Switch in Time 37
Everybody's a Critic 38
Radio Activity 40
Signs of Life 41
Mummy Dearest 42
Making Tracks 44
Meters & Gauges 46
Twelve Brats of Christmas 47
Inferior Decorator 48
Class Reunion 50
Stories from the Safari 51

3

NUMBER CRUNCHING AND LOGIC CHOPPING 53

Alternating Currency 53
Untrue Confessions 54
Can You Think Under Pressure? 56
Polish Your Wits 57
Cutting a Rug 58
Word Division 58
Slugfest on Proteus 59
Training Exercise 60
Letter Logic 61
Cross Math 61
Coin-Op Puzzlers 62
Nine Psychic Guesses 64

4

A COLORFUL PARADE OF GAMES 65

Riddle Maze 65
Making Connections 66
Which Two Butterflies Are Exactly Alike? 68
Bringing Up Baby 69
The Egg Hunt 70
Murder for Breakfast 72
Good Heavens! 74
Scenic Route 76
Final Curtain 78

5

WORDPLAY AND OTHER FORMS OF VERBAL ABUSE 81

Wumble's Candy 81
Wit Twisters 82
Alphaswitch 82
Caveat Emptor 83
Knight Moves 84
Rebusiness 85
Pro Test 86
Half and Half 88
Opposites Attract 89
Evolution 90
Limbericks 92
Wacky Wordies 93
Word Ladders 94
Two by Two 94
Alphabet Soup 95
Literary Connections 96
Solitaire Hangman 97
Word Golf 98
Analograms 99

Moonlighting . . . 100
Dszqtionary . . . 101
Added Attractions . . . 102
Blankety-Blank . . . 103
Egyptograms . . . 104
Rhyme and Reason . . . 106
Tom Swifties . . . 107
The Last Word . . . 108

6

TRIVIA MANIA AND QUIXOTIC QUIZZES . . . 109

Hairdos and Hairdon'ts . . . 109
Twisted Television . . . 110
Picture Quiz . . . 112
Second Guessing . . . 114
A Herculean Atlas Quiz . . . 116
Comic Relief . . . 118
Off and Running . . . 120
What's the Difference? . . . 122
Quizword Puzzle . . . 123
Take the Day Off . . . 124
Number, Please! . . . 126
Famous Footsteps . . . 127
When the Boomers Were Babies . . . 128
The Melting Pot Quiz . . . 130
Can You Answer This? . . . 132

7

ACROSS, DOWN, AND ALL AROUND . . . 133

Round and Round . . . 133
Pencil Pointers . . . 134
Spell-Weaving . . . 135
Going Places . . . 136
Trio . . . 137
Jumbo Crossword . . . 138
Square Routes . . . 140
Wraparounds . . . 141
Word Geometry . . . 142
Boomerangs . . . 144
Cross Anagram . . . 144
Missing Links . . . 145
To the Nines . . . 145
Cross Comics . . . 146
Left and Right . . . 148
Split Ends . . . 149
Marching Bands . . . 150
Pathfinder . . . 151
A to Z . . . 152

8

WARNING: TOP SOLVERS ONLY . . . 153

Magic Rings . . . 153
Card Addition . . . 154
Figure Eights . . . 155
Baseball Lineup . . . 156
Mystery Theme . . . 157
How Far to Zequop? . . . 158
Spoonerisms . . . 159
Word Quest . . . 160
Full House . . . 161
Locker Room Mystery . . . 162
Pentathlon . . . 163
Word Games . . . 164
Crytpic Crosswodr . . . 165
Puzzle Decathlon . . . 166
  Ten Takeaway . . . 166
  Crisscross . . . 166
  Double-Crostic . . . 167
  Complete This Sequence . . . 167
  Count the Triangles . . . 168
  Word Search . . . 168
  Digititis . . . 168
  Cryptogram . . . 168
  Crossword . . . 169
  Pinball Maze . . . 169

The Last Roundup . . . 170

?

ALL THE ANSWERS . . . 171

ACKNOWLEDGMENTS . . . 191

PUZZLE DIFFICULTY RATINGS

★Smooth Sailing ★★Uphill Climb ★★★Proceed at Your Own Risk ★☆Mixed Bag

1 TEASERS TO GET YOUR MIND IN GEAR

Where in the Whorl? ★

by Gabriel Giurgea

If you find prints charming, you'll enjoy this maze. Start at the arrow and journey to the center of the whorl by the shortest possible path. Your route may not go outside the thumbprint.

Answer, page 172

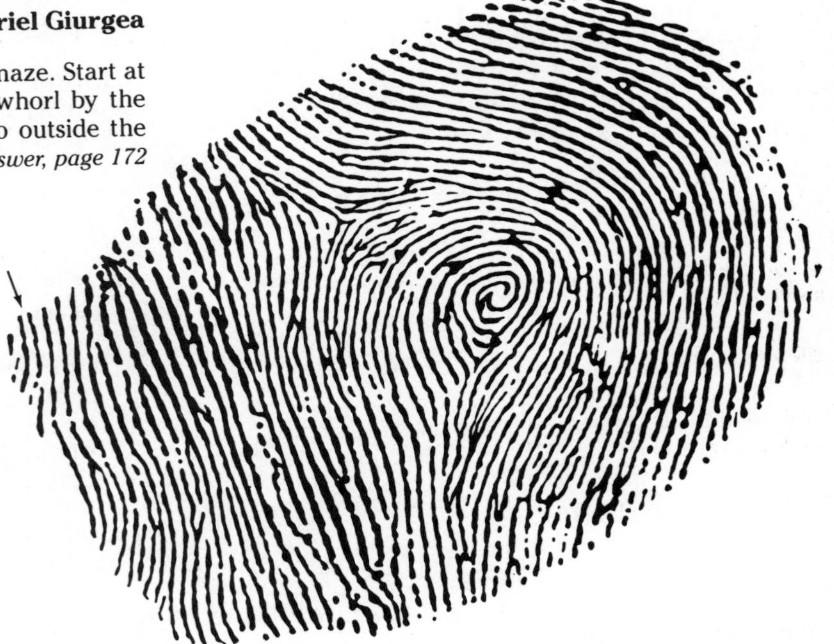

Quote Boxes ★

by Lewis Pince

To solve Quote Boxes, drop the letters from each vertical column—not necessarily in the order in which they appear—into the empty squares below them to spell a quotation reading from left to right, line by line. Black squares indicate ends of words. A word not stopped at the end of one line is continued on the next. The author of each quote is given above the grid.

Answers, page 172

1. GEORGE ORWELL

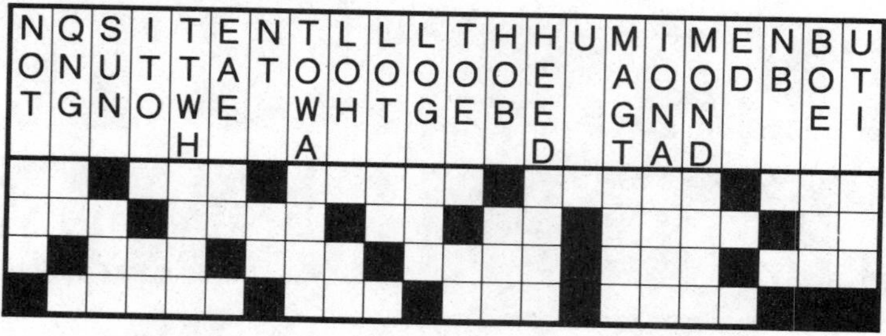

2. RONALD REAGAN

Compound Interest ★☆

by Stephen Sniderman

Each sentence below tells a little story about a famous person whose first name begins the sentence. By breaking the celebrity's last name into two pieces, each a word, you'll be able to fill in the blanks to complete the story. For example, given the sentence "Rita can't find freshly cut _____ _____ half the money charged," you'd fill in HAY WORTH (Rita Hayworth). Though spelling of the last name is unchanged in the blanks, pronunciation may vary.

Answers, page 172

1. Neil considered his right __________ __________ but the rest of his body weak.

2. Maria made the phone __________ __________ soon as she could.

3. Glen rang the __________ __________ every morning.

4. Wilt found his clothes in the __________ __________ neatly on the bed.

5. Norman will be able to __________ __________ when his special chair is fixed.

6. Vanessa noticed the __________ __________ marker as soon as she entered the cemetery.

7. Jayne stood in the red-haired __________ __________ with a dozen cows.

8. Frederic ordered a pork __________ __________ the restaurant.

9. Bruce gets annoyed when his 15-year-old __________ __________ problems on him.

10. Johnny envisioned each apartment __________ __________ a means of making a profit.

11. Dorothy and I felt like we were on the __________ __________ entire vacation.

12. Karen watched the huge __________ __________ an underwater cave.

Directory Assistance ★☆

by Keith Glasgow

Can you identify the type of store, product, or service being advertised in each of these excerpts from the yellow pages?

Answers, page 172

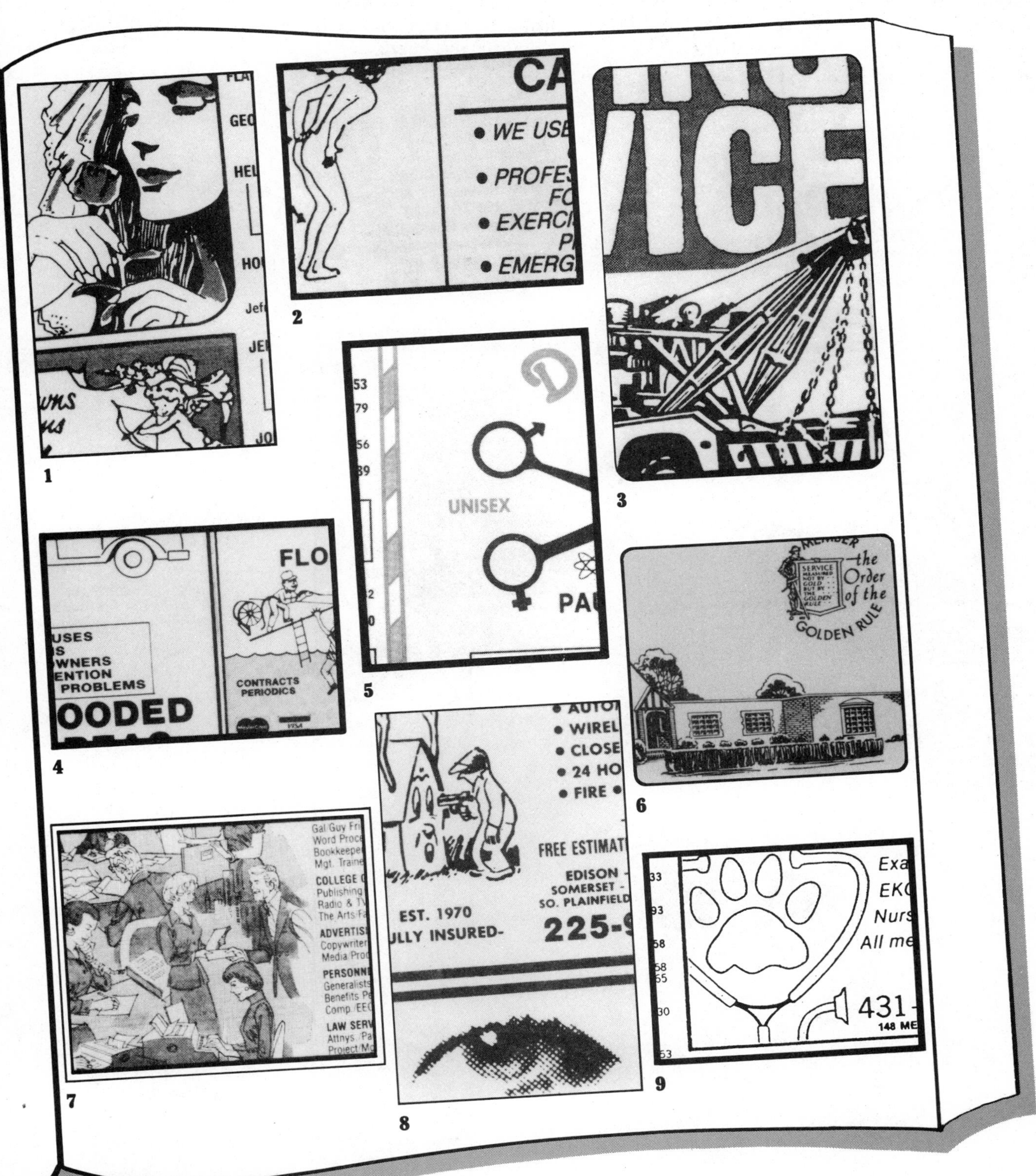

Initial Reactions★☆

by Robert Leighton

If you found out that a friend had just joined a group with the initials D.C.O.A., what would you think? That depends. Has the friend become part of Decent Citizens of America? Disgustingly Cheap Overeaters Anonymous? Dentists Cleaning Out Attics?

Below are 12 common acronyms (A.S.P.C.A., B.M.O.C., etc.) and 12 uncommon ideas of what they might stand for. Can you describe each illustration so that it matches one of the sets of initials? Get all 12 and you're S.T.P.—Some Terrific Puzzler.

Answers, page 172

8

9

10

12

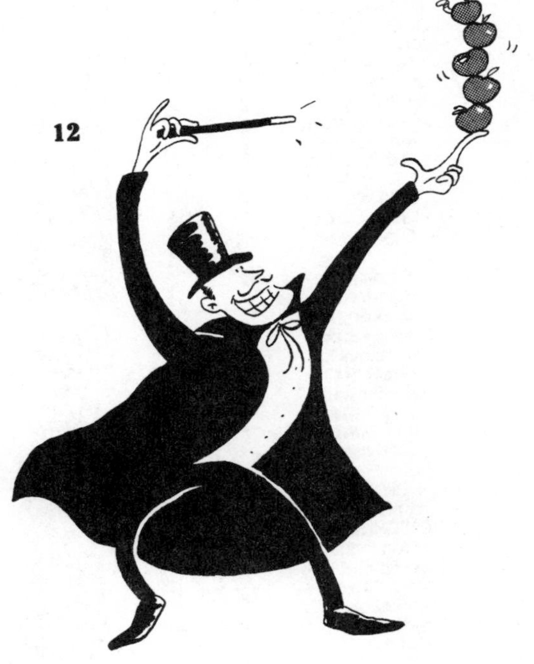

11

ACRONYMS

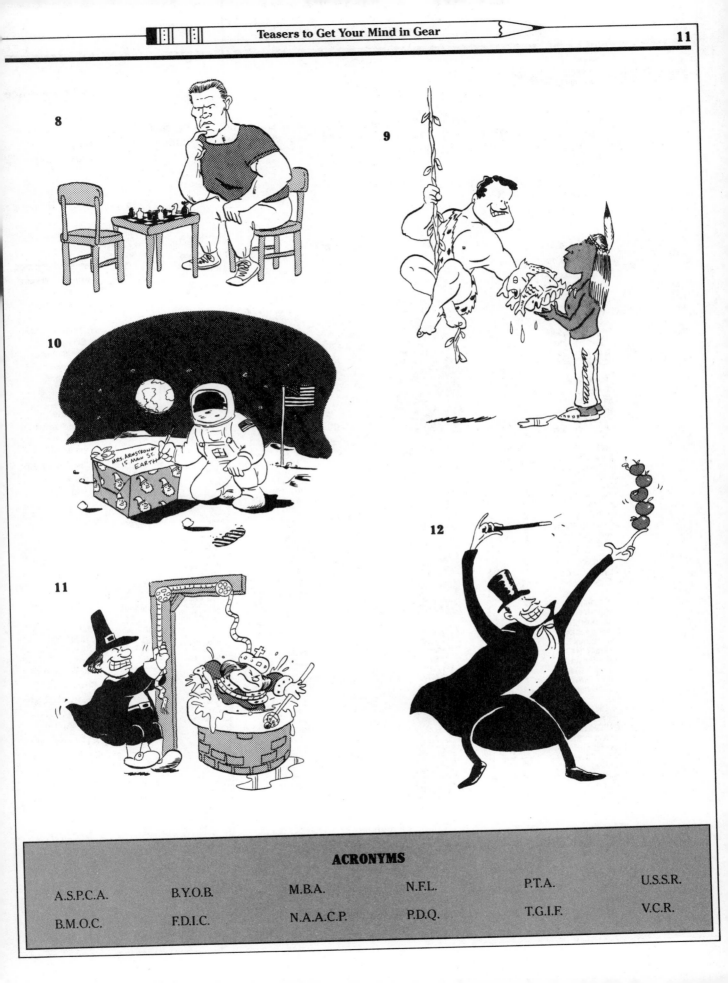

A.S.P.C.A.	B.Y.O.B.	M.B.A.	N.F.L.	P.T.A.	U.S.S.R.
B.M.O.C.	F.D.I.C.	N.A.A.C.P.	P.D.Q.	T.G.I.F.	V.C.R.

Strip Tease ★☆

by Lewis Pince

That does it. We're never leaving the kittens alone in the house again. When we got home the other evening we found these torn strips of reading matter lying all over the place, and since then we've racked our brains trying to figure out where each one came from. Can you help?

Answers, page 172

1

., F Hls
lls
ATED
R
uses, Apartme
Management
793
Metropolitn Av, F Hls
nd Av, F Hls
Rd, F Hls
Pk
2 Queens Bl, F Hls
., Inc.
ogy)
st.
eaning)
327-211
politn Av, F Hls
F Hls
F Hls
ueens Bl, F Hls
F Hls
lls
ne Bl, F Hls
F Hls
Hls
08th, F Hls
Hls
113th, F Hls
rd Rd, F Hls
on Tpk, F Hls
lls
Hls
ls
ls
F Hls
F Hls
Rd, F Hls
Bl, F Hls
Av, F Hls
ls
ls
s Bl, F Hls
s Bl, F Hls
ls
Rd, F Hls

2

hart is on A-1
vie details be
LAND FAMILY—
T ME NOW!—C
CHOOL SPORT
OUNTRY
RACKS POW
NE
SHOW—Joan
azz artist Davi
BURNETT AND
Berry plays
Garland.
ximate after b
MOVIES—Revi
"Street S
glar" (Whoop
."
REET WEEK—
D PEACE—Dr
NTE—Novela; 6
STAR—Musica;
R WHO—Scienc
EEL—Fishing
OF THE UNEXPE
oy friend ann
oman in Austr
an unusual w
O BILL—Come
ASTLE AND M
; 60 min.
UNE—Lou Do
CC)—Comed
. . . The M
Comedy-Dra
Murders." (
bumbling g
tes a suspic
a tranquil to
WINSTON C
6—Drama
N BE A STAR
RK SPORTS
(CC)—Come
k."
LIGHT; 60
ments and
F HIGHLIGH
action in the
ip, taped at P
IGHT; 60 min.
Animal expe
nny Carson,
HTLINE (CC)-
G; 60 min.
: Virgil Hill vs
a 12-round l
lantic City.
MOONERS (F
Carney) trie
PING SERVIC
New

3

28
Lands
gos' partne
hurible
Undergrowth
Type faces
Possessive
pronoun
Odd: Scot.
Raccoon
relative
Proofreader
direction
5 6
15
28
33
36
39
4 55
7
60

4

AND JUST B
IY IDEA IS...SINC
CAN TELL A LIE WH
R A TRUTH BEA
A TRUTH BEA
NG IT INTO CO
TIFY, STANDIN
ESIDE IT!
E
ME
ION,
SUPE
OF MA
AND C
FLOWE
GAVE H
AND T
WHILE
THAT DES
YOUR
"TEMPORA
INSANITY
PLEA! N
MORE
QUESTIO

5

APPE
g Roll ......
rimp Toast
umpling [Fr
ntail Shrim
r-B-Q Spar
sorted Ho
odle Pekin
Noodle
ed Chick
SO
cken Egg D
nton Soup
and Sour
dded Pork
Curd
d Chick
POU
o Goo Gai
ced Chicke
inbow Chi
ced Chick
ed Chicke
ed Chicke
d Peanut
lden Cris
veet and
icken wi
emon Chic
hicken an
Szechuan F
Ta Chien C
Sliced Chi
F
oo Shu P
veet and
uble Sau
redded F
nredded F
liced Pork
liced Pork
liced Por
ced Pork

6

st
which was
was the
of Jĕs'-sĕ,
hich was t
son of Săl
ā-ăs'-sŏn,
of Ā-min'-
ăm, whic
a was the
on of Jŭ'-
Jā'-cŏb
ich was
was the
on of Nā
of Să
găū, whic
a was the
on of Să'-
n of Că-
phăx'-ăd,
h was the
of Lā'-m
n of M
on of E
r'-ĕd, whic
hich was t
of Ē'-nŏs,
h was the
n of Go
4
ll of the
n Jôr'-dă
the wilde
ted of the
d eat no
d, he afte
to him,
mand thi
l him, sa
all not l
y word of
him up i
unto him
in a mom
to him,
d the g
unto m
ve it.
worship
i and said
, Să'-tan:
rship the
alt thou
Jĕ-rŭ'-s
of the t
be the
om henc
shall g
keep t

7

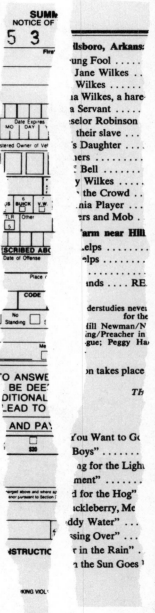

Kell
SM
NUTRITION
RVING SIZE:
CUP) HONEY SM
CUP VITAMIN
RVINGS PER PA
LORIES
OTEIN
RBOHYDRATE
LESTEROL
IUM
ASSIUM
CENTAGE OF
DAILY ALLOW
OTEIN
AMIN A
AMIN C
IAMIN
BOFLAVIN
ACIN
CIUM
MIN D
MIN B
ACID
SPHORUS
NESIUM
ER
LE MILK SUPPLIES
RIES, 4 g FAT, AND
AINS LESS THAN 2
UTRIENT.
IENTS: SUGA
HONEY, HYD
, CARAMEL
AND IRON: V
TE), VITAMIN B
AMIN A (PALMI
NE HYDROCH
LAVIN), VITAMI
ORIDE), FOL
D.
KELLOGG COMPAN
CREEK, MI 49016, U
KELLOGG COMPANY
LOGG COMPANY
CARBOHYDRATE
PLEX
ARBOHYDRATES
ROSE & OTHER
GARS
L
BOHYDRATES
ARANTEE

8

SUMM
NOTICE OF
5 3
First
Date Expires
MO DAY
stered Owner of Veh
6 7
S BUICK V.W.
TLR Other
5
ESCRIBED ABO
Date of Offense
Place
CODE
No Standing
Me
TO ANSWE
BE DEE
DITIONAL
LEAD TO
AND PA
$20
NSTRUCTIO
KING VIOL

9

llsboro, Arkans
ung Fool . . . . .
Jane Wilkes . .
Wilkes . . . . . .
a Wilkes, a hare
a Servant . . . . .
selor Robinson
their slave . . .
s Daughter . . . .
ers . . . .
Bell . . . .
y Wilkes . . . . .
the Crowd . .
nia Player . . .
rs and Mob .
arm near Hill
elps . . . .
elps . . . .
nds . . . . RE
derstudies neve
for the
Hill Newman/N
ing/Preacher in
gue; Peggy Ha
n takes place
TH
You Want to G
Boys" . . . .
ng for the Ligh
ment" . . . .
d for the Hog"
ckleberry, Me
ddy Water" . . .
sing Over" . . .
r in the Rain" .
the Sun Goes

10

iato. A 6-lb
ato was grow
rence Dailey c
Wis. in Aug
longest tomat
ft, grown by
Graham of Ec
, in 1984.
e greatest wei
342 lb 2 oz on
y-tomato hyb
grown by C
Vilber of Cran
in 1985, in a
plants whose
ed 1,368 lb.

nip. A turni
ghing 73 lb w
ted in Dec 17
dern times the
lb 4 oz for
vn by C. W.
Terton, Hum
and. A turni
as reported
ka in 1981.

'ORLD

11

E ENDG

B6ch!!, K×
win.
ys a win,
ns.
tical difficu
ave a fligh
o avoid a b
ote A.), R—
, R—QR6,
R8ch; 8 R—
5ch, K—Kt
35, R—KR
R—B8ch; 17
—KKt8; 2
—R6; 23
R4ch; 26 R
R—Q6,
Q7, R—R

om checks
R—B5ch
B5 and v
now giv
any mov
ced).
e one Pa
. 139B W
giving
K—B3; 2
K—Q5, K
R—QKt8
K—B5;
R—B8ch;
so be all w

No. 139C
sacrificing
—Kt5, R
—Q6, K—

be brok
R7; 3 P
K×P c
-Q6; 10

12

13

unclarity, u
indistinctne
ess, shapele
ness, murk,
g, darkness,
egibility, un
indecipher
xpressivenes
lessness, in
l pan [slang
pplicability,
retability,
unaccoun
xtricability;
ness, myster
mething un
, double Du
, gobbledyg
jumble, ga
language,
er, crypto
ues.
ma, myst
nese puzzle,
le; problem
lem, why;
d *or* perple
tion, sixty-f
l]; perple
, point to
n twister
ng]; mind
informal]
to crack
j, "a perfe
nan under
le, conun
, anagram
BS be in
e, be too
beyond c
le *or* escap
ation *or*
Greek to,
tanding,
514.13, ric
les; spea
ch, babb
underst
d, not h
get into c
ll; be out
; not kno
hing of,
be able
ble to see
s; give up,
e unintel

14

T REFEREN
urchase
ng
e
e
ebts as Borrow
sheet if more s
C
A
O
A
dit Card
ner Credit Car
ICAN EXPRE
nt ☐ Former
bill to office
ITIONAL CAR
nly $30 per
bership fee)
members of
at least 18 ye
use the Gold
Credit. Card n
credit informat
nted above th
(optional): ☐ Mr. ☐
in the boxes be
he Gold Card. S
te of
rth
X
gnature of Additic
N APPLICANT.
am asking A
ny, Inc. or it
count and iss
ase enroll me
press® Card
less I so requ
rd account, a
rds issued fo
ent accompa
nd return it to
rd, all Card
lly. I am ask
rticipating fir
quest for a L
y application
he financial
e of Credit
t to me by
nied, my s
merican Ex
tion reques
n Express
plied on th
rmation ab
gnature of Appli
stitution No.
| 23 | 22 | 21
edit No.

15

olors
pider Plant
attractive, f
background
es of graceful
and purple
rs early sum
ds. Ht. 4 ft.
Pkt 75¢ H
Grow a
ucer Vine
limbing vine for
d blooms open cl
large plum-shap
s. Ht. 20 ft.
Seed Pkt $1.50,
ilegia F
om spring to eart
the perennial bord
l in sun or semi-s
Colors *All-A*
oms with long
eep yellow, prim
for cutting. Ht.
103.)
d Pkt 95¢
S AVAILABLE—see
d Colors Smaller p
color range. Ht. 1½
Seed Pkt 85¢, 2
Greenho
Colors Beautif
mine, rose, cri
g variety gives
wing. Ht. 11 in
seeds) $1.50,
THE POSTAGE!

16

, Scot., ...*C5
Ont., Can., ...B9
Ga., 1,201 ....C2
Mass., 900 ....B1
Mich., 1,097 ....F6
ex., 1,111 ..E4, k8
Aus., 11,853 ....D8
Swe.,
0) H8, i36
o., Swe.,
....*H8
., 140,000 ..D5
950 ......E2
,000) D3, h10
800 ......A3
., 2,073 ....C4
., 838 ......D4
, Mo.,
......E8
ent., Eng.,
*450,000) D5
N.C., 22,314 ...A2
N.C., 900 ......A3
801 ....p28
., 39,300 ......C3
0 ....C7
, 6,294 ......B3
., 7,013 ......E4
, 8,176 ......E4
1,267 ....D1
00 ....f9
., 22,300 ...g11
N.J., 834 ......E3
., 4,500 ......B5
8,000 ....*B4
Ga.,
C2, h8
4,242 ......*B6
nes,
......*B5
., 968 ......A3
an., Can.,
......D3
., 1,126 ......C5
Tex.,
......C2
Ont., Can.,
......D5
onn.,
......D9
1,076 ......D4
aine, 800
......D4
N.Y.,
......*n15
ills, Pa.,
......*F10
, Can.,
......D3
, Can.,
......C3
2,000 ..A5
1,300 ..B1
o,
......*A2
568 ......B2
a. 7,728 ..B2
nt., Can.,
......B9
5,400 ......A3
n.,
......G5
0 ......B7
49,327 ......B4
1,943 ......B4
1,040 ......C7
Can.,
D5, k15
Can.,
......H4
B5, h11
......F4
......A3
......C4
......A4
......F10
Pa.,
......*E2
C., Can ..E7
7,780 ......C1
940 ......I1
400 ......D4
2,500 ......*G10
N.H.,
......E5
zech.,
......D2
5,448 ......D8
70,700 ......A6
8,300 ......E3
9,300 ......C1
, Can.,
......F3

17

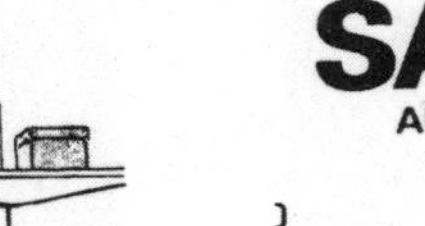

LE JACK
k Horner
e corner,
ng of Chr
n his thur
ed out a
said, "W
n I!"

BIRD

ds, away!
ttle and l
ot come
u do,
ot you th
will be

18

SA
AN

LEY
R PL
A 9270

ITH WORLD'S
MPOUNDED

CHEC

POSITS/
CREDITS
65.00

NUMBER
471*
472
473

NTIAL CHECK

CHECK

ITE
BEG.
CHE
CHE
CHE
DEP
CHE
CHE
CHE
CHE
CHE
CHE
CHE
CHE

Character Study★☆

Everyone knows that *I* is egocentric, *O* is surprised, and *?* is curious. But when these symbols get together in social situations, their attitudes become more complex, even as ours do.

For example, *S* remarks to *XL*, "You really ought to lose weight"; *mp* says he can't get much of anywhere without *h*; and $>$ accuses $<$ of consistently minimizing things.

We think there's a lot more conversation to be overheard among the letters, numbers, punctuation marks, and other symbols that surround us. Here are 12 groups of symbols engaged in witty repartee. Can you pick the conversational gambit (a–l, below) that goes in each balloon?

Answers, page 172

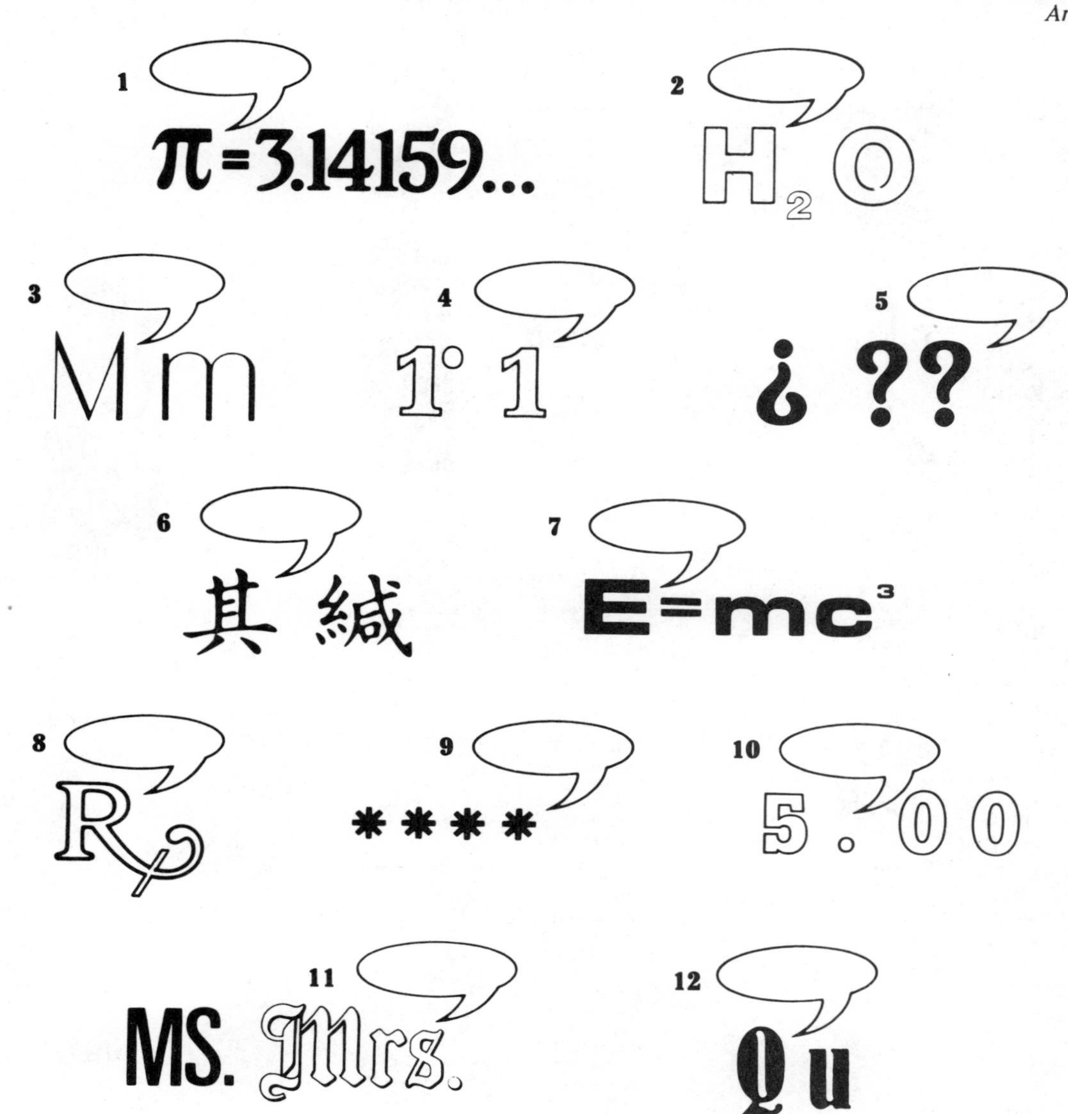

a. "What dirty word are we this time?"

b. "Come on over here. I'm thirsty."

c. "Why are you always following me?"

d. "Don't worry, it's only baby fat."

e. "How can you be hungry? We just ate an hour ago."

f. "Enough already!"

g. "I'd like you to meet my friend Pedro."

h. "I have an idea that will make us all 10 times richer."

i. "Someone here is an impostor."

j. "Sick people. Nothing but sick people."

k. "I guess I'm just old-fashioned."

l. "So you're a college man. Big deal!"

Family Pictures★★

by L. M. Wilkie

The 15 pictures below can be grouped into five "families" of three members, each family containing some common element. Can you pick out the five triplets and determine what ties each set together? (Hint: Think about the words the pictures represent.)

Answers, page 172

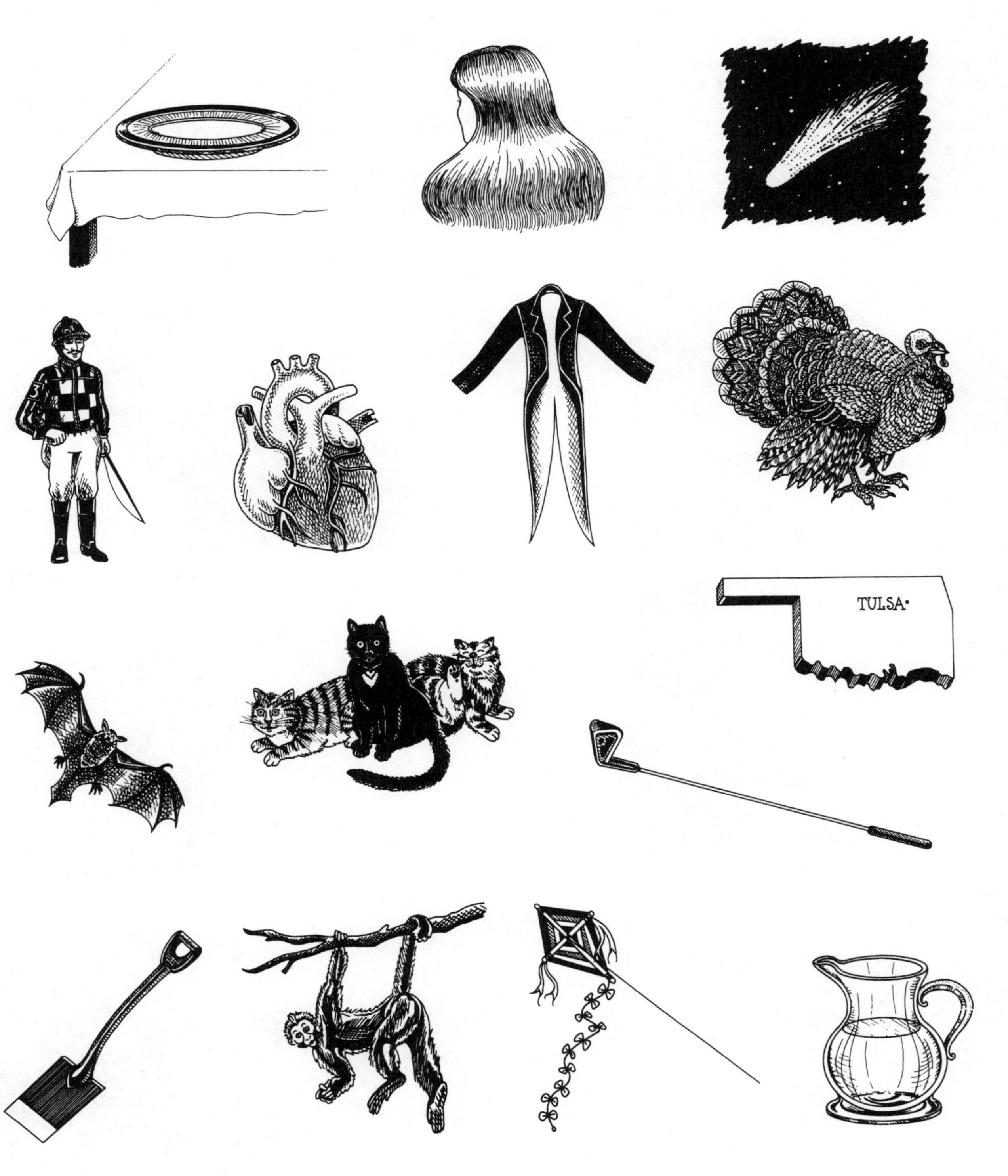

Cartoonerisms ★☆

by Greg Scott

If you've ever said something like "bee throttles" when you meant to say "three bottles," then you're already familiar with the spoonerism. That's the accidental switching of the initial sounds of two words to make a new and often silly-sounding phrase. Each pair of drawings on these two pages suggests such a set of spoonerized words. For example, picture 1a shows a *weeping lizard,* while picture 1b shows a *leaping wizard.* The other pairs are equally likely to bend your mind... or, if you prefer, mend your bind.

Answers, page 172

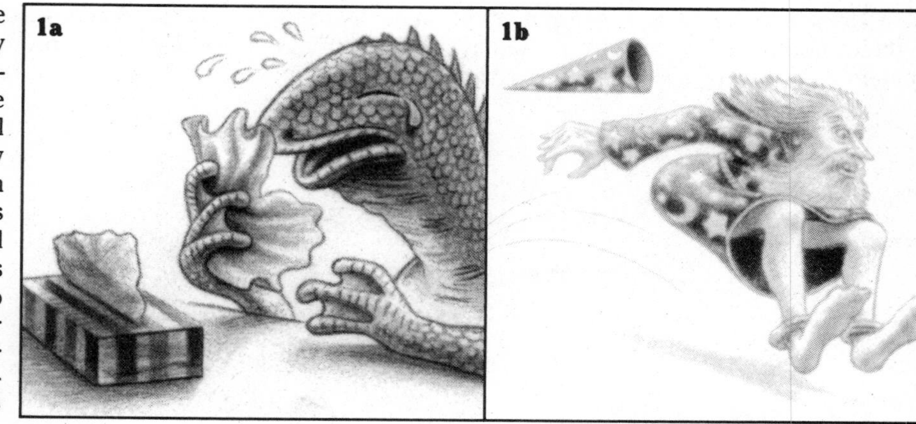

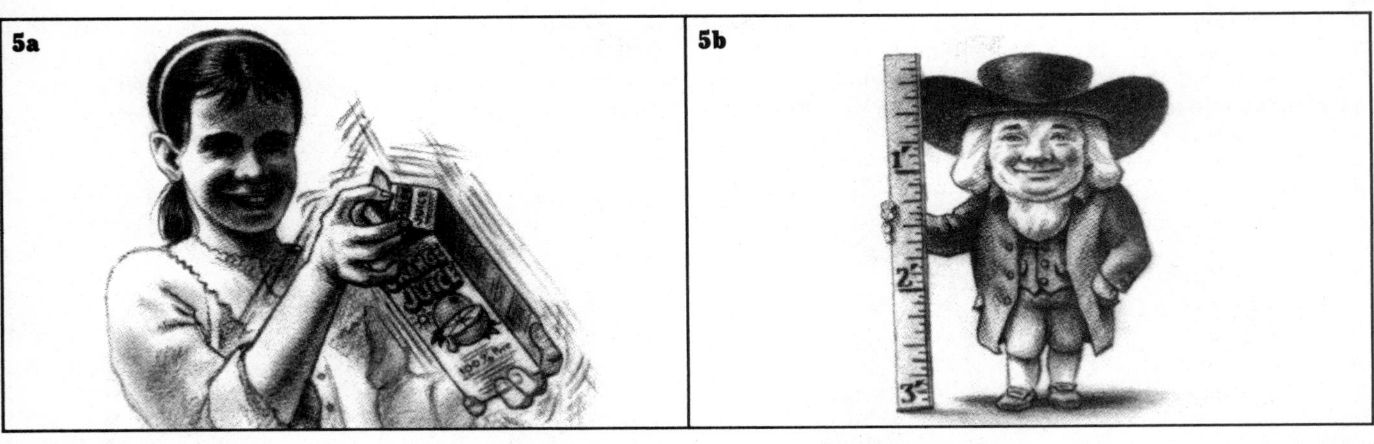
5a
ORANGE JUICE
5b
1'
2'
3'

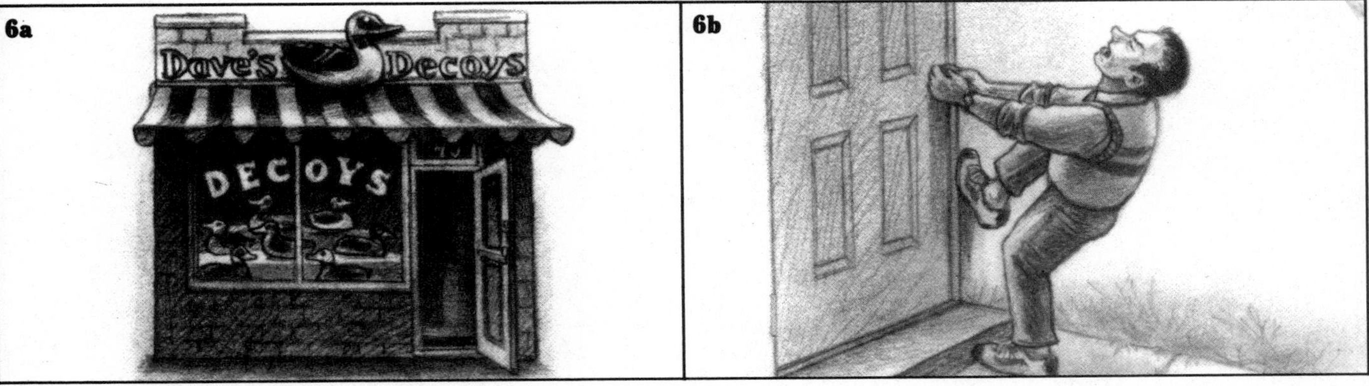
6a
Dave's Decoys
DECOYS
6b

7a
7b

8a
COMIX
8b

Address Correction Requested ★☆

by Carol Hines

The Television Characters Association is about to mail out its monthly newsletter, but it seems that the secretary, Miss Cast, has—in her usual incompetent manner—managed to mismatch the names and addresses of the members. Can you remedy the situation by rearranging the characters' names so that they appear on the correct envelopes? And for extra credit, name the television series that each one comes from.

Answers, page 172

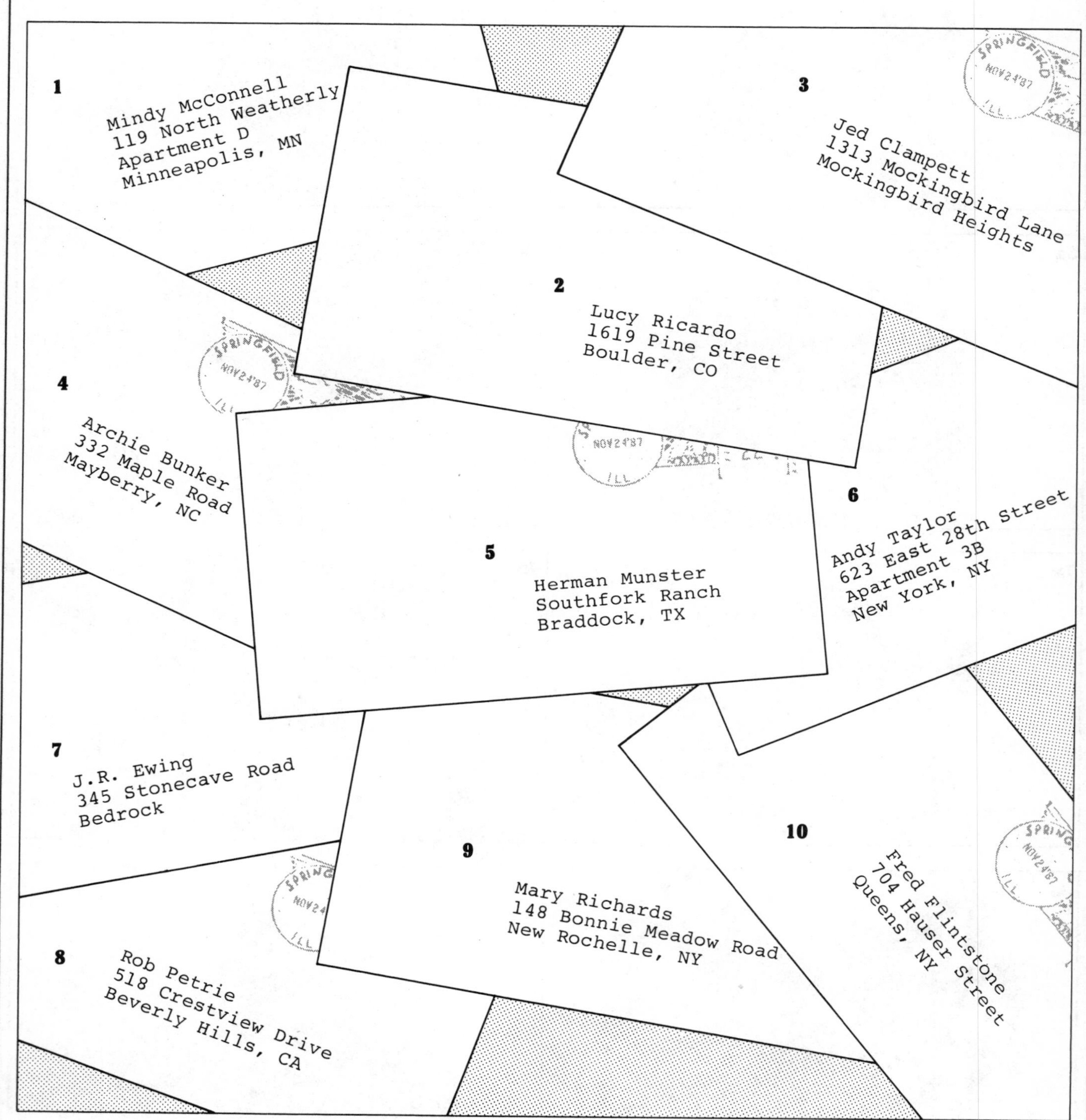

1
Mindy McConnell
119 North Weatherly
Apartment D
Minneapolis, MN
2
Lucy Ricardo
1619 Pine Street
Boulder, CO
3
Jed Clampett
1313 Mockingbird Lane
Mockingbird Heights
4
Archie Bunker
332 Maple Road
Mayberry, NC
5
Herman Munster
Southfork Ranch
Braddock, TX
6
Andy Taylor
623 East 28th Street
Apartment 3B
New York, NY
7
J.R. Ewing
345 Stonecave Road
Bedrock
8
Rob Petrie
518 Crestview Drive
Beverly Hills, CA
9
Mary Richards
148 Bonnie Meadow Road
New Rochelle, NY
10
Fred Flintstone
704 Hauser Street
Queens, NY

Sketchwords ★☆

by Robert Leighton

The pictures below are doing double duty. On the one hand, they represent letters of the alphabet, and, on the other, they provide visual clues to the words in which they appear. To solve, first determine the letter that each sketch resembles. Then find a word suggested by the picture or pictures that fits the blanks. In the example, the Eiffel Tower suggests the letter A and the word PARIS.

Answers, page 172

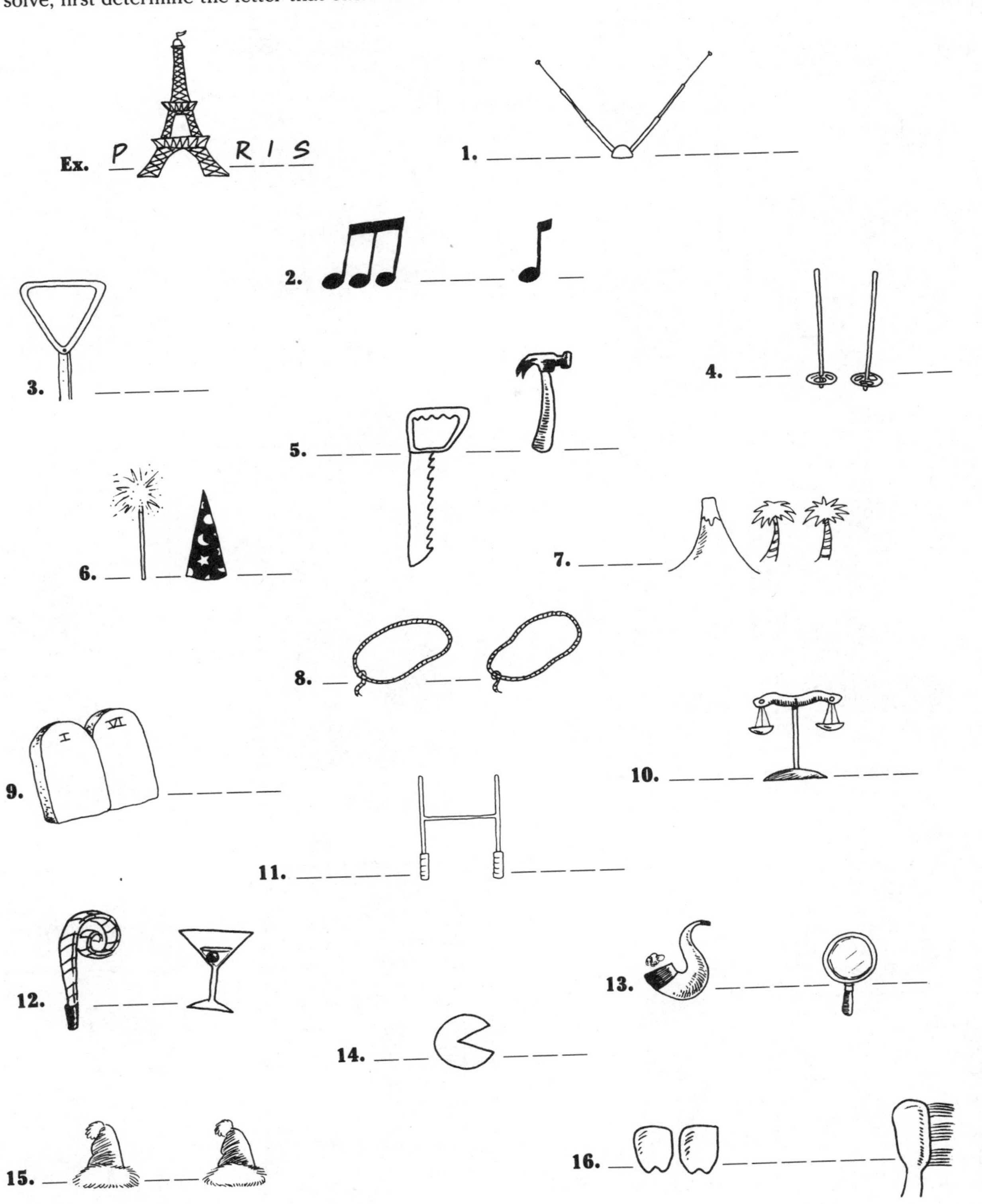

Scrambled Comics★★

No one would have found Henny Youngman funny if he had stood on stage and said "Please—take my wife." What makes a joke funny is the surprise punch at the end. But when the punch line comes ahead of the story, there's no surprise, no humor, and no joke. The three comic strips on these pages suffer from a similar problem—the panels have been jumbled,

BLOW-UP

A

B

C

D

ABOUT A BOUT

A

B

C

D

BUY LINES

A

B

C

D

by Robert Leighton

making the punch lines punchless. Can you put them back in order? You may find more than one way to arrange a set in a logical sequence, but only one route leads to the joke. *Answers, page 172*

E

F

G

1. ______
2. ______
3. ______
4. ______
5. ______
6. ______
7. ______

E

F

G

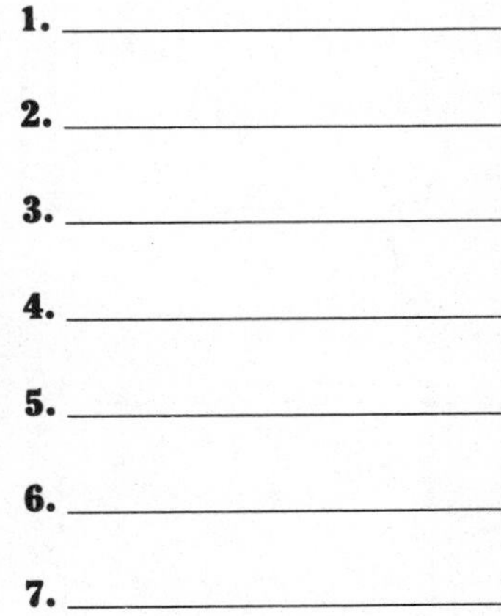

1. ______
2. ______
3. ______
4. ______
5. ______
6. ______
7. ______

E

F

G

1. ______
2. ______
3. ______
4. ______
5. ______
6. ______
7. ______

Picture Dominoes★★

by Robert Leighton

The dominoes below, like their spotted everyday counterparts, can be linked to form a continuous chain. But the difference is that these dominoes are to be linked according to story lines suggested by the pictures: The bottom half of each domino begins a story that continues in the top half of another. For example, the bottom of domino A (man being photographed with gorgeous woman) leads to the top of domino C (photo showing just the woman). The bottom of C, starting a new story, leads to the top of . . . ? Eventually, the chain will end up with the top of domino A. Get the picture?

Answer, page 172

A

B

C

D

E

F

G

H

Signs of Trouble★★

by Steve Coughlan

To help tourists find their way around town during the upcoming Ragweed Festival, the Ragville Chamber of Commerce has bought 15 new signs, to be erected at various intersections around town (in the positions indicated by dots on the map below). Each will be placed so that drivers approaching an intersection will see the sign on their right. The holes have all been dug, but no one can remember which sign goes where. Can you save the Ragweed Festival by placing each sign in its correct position?

Answer, page 173

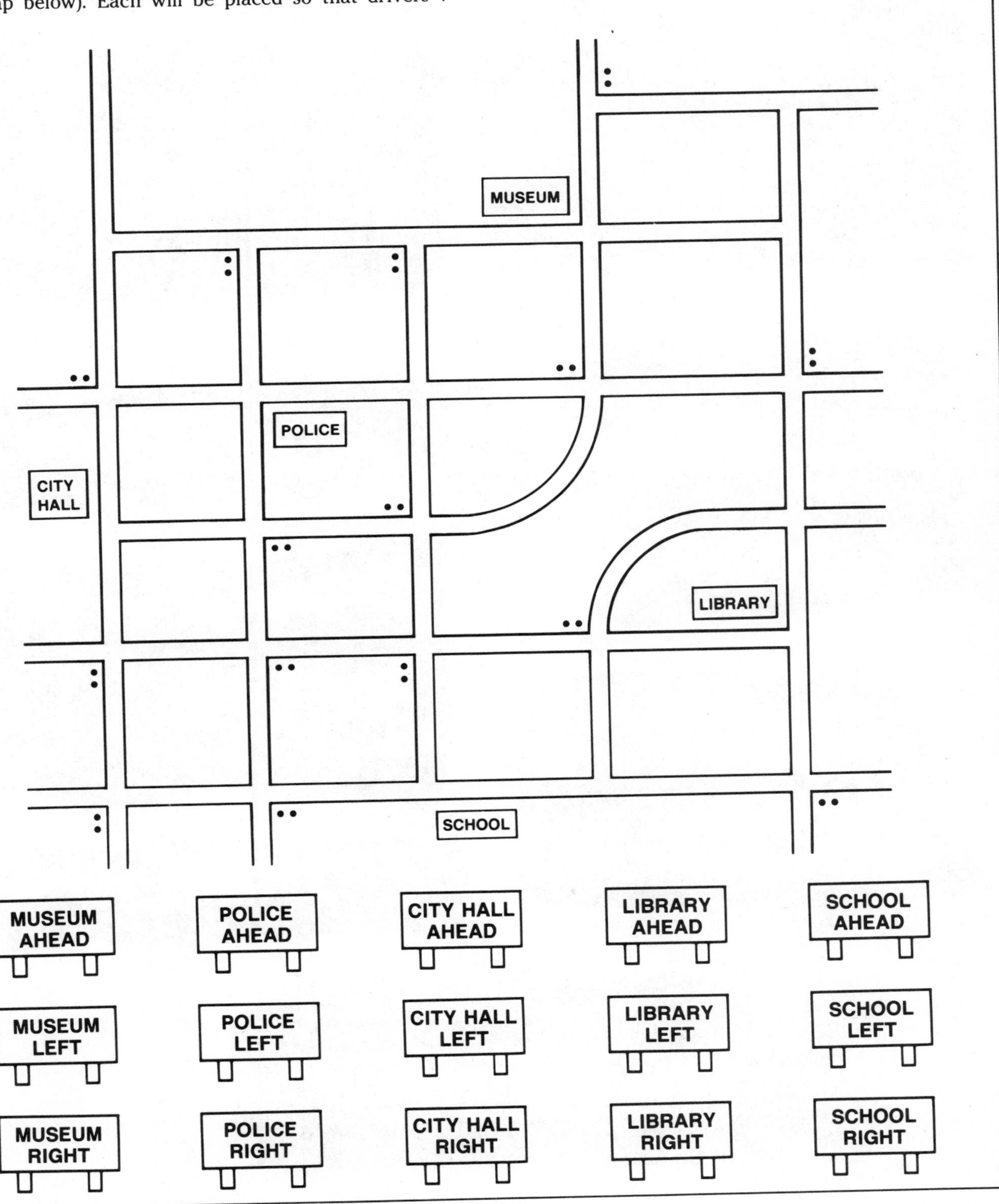

Bon Appetit! ★☆

by Ingrid Yentz

It's elementary. Or should we say alimentary? Here are the ingredient labels of 17 familiar foods, which we bought at the corner grocery. How many can you identify? (Brand names aren't required.)

Answers, page 172

1

INGREDIENTS: BEEF STOCK, TOMATOES, CARROTS, POTATOES, CELERY, PEAS, ZUCCHINI, GREEN BEANS, CABBAGE, WATER, MODIFIED FOOD STARCH, SPINACH, SALT, VEGETABLE OIL (CORN, COTTONSEED OR PARTIALLY HYDROGENATED SOYBEAN OIL), DEHYDRATED ONIONS, HIGH FRUCTOSE CORN SYRUP, MONOSODIUM GLUTAMATE, YEAST EXTRACT AND HYDROLYZED VEGETABLE PROTEIN, BEEF FAT, CARAMEL COLOR, NATURAL FLAVORING, DEHYDRATED GARLIC AND OLEORESIN PAPRIKA.

2

INGREDIENTS: GOLDEN ROASTED PEANUTS, SUGAR, PARTIALLY HYDROGENATED VEGETABLE OILS, SALT, MONO AND DIGLYCERIDES.

3

AN ULTRA-PASTEURIZED BLEND OF CREAM, NONFAT MILK SOLIDS, SUGAR, CORN SYRUP, MONO- AND DIGLYCERIDES, ARTIFICIAL FLAVOR, CARRAGEENAN, WHIPPING GAS-NITROUS OXIDE.

4

INGREDIENTS: TOMATOES, SOYBEAN OIL, SALT, SUGAR, CORN SYRUP, DRIED ONIONS, ROMANO CHEESE MADE FROM COW'S MILK, OLIVE OIL, SPICES, GARLIC POWDER.

5

INGREDIENTS: SOYBEAN OIL, WATER, WHITE DISTILLED VINEGAR, SALT, SUGAR, DRIED GARLIC, HYDROLYZED VEGETABLE PROTEIN, SPICES, XANTHAN GUM (IMPROVES MIXING), CALCIUM DISODIUM EDTA (A PRESERVATIVE), OXYSTEARIN (PREVENTS CLOUDINESS UNDER REFRIGERATION), ARTIFICIAL COLORING.

6

INGREDIENTS: UNBLEACHED ENRICHED WHEAT FLOUR [FLOUR, MALTED BARLEY FLOUR, NIACIN (A "B" VITAMIN), REDUCED IRON, THIAMINE MONONITRATE (B1), RIBOFLAVIN (B2)], RAISINS, WATER, BUTTER, YEAST, NON-FAT MILK, GRANULATED SUGAR, RAISIN JUICE, WHEAT GLUTEN, SALT, CORN SYRUP, LECITHIN, LEMON POWDER, CINNAMON.

7

INGREDIENTS: PEACHES, WATER NECESSARY FOR PREPARATION AND VITAMIN C.

8

INGREDIENTS: Figs, sugar, enriched wheat flour (contains niacin, reduced iron, thiamine mononitrate [vitamin B_1], riboflavin [vitamin B_2]), corn syrup, animal or vegetable shortening (lard or partially hydrogenated soybean oil with hydrogenated cottonseed oil), high fructose corn syrup, whey, salt, yellow corn flour, baking soda and artificial flavor. Figs may be preserved with sulfur dioxide by the grower.

9

INGREDIENTS: TOMATO JUICE FROM CONCENTRATE (WATER. TOMATO CONCENTRATE), RECONSTITUTED JUICES OF CARROTS, CELERY, BEETS, PARSLEY, LETTUCE, WATERCRESS, SPINACH, WITH SALT, VITAMIN C (ASCORBIC ACID), NATURAL FLAVORING AND CITRIC ACID.

10

INGREDIENTS: RICE, SUGAR, SALT, CORN SYRUP, MALT FLAVORING.

11

Ingredients:
Meat By-Products, Water sufficient for processing Horsemeat, Beef By-Products, Poultry By-Products, Soy Flour, Salt, Potassium Chloride, Guar Gum, Methionine Hydroxy Analogue Calcium, DL-Alpha Tocopheryl Acetate (Source of Vitamin E), Citric Acid and Ethoxyquin (Preservatives), Magnesium Oxide, Choline Chloride, Sodium Nitrite (To promote color retention), Iron Carbonate, Copper Oxide, Cobalt Carbonate, Vitamin A Palmitate (Stability Improved), Manganous Oxide, Zinc Oxide, Ethylenediamine Dihydroiodide, Thiamine Mononitrate, D-Activated Animal Sterol (Source of Vitamin D-3) and Vitamin B-12 Supplement.

12

CONTAINS WATER, TOMATO PASTE, DISTILLED VINEGAR, CORN SYRUP, RAISINS, SALT, HERBS AND SPICES, ORANGE BASE, ORANGE PEEL, CARAMEL, DEHYDRATED GARLIC, DEHYDRATED ONIONS.

13

INGREDIENTS: SOYBEAN OIL, PARTIALLY HYDROGENATED SOYBEAN OIL, WHOLE EGGS, VINEGAR, WATER, EGG YOLKS, SALT, SUGAR, LEMON JUICE AND NATURAL FLAVORS. CALCIUM DISODIUM EDTA ADDED TO PROTECT FLAVOR.

14

WHITE WINE, PASSION JUICE, PINEAPPLE JUICE, GRAPEFRUIT JUICE, WATER, SUGAR, CITRIC ACID, NATURAL FLAVORS, CARBONATION, SULPHUR DIOXIDE, POTASSIUM SORBATE, AND SODIUM BENZOATE ADDED TO PROTECT FLAVOR, AND ARTIFICIAL COLORS.

15

CULTURED PASTEURIZED GRADE A MILK, SKIM MILK, STRAWBERRIES, SUGAR, CORN SWEETENERS, NONFAT MILK SOLIDS, PECTIN, NATURAL FLAVORS, AND LEMON JUICE.

16

INGREDIENTS: KIDNEY BEANS, GROUND BEEF, TOMATOES, WATER, TOMATO PUREE, GREEN PEPPERS, MODIFIED CORNSTARCH, SUGAR, SALT, DEHYDRATED ONIONS, ENRICHED WHEAT FLOUR, CHILI PEPPERS, BEEF, NATURAL FLAVORINGS, MONOSODIUM GLUTAMATE, SPICES, CORN OIL, CHICKEN FAT, CARAMEL COLORING, DRIED BEEF STOCK, DEHYDRATED GARLIC, ERYTHORBIC ACID.

17

INGREDIENTS: FLOUR, LOW MOISTURE MOZZARELLA CHEESE (PASTEURIZED MILK, CHEESE CULTURES, SALT, CALCIUM CHLORIDE, ENZYMES), TOMATO PUREE, WATER, PARTIALLY HYDROGENATED VEGETABLE OIL (SOYBEAN AND/OR COTTONSEED AND/OR PALM OIL) WITH LECITHIN, ARTIFICIAL FLAVOR AND ARTIFICIAL COLOR (BETA CAROTENE), YEAST, SALT, SOYBEAN OIL, GREEN PEPPERS, SUGAR, DOUGH CONDITIONER PRODUCT (DRY WHEY, L-CYSTEINE MONOHYDROCHLORIDE), SPICES, FOOD STARCH—MODIFIED, CORN OIL, CALCIUM PROPIONATE ADDED TO RETARD SPOILAGE OF CRUST, XANTHAN GUM, GARLIC POWDER.

What's So Funny? ★☆

by Robert Leighton

Did you ever tell a joke and forget the punch line? The artist here has drawn 12 cartoon gags and forgotten to include the part that makes each one funny. To complete the gags, place each of the missing objects (labeled A–L) into the appropriate cartoon (1–12). The gray squares indicate roughly where each object belongs in the picture. *Answers, page 173*

1

2

3

4

5

6

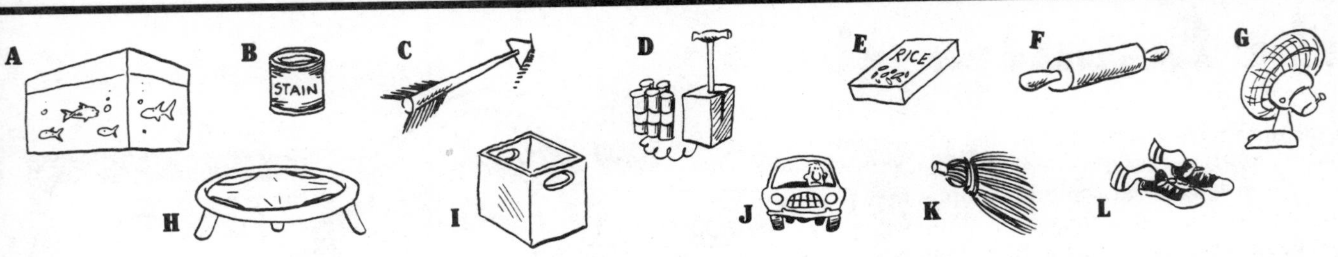

7

8

9

10

11

12

The Beadless Abacus*

by Mel Stover

You may have heard claims that an abacus, used properly, can enable you to perform lengthy arithmetic computations as quickly as a calculator. With the "beadless abacus" shown here, you can impress your friends without resorting to a computing device of any kind.

Show a friend this diagram, in which each hexagon-shaped cell contains an arithmetic operation. Now, perform the following feats:

1. Ask your friend to designate, by laying a matchstick across them, any *three* cells that lie in a straight line. (Each cell must touch the next along an entire edge.) Tell your friend in advance that you will perform the operations in each of the three designated cells and add together the three results, giving the total out loud almost immediately after the matchstick is placed.

2. Next, ask your friend to designate any *four* consecutive cells in any line. This time, you will perform the operations and add up the results even faster than in the first trick.

3. For your grand finale, have your friend choose a cluster of *seven* cells—any cell not on an edge, plus the six surrounding cells—by covering them with a shot glass. You will then glance through the shot glass, look away, and a moment later give the sum of the results of all seven operations.

Answers, page 173

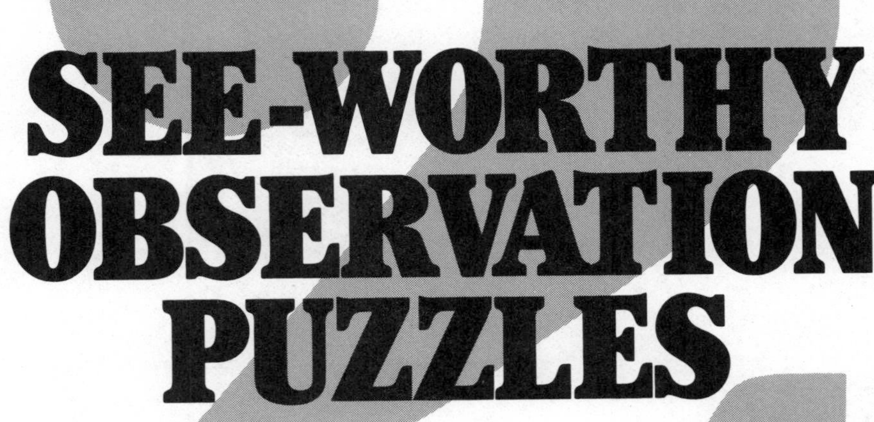

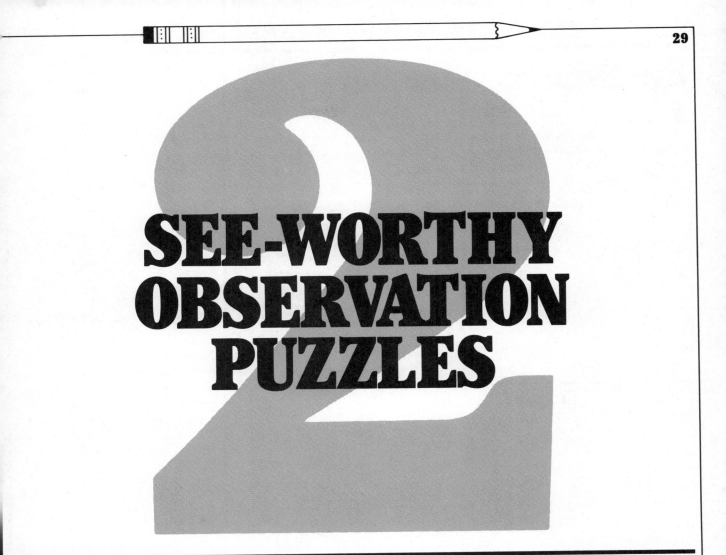

SEE-WORTHY OBSERVATION PUZZLES

Terror Incognitus ★☆

by Patricia Wynne

Is this nightmarish beast a fugitive from a medieval myth? Or is it the result of some disastrous gene-splicing experiment? All we know for sure is that the creature contains parts of 22 different types of animals. How many can you identify? Be as specific as possible; for example, don't give "bird" as an answer if you can determine the particular type of bird. *Answers, page 173*

Eye Exam ★☆

by Dr. Seymour D. Tayle

Are you observant? Here's a test to help you find out. Carefully study the seven observation problems on these two pages and solve as many of them as you can. But don't spend too long on any one problem—the test is designed to be completed in 15 minutes or less.

Have a watch ready? Go!

Answers, page 173

1. Which face is made up of the most common elements in the six pictures?

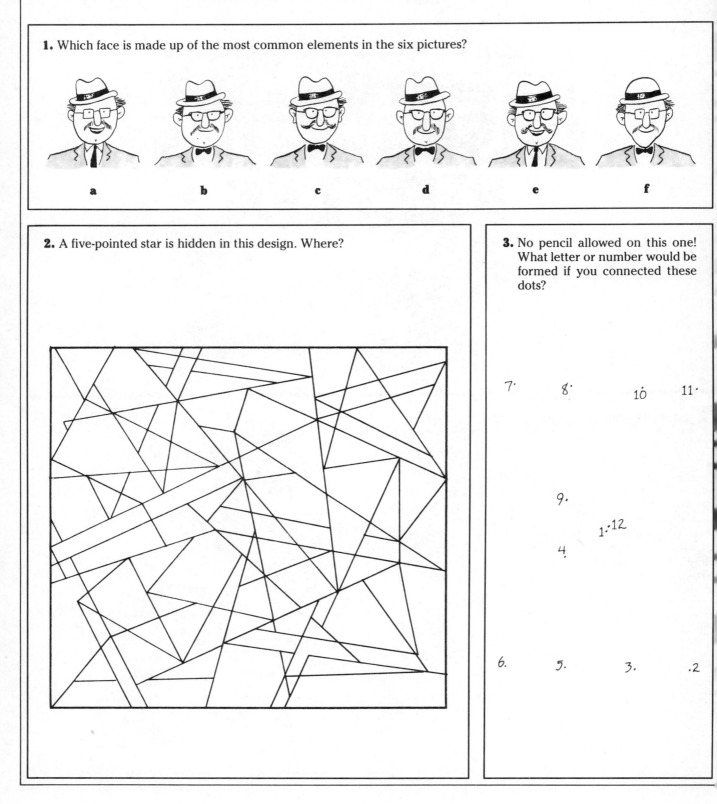

2. A five-pointed star is hidden in this design. Where?

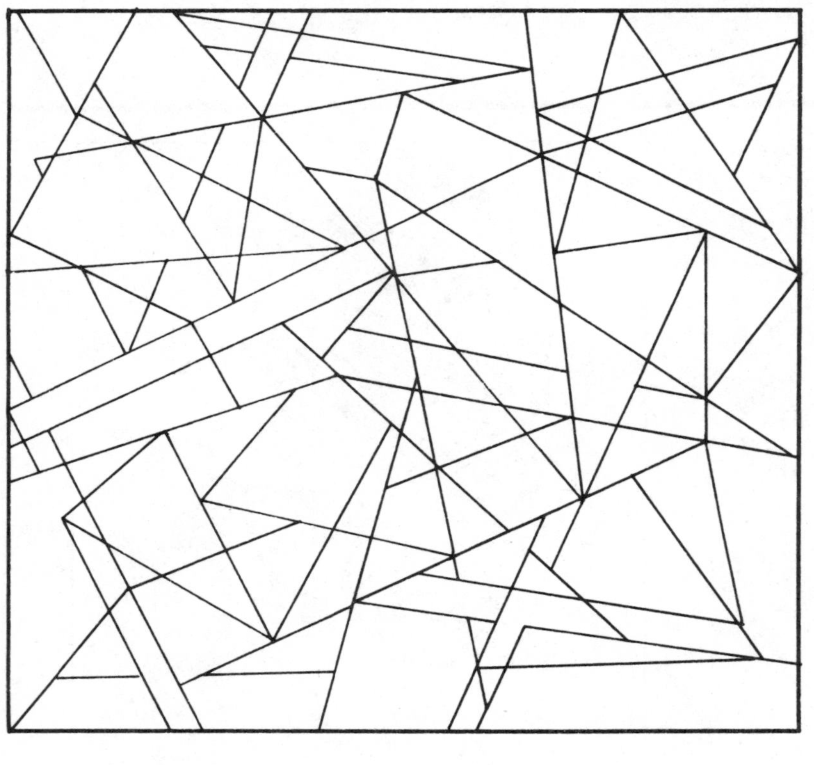

3. No pencil allowed on this one! What letter or number would be formed if you connected these dots?

7· 8· 10 11·

9·

1·12

4

6. 5. 3. .2

4. Which circles are the same size as a) a dime, b) a penny, c) a quarter?

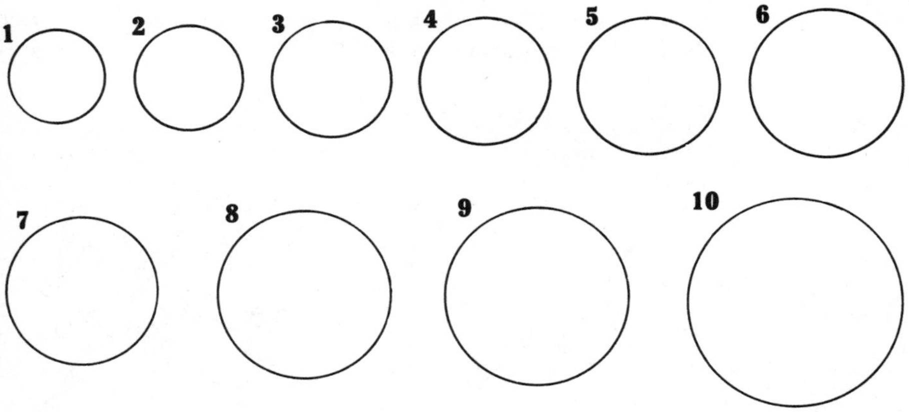

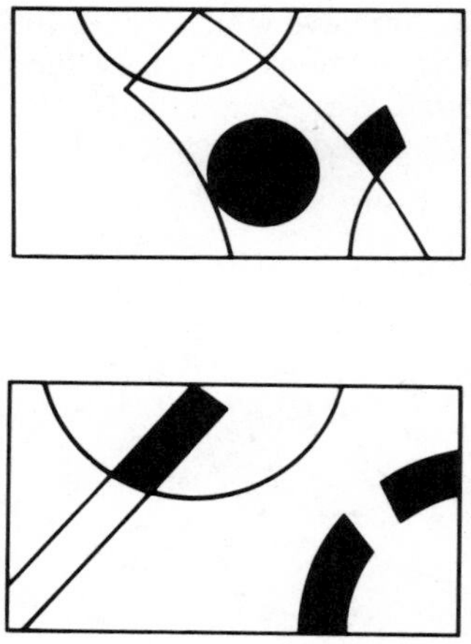

1 2 3 4 5 6

7 8 9 10

5. Which of the following pieces fits the empty square in the picture?

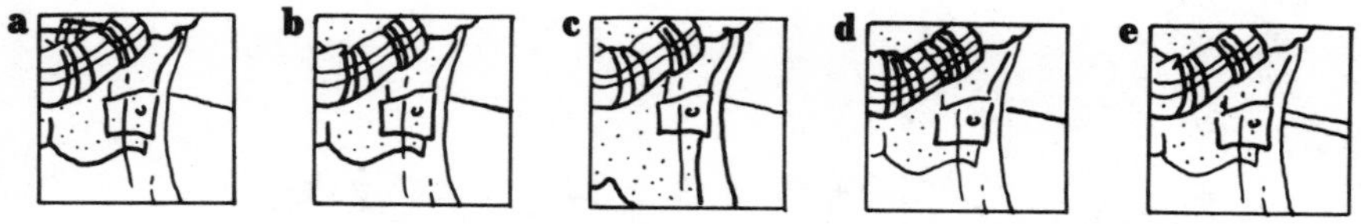

a b c d e

MA + PA 6 HR CLEANING

"Well, we got all the stains out, but we really think you should sit closer to the table when you eat."

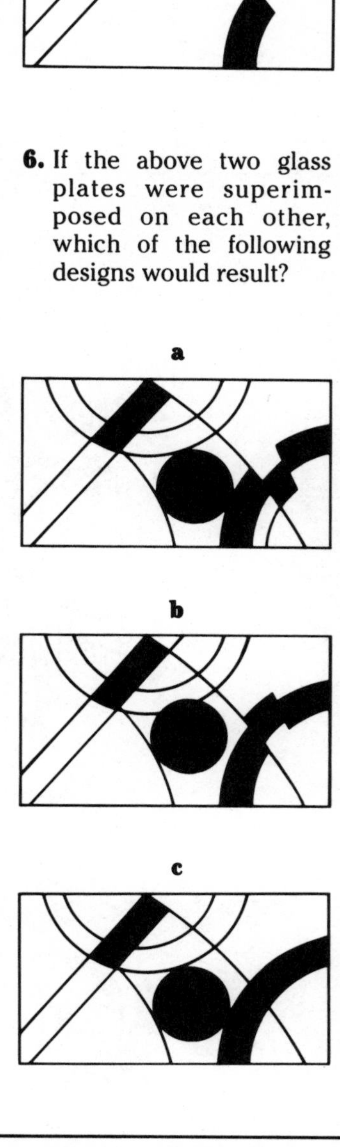

6. If the above two glass plates were superimposed on each other, which of the following designs would result?

7. How many perfect circles appear on these two pages? (You can ignore periods, dots, and letter o's.)

Match Play★

by Mark Mazut

"Do you have what it takes to be a commercial artist?" asks the matchbook. "Just sketch Jollo the Jester for a FREE professional evaluation. No obligation!"

That's what 11 hopeful artists did here. Unfortunately, only one of the sketches is correct in every detail. Each of the others contains exactly one small error. Can you find the errors and determine, by process of elimination, which sketch is perfectly rendered? *Answer, page 173*

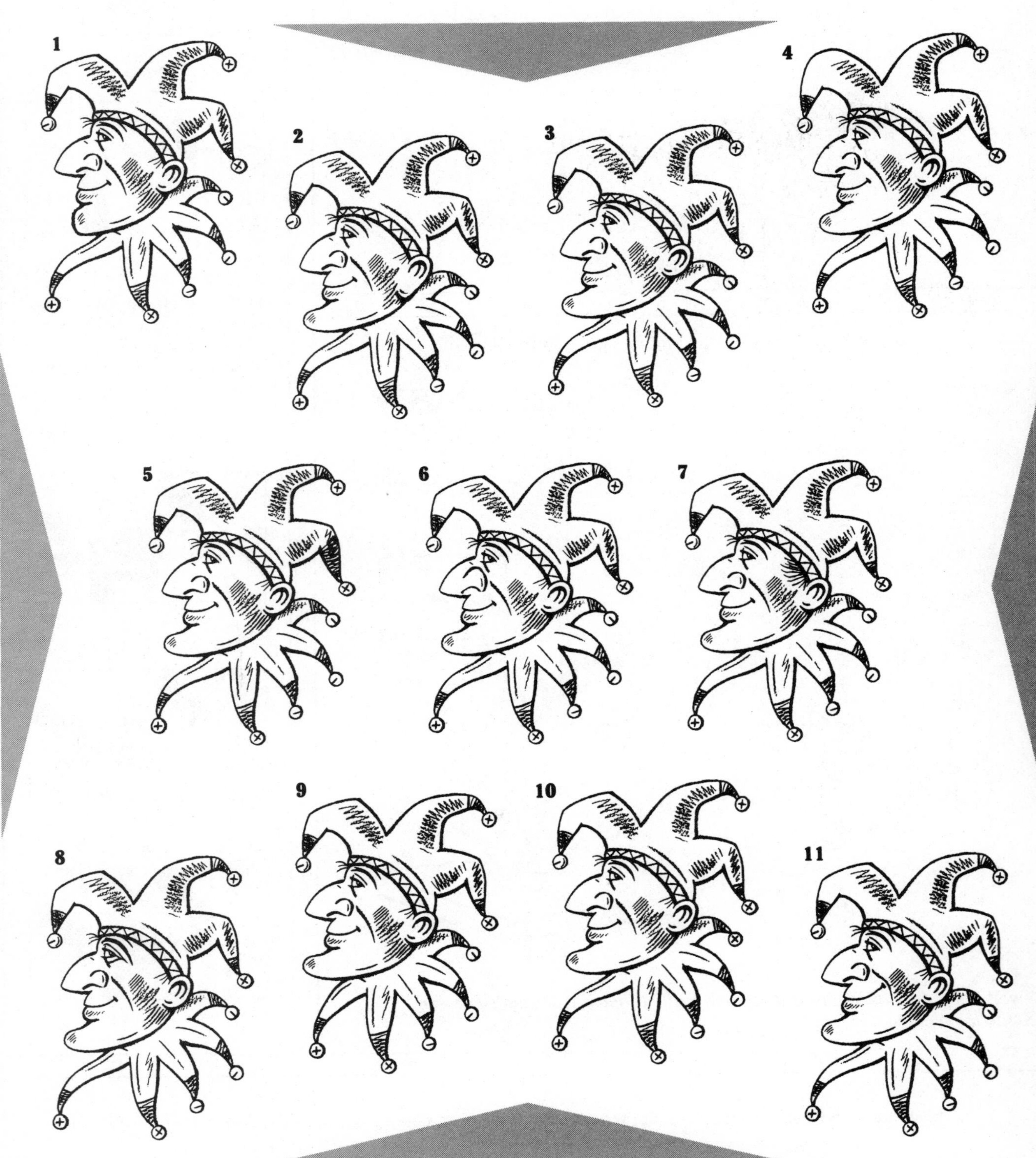

Out of This World ★☆

by R. Wayne Schmittberger

Simply put, the challenge—which may not be so simple—is to identify each of the nine map details below. For street maps, name the city. Otherwise, name the state, province, or territory (for places in the United States or Canada) or foreign country. If none of these identifications applies, use any reasonably accurate designation of what the map shows. Caution: Not all the maps may be current (but you don't have to identify how old they are!). *Answers, page 174*

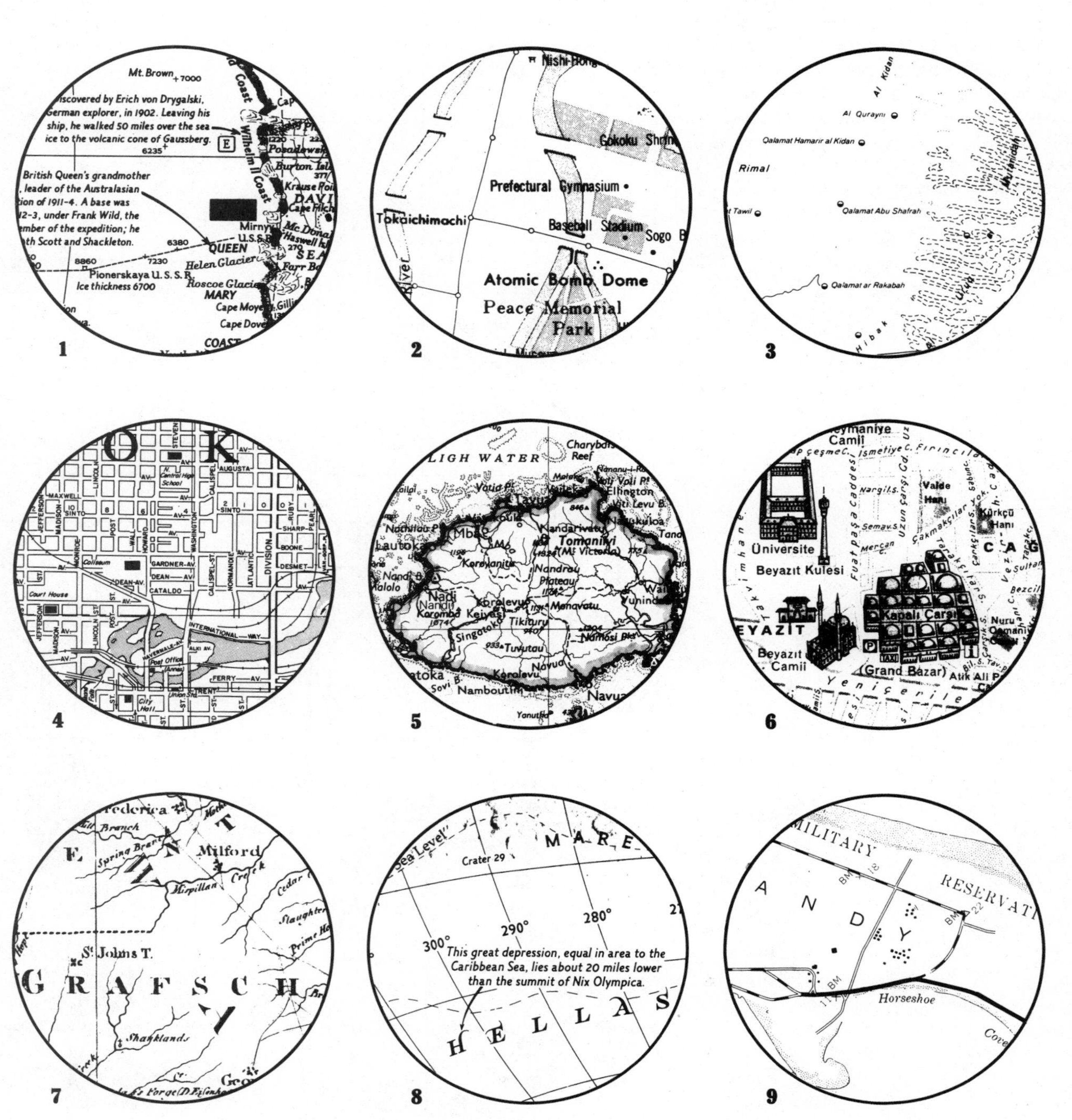

A Better Mousetrap★★

by William Perry

No one's beating a path to this inventor's door, but someone may come around when his "better mousetrap" is properly assembled. Each row of this Rube Goldberg-style mousetrap has been cut apart and its pieces scrambled. The parts in each row always remain in that row. Can you return them to their proper order so they form a working mousetrap?

Solving hint: In the solution, each action pictured causes a reaction in an adjacent box (above, below, or at the side). Try to fit the jigsaw pieces together to form a coherent series of events. The first piece has been placed for you. *Answer, page 174*

C

B

A

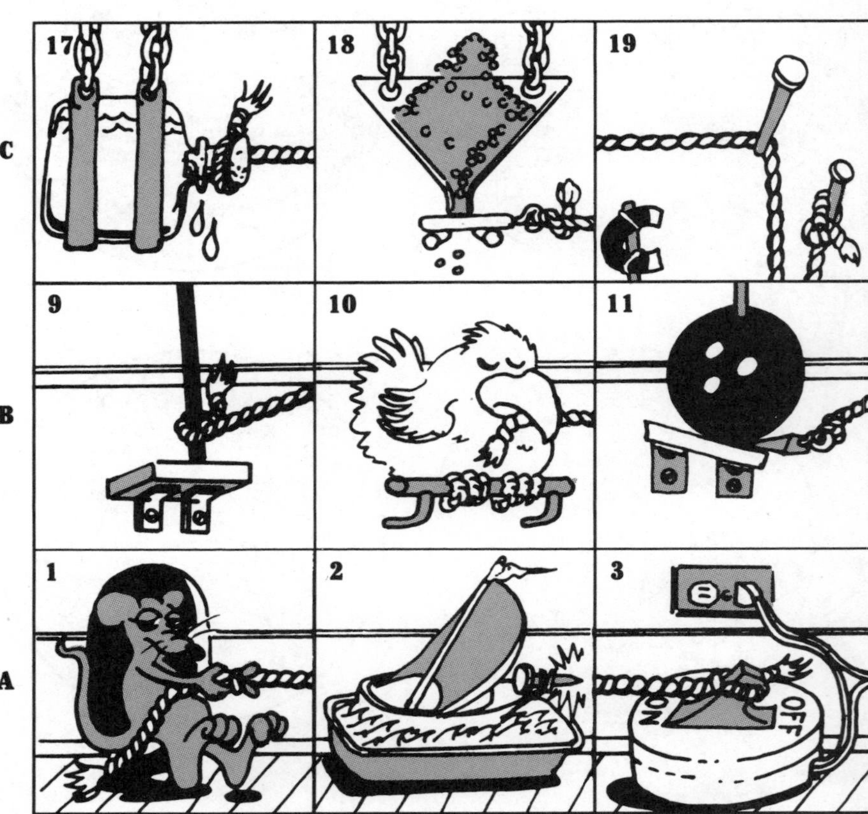

20
21
22
23
24
12
13
14
15
16
4
5lb
5
6
7
8

The Buck Starts Here★★

by John Chaneski

Who says making money is hard? Below are blank front and back views of a $1 bill, each view divided into regions. Below them are numbered pieces that fit into those regions, one piece per region. Some pieces belong on the front of the bill, others on the back. If you can put it all together without checking your wallet, you're on your way to your first million.

Answer, page 174

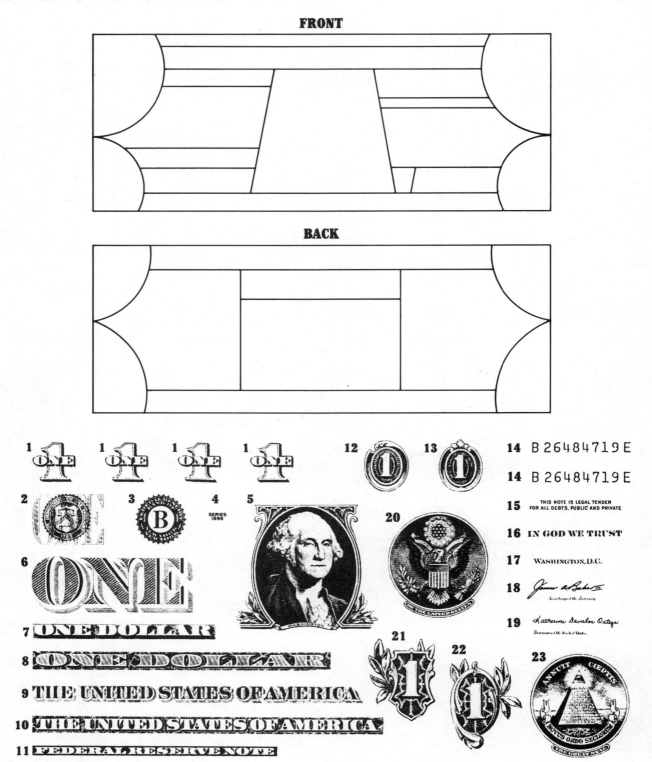

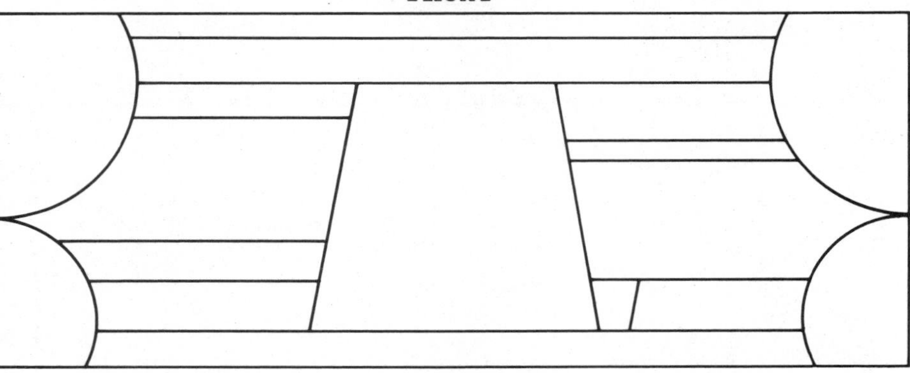

BACK

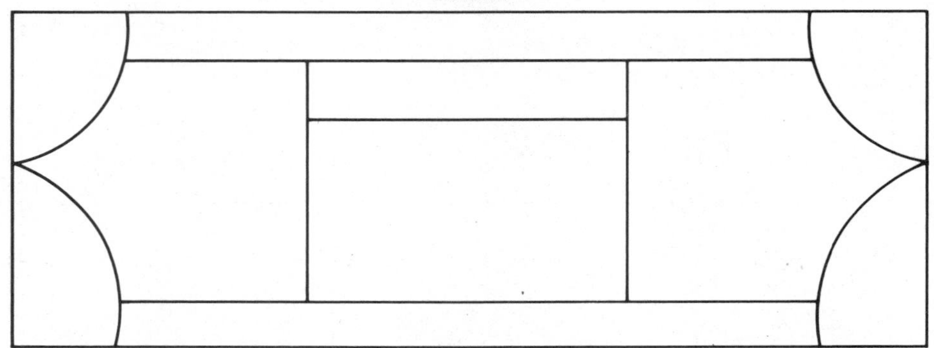

1 
1 
1 
1 
12 
13 
14 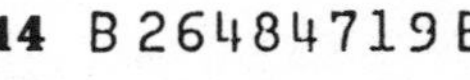

14 

2 
3 
4 

5 

15 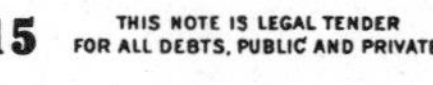

6 

20 

16 

17 WASHINGTON, D.C.

18 

19 Katherine Davalos Ortega

7 

8 

9 

10 

11 

21 

22

23 

A Switch in Time ★☆

by Margot Seides

"If you're going to illustrate our story on Betsy Ross, the homemaker," said the editor of *Colonial Kitchens* to the artist, "take these old woodcuts for reference. The year is 1788."

She attempted to push some musty books into his hands.

"Don't need 'em," the artist said. "I know that period as if I lived it myself."

The editor's fears proved to be justified, however, when the drawing came back full of errors. Right away she noticed the zipper on Ross's dress—an item not invented until more than a century later. As she looked further she spotted 21 other anachronisms—things that didn't yet exist in America 200 years ago. How many can you find?

Answers, page 174

Everybody's a Critic ★

by Andrea Carla Michaels and Robert Leighton

Sometimes the best dialogue at the movies can be heard in the audience. At least, that's what's happening here during the 8:30 showing of *Commie Love Slaves from Mars.* All the witty rejoinders to the comments in the picture are listed, in no particular order, in the column at the left. How many of them can you correctly place in the scene? *Answers, page 175*

REJOINDERS

A. I have to! My feet are completely stuck to the floor!

B. You're right—we should learn it from you and Dad at home!

C. Uh-oh. This is supposed to be an intense drama!

D. Not so loud! That's Siskel and Ebert!

E. Like "I don't know how to work this camera."

F. Let's see . . . Redford, Eastwood, and Shlobotnik. I wonder which actor gets killed first?

G. That explains why the ad claims it's "explosive!" and "a feast!"

H. Too bad the popcorn tastes like Styrofoam!

I. Those aren't stars—they're asterisks! Newspapers can't print those words in a review!

J. And that was just in the ticket-holders' line!

K. No, No . . . listen carefully. That's just the way Stallone talks!

L. Exactly! I want him to turn it off!

M. Yes, it's called "The Return of My Investment!"

EXIT
WHY DO YOU KEEP SHOUTING "SOUND!" O THE PROJECTIONIST? E CAN HEAR JUST FINE!
I DON'T WANT MY KIDS HEARING SUCH FOUL LANGUAGE IN THE MOVIES!
OH NO! ALL THREE GUYS ARE WALKING INTO THAT ABANDONED WAREHOUSE! THIS DOESN'T LOOK GOOD!
WOW! FOUR HUGE FISTFIGHTS, A CAR CRASH, AND A KNIFING-- ALL IN THE FIRST TEN MINUTES!
THE REVIEWERS ALLED THIS MOVIE BOMB" AND "A TURKEY."
I HEAR THE PRODUCERS ARE PLANNING THE SEQUEL ALREADY.
BY FILMING THESE SCENES AT ODD ANGLES OR OUT OF FOCUS, THE FILMMAKER IS SAYING SOMETHING TRULY IMPORTANT.

Radio Activity ★☆

by Mark Mazut

Radio deejay Ron Rocker has locked himself in the studio to protest his station's call letters—WIMP. "I'm not leaving until management approves a new name," he's saying right now at typical breakneck speed. "Let's open those phone lines for some suggestions."

Actually, phone calls won't be necessary. Located around the studio are 20 things with four-letter names starting with W, all of which could be used as station call letters. For example, the Los Lobos album cover near the mike suggests WOLF. How many of the other "Top 20" possibilities can you find?

Answers, page 174

Signs of Life★★

by Emily Cox and Henry Rathvon

American Sign Language, or AMESLAN, is a system of communication using the hands and fingers to express words, letters, and thoughts—often through signals that describe or suggest the things they represent. Each of the 12 illustrations below, for example, shows the official AMESLAN sign for a particular kind of animal. Arrows indicate movement of the hands. Can you match each sign (A–L) with the corresponding animal name (1–12)?

Answers, page 174

ANIMALS

1. Butterfly	**3.** Deer	**5.** Elephant	**7.** Kangaroo	**9.** Owl	**11.** Spider
2. Cat	**4.** Duck	**6.** Giraffe	**8.** Monkey	**10.** Snake	**12.** Turtle

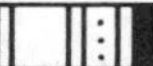

Mummy Dearest★★

by William Perry

These labyrinthine walls haven't echoed with footsteps for 4,500 years. Now archeologists believe they've found the long-sought tomb of King Atsalottalute. The 12 pictures show a series of views on the winding path from the entryway (G) to the pharaoh's chamber (F). Can you peer amid the visual clues to put the pictures in order? *Answer, page 174*

D

E

F

J

K

L

Making Tracks★★

by Mark Mazut

The circus parade took an unexpected detour one afternoon when a stray mouse (see tiny tracks, below left) attempted to dart in front of the parade's lead elephant. Fortunately, the mouse was not injured. Unfortunately, the crazed elephant jumped onto the freshly paved sidewalk, leading the entire circus parade through a block-long stretch of wet cement. By examining the overlapping tracks left in their wake, can you identify the marks of the kangaroo, the ostrich, and eight other circus performers—and then determine the order in which they stomped through town?

Answers, page 174

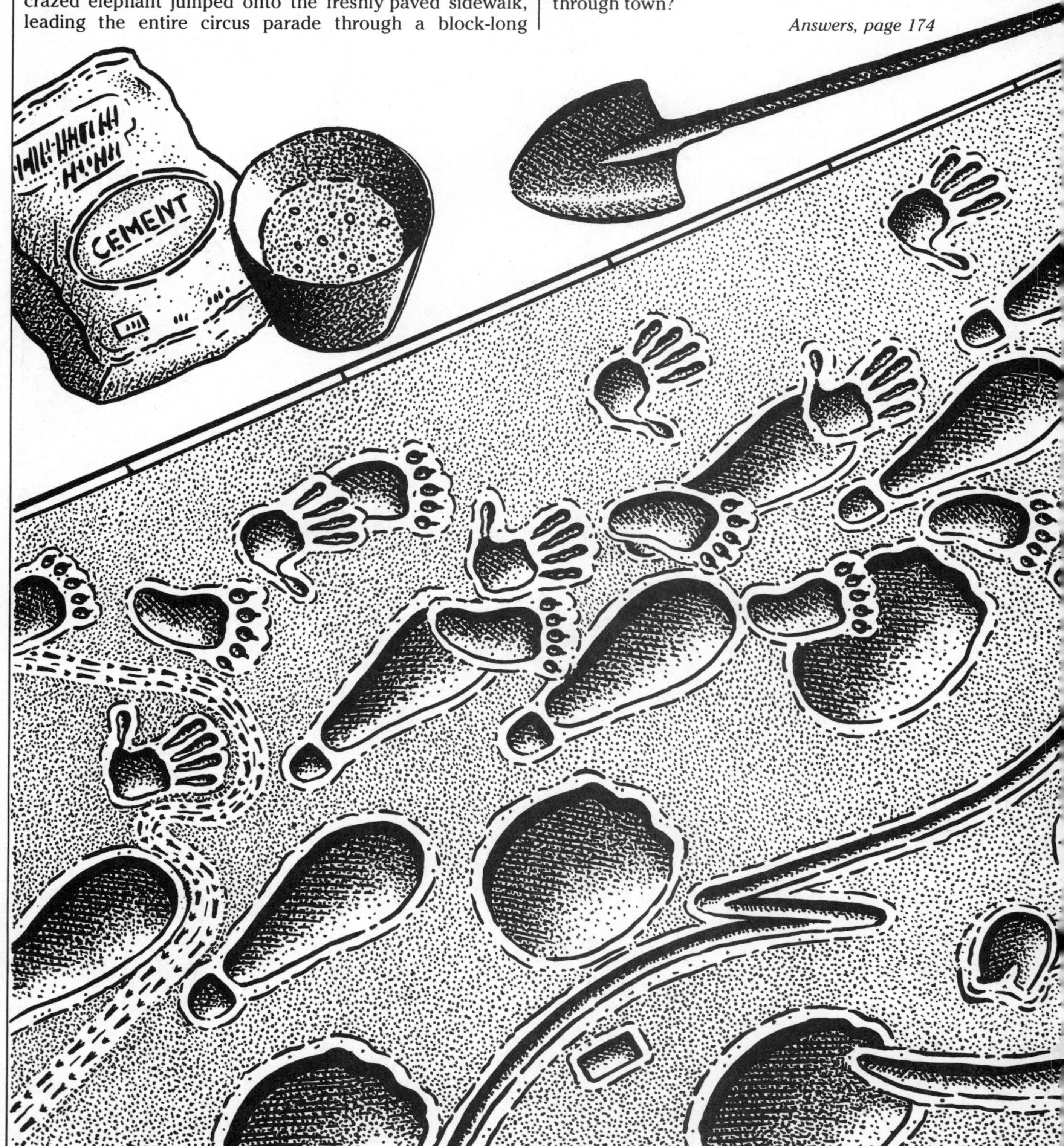

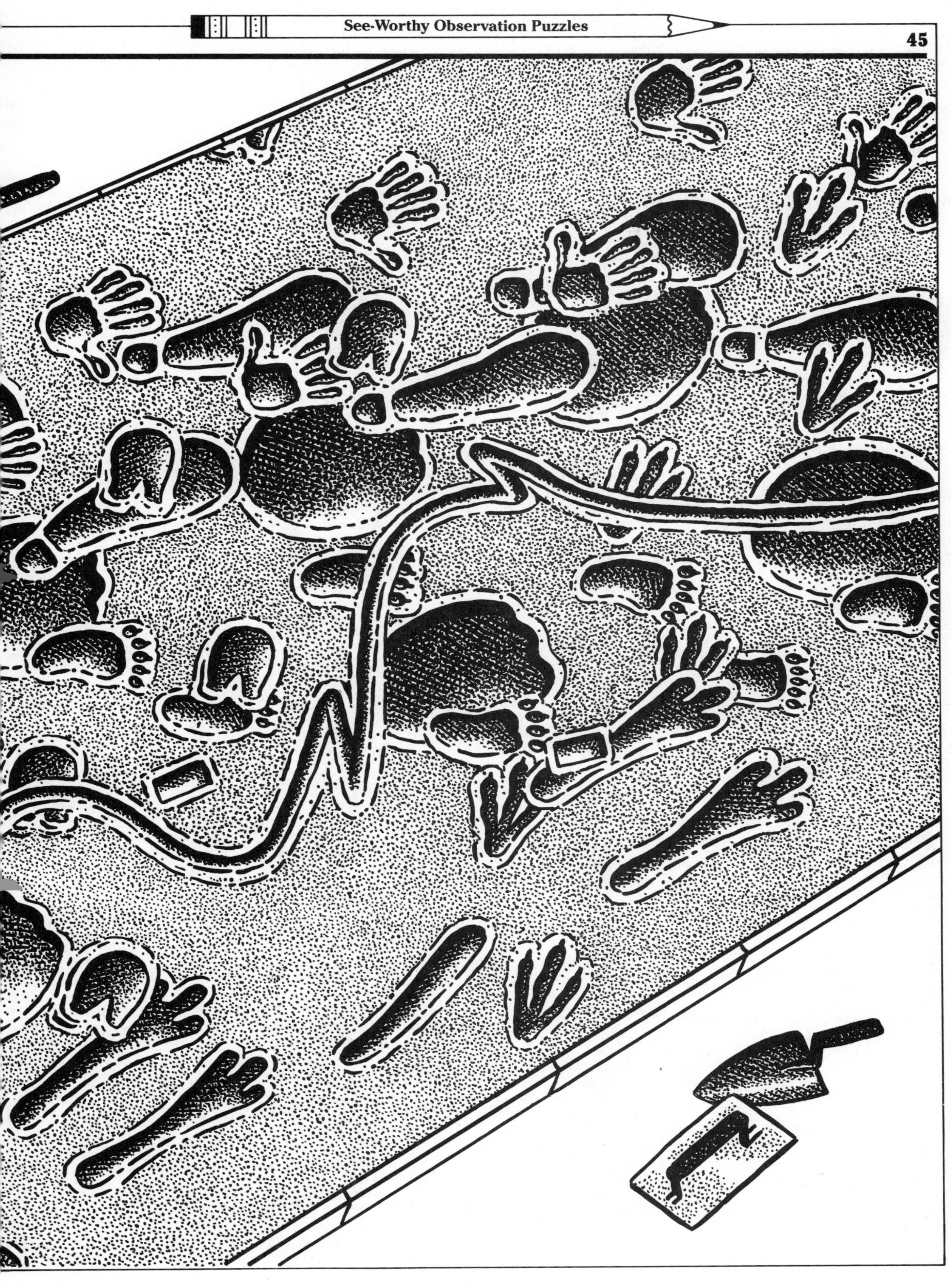

Meters & Gauges ★☆

by Keith Glasgow

On what devices can these calibrated close-ups be found? *Answers, page 175*

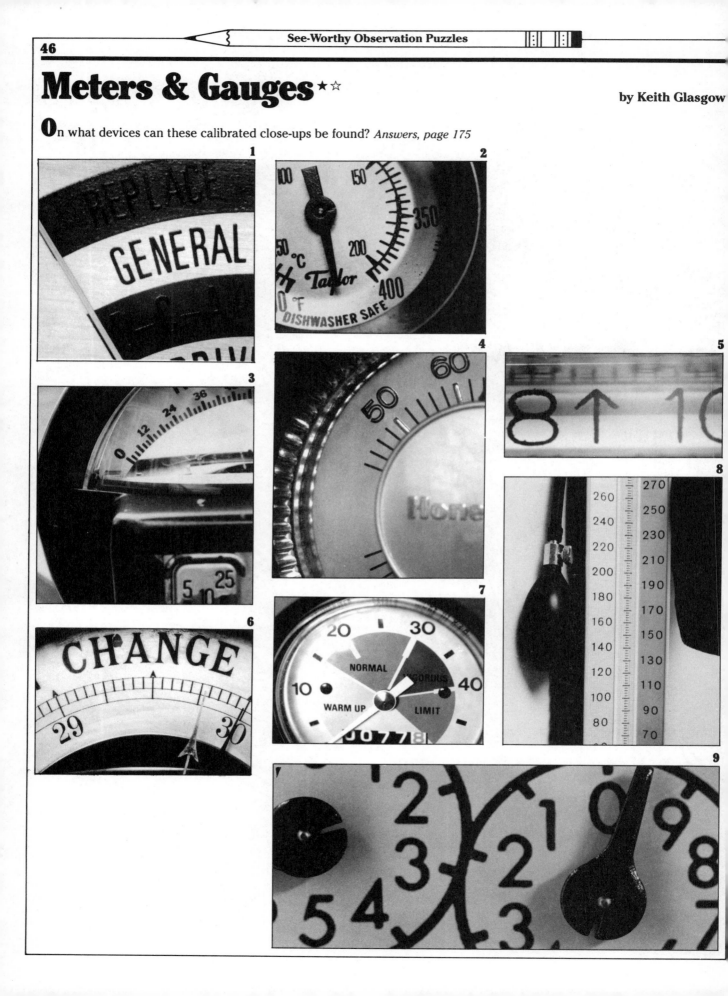

1

2

3

4

5

6

7

8

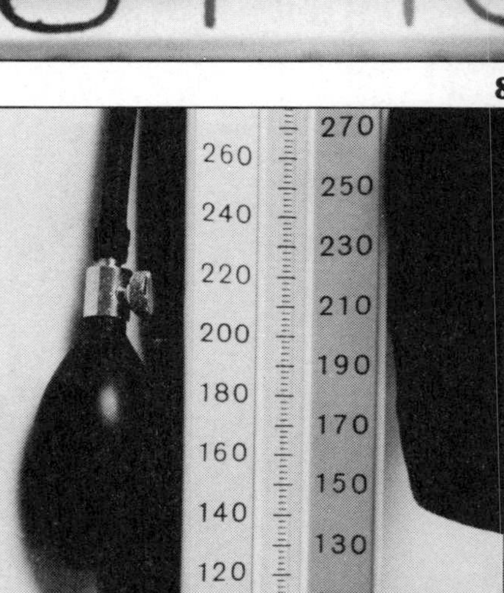

9

Twelve Brats of Christmas★★

by Robert Leighton

One of the drawbacks of being Santa Claus is that you have to bring gifts to kids who are technically "good" but still basically unpleasant. As a rule, these kids don't get the gifts they ask for. Instead, Santa goes through his leftovers and pulls out something he couldn't get rid of last year.

By coincidence, Santa has a system that will neatly pair the 12 kids below with the 12 leftover gifts. To start, we'll tell you that Roz gets the theater passes. Can you figure out the rule behind Santa's system and assign the other 11 gifts? Hint: The kids' names have nothing to do with the answers.

Answer, page 175

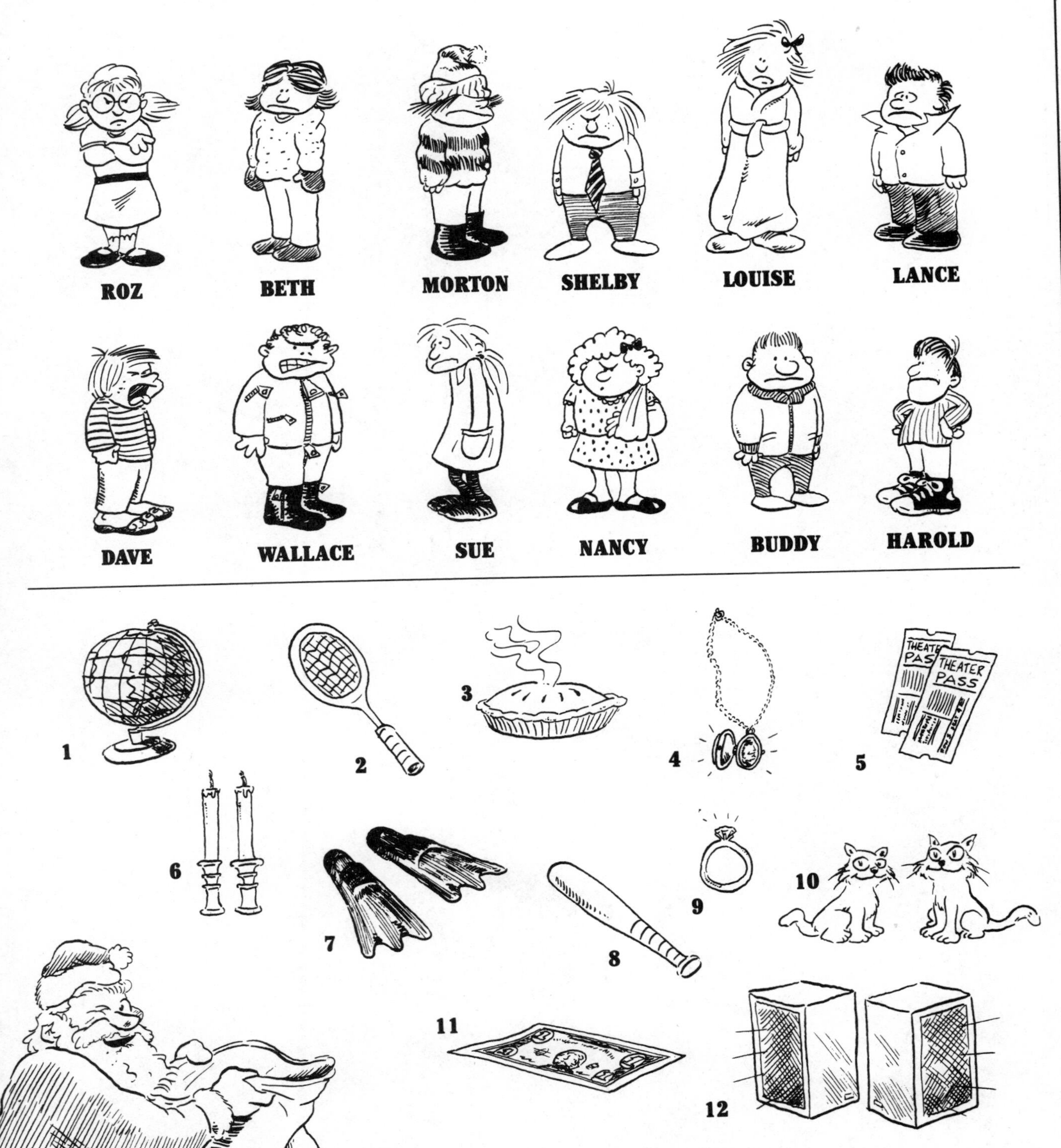

Inferior Decorator ★☆

Are the filthy rich above the law? The eccentric billionaire who lives here certainly seems to be—he's decorated his sprawling home with complete disregard for the laws of logic, physics, or perspective. Even Jeeves, his electronic butler,

by Greg Scott

blows an occasional fuse trying to make sense of everything. Jeeves's well-ordered mind has detected 30 implausibilities in this room alone. While lunch is being served, see how many you can find.

Answers, page 175

Class Reunion ★☆

by Mark Mazut

Class reunions are the pits. You've just arrived at yours, and you don't recognize a single face, even though all these people were friends way back when. Worse, no one's wearing a name tag, and the list of attendees (below) provides only last names.

To avoid a social gaffe, realize this: Each classmate has a common first name which, when combined with his or her last name, forms a word that describes that person. For example, the heavy smoker is Nick O'Teen. Can you figure out the first names of the other 10 classmates?

Answers, page 175

Ex. NICK O'Teen

1. ____________ Adohr

2. ____________ Graff

3. ____________ Harmonick

4. ____________ Hawk

5. ____________ Nast

6. ____________ Nette

7. ____________ O'Fone

8. ____________ Tator

9. ____________ Veneer

10. ____________ Voyent

Stories from the Safari (Part 1) ★☆

by Will Shortz

How good is your memory and eye for detail? Study this scene for up to three minutes . . . then turn the page to read the hunter's account of what happened. Once you turn you will be relying solely on your memory of what you've seen.

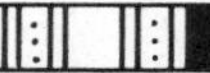

Stories from the Safari (Part 2)

On the previous page you were witness to an attack on a hunter in Africa. It was a dangerous encounter, to be sure, but somehow back home the hunter's account of the attack has improved in the retelling. How many misrepresentations or other errors can you find in his story below?

Answers, page 175

I've had many harrowing adventures while on safari in Africa, but my closest call was wrestling with a tiger when I was armed with only a knife.

The attack occurred around noon along a deserted road in Tanzania, two miles from the village of Bukwimba. I was all alone at the time. My throat was dry because I had left my canteen back at camp. A pride of lions could be seen to the left of the road ahead, and a snake was coiled on a branch above me.

Suddenly a twig snapped. I turned and saw a tiger leaping toward me. I slipped my pistol from its holster and raised my arm to shoot, but—click!—the gun wasn't loaded!

The tiger was still charging. In one more leap it would be at my throat.

In a flash I whipped out my knife and wrestled the tiger to the pavement. I repeatedly stabbed him as he bit and clawed me. Eventually I subdued him, but not without a terrible struggle. You can still see the scar where he gashed me on the arm.

Fortunately, I have another, better memento of the occasion—his head mounted on the wall behind me.

NUMBER CRUNCHING AND LOGIC CHOPPING

Alternating Currency★★

by Keith Ringkamp

The distant kingdom of Azalia has recently issued three new coins. Each coin has a different value (17, 36, or 55 pengos), a different color (olive green, maroon, or turquoise), and a different shape.

If you randomly select a coin, it will be either olive green, a circle, or the 17-pengo piece. If you randomly select another coin, it will be either turquoise, a triangle, or the 36-pengo. The triangular coin is worth more than the square coin.

What color and what shape are the different values of coins?

Answer, page 175

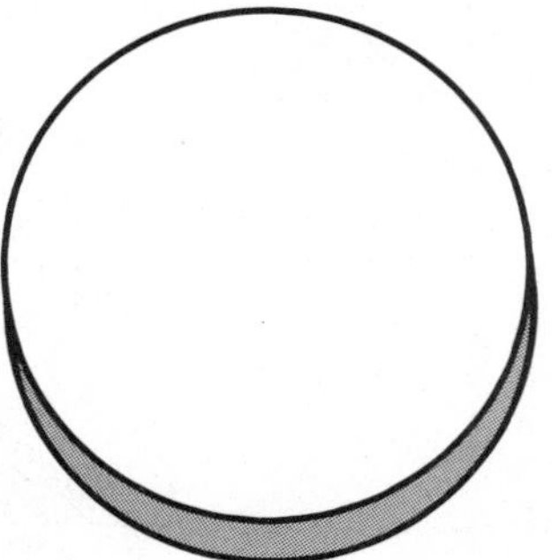

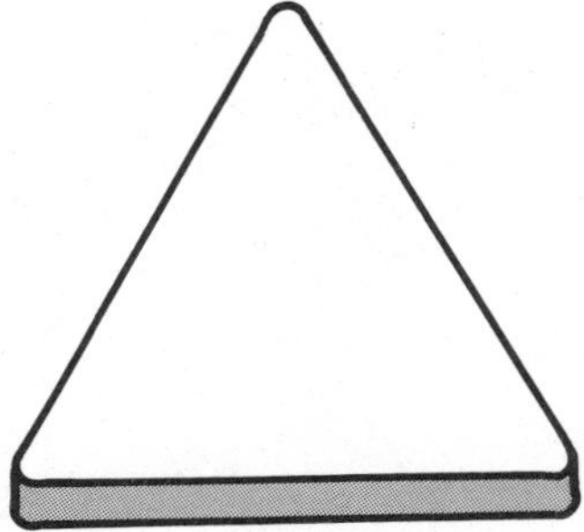

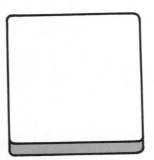

Untrue Confessions★★

by Emily Cox and Henry Rathvon

A frightful homicide has just been committed at the Placid Hills Asylum for Peculiarly Unbalanced Persons. This progressive hospital, which treats people with some of the most exotic mental afflictions known to science, has the world's only ward set aside for patients who think they are pneumatic drills, and an entire meadow reserved for one woman who imagines herself to be a 15th-century cathedral.

The hospital's leading therapist, Dr. Fred Shrynker, has been found murdered in his study, a room on the second floor of a cottage restricted to Shrynker and the patients under his care. It is known that the crime was committed by one of Shrynker's patients—which simplifies matters. But the special division headed by Shrynker is the Ward for Patients Suffering from the Delusion That They Are Murderers—which complicates matters. For eight different patients have eagerly confessed to the killing!

A sleuth with a sharp eye for detail can solve this case by studying the picture below, which shows the scene of the crime just minutes after the murder, and comparing it with the eight confessions on the facing page. (For a three-star challenge, study this page for five minutes before reading the confessions, and do not refer back to the picture while solving.) By careful analysis, you will find that seven of the eight confessions do not hold water, based on details from the picture. By elimination, the eighth confession will reveal the murderer.

Answer, page 176

Louise Bonkers:

"I *had* to kill Dr. Shrynker. First, he was a Yankees fan. Second, it was the 15th of November. Third, I had a toothache. So what I did was drop by his office on the pretext of borrowing some records, and then grab the phone from the desk and strangle him with the telephone cord. I guess that'll teach him to root for Dave Winfield! I still have a toothache, though."

Gerald McNutt:

"Yes, I assassinated President Shrynker. Did you know he was planning peace talks with the Soviets? I knew that to keep our country strong I must act swiftly, so I confronted him in his study. There he was calmly sipping brandy, as if our national defenses were not on the verge of total collapse! He had just raised the cup to his traitorous lips when I snatched one of his bowling trophies from the wall and brought it down on his head. It was civic duty, pure and simple."

Dotty Noodleton:

"Dr. Shrynker has always loved me with a passionate, all-consuming desire. Tonight we were to elope together! I leaned a ladder against the building and climbed to his room. But when I stepped into the study and saw him reading a letter from his wife, I knew he had betrayed me! I struck him with a large heart-shaped ashtray beside his chair, then quickly left the way I had come. It was an act of passion, like all my acts toward him!"

Leopold Looney:

"Now that our invasion is under way, it is safe to confess that I am not the Earthling I seem to be. I have mingled among you people for years, planning the takeover of your puny planet. Dr. Shrynker knew this but could not prove it. Tonight he caught me in this office telepathically beaming signals into space through the window. He tried to jam my transmission by blowing on the harmonica he keeps next to his chair, but in two steps I'd grabbed the globe-shaped paperweight from the desk and killed him. It doesn't matter what you do to me now. Our ships will arrive very soon."

Griselda Cracklin:

"Shrynker's name has eight letters in it, did you know that? I was 56 eight days ago. And there are eight panes in the window of Shrynker's office. Eight times eight is 64, minus eight is 56, you see? So I took eight steps around Shrynker's chair, then strangled him from behind four times with my scarf. I burned the scarf in the fireplace, which took three minutes. That meant I had to drink five glasses of brandy and spin the globe in the corner three times. This is my 47th murder, so I need one more."

Corker Mayhem:

"Frankly, Shrynker was one of my least promising patients, practically a hopeless case. I decided to resort to my most extreme therapy, which I call 'Mayhem's Sudden Surprise Method.' I went to Shrynker's office before he got there, hid behind the door when he came in, waited until he was comfortably seated, then tiptoed over and, for a surprise, suffocated him with a cushion. I believe this technique will effectively terminate any future behavior on his part."

Mabel Fogpate:

"We must not leave things undone. So many holes must be filled, so many loose ends must be tied! I told Dr. Shrynker just tonight that his typewriter was uncovered, but he ignored me. Then I saw that his shoelace was untied. That, of course, cannot be tolerated. He bent to tie it, when I noticed that his entire bookshelf was out of alphabetical order! I struck him with a golf club to put a stop to his insufferable oversights, and he died. At least that's all done with!"

Cootie Bananaman:

"I know Dr. Shrynker was jealous of me because of my cloak of invisibility. It is my special gift, bestowed upon me by the Immortal Being, and no one can take it from me. I had the cloak on when I entered his office, so I didn't worry about him seeing me. But as I stepped in, I made a floorboard creak, and the doctor looked up abruptly in alarm. To get the job over with quickly, I just throttled him with my invisible fingers. Ha ha! Now my cloak is safe forever!"

Can You Think Under Pressure? ★☆

by Scott Marley

This test measures your ability to follow directions and think clearly under pressure. Switchboard operators and short-order cooks may have an advantage here. You have exactly 10 minutes to read and answer the following questions. Have a pencil ready, and a clock or stopwatch handy to time yourself. When the 10 minutes are up, stop working, whether or not you're finished.

On your mark, get set, go! *Answers, page 176*

Draw a line under the third H within this sentence. Then write the numbers 5 through 1 in backward order here ______ ______ ______ ______ ______. Now strike out every baseball term in this sentence, unless a bat is a type of fowl. Circle the word that doesn't belong: China, Peru, India, Africa, Luxembourg. Cross out four matches in diagram "A" at right so as to leave only two squares, unless there would be eight matches left, in which case cross out four matches so as to leave only one square. If cows don't give milk, write BULL in this space ________. Draw a wavy line under the fraction that is not equal to one half: 2/4, 3/6, 8/18, 17/34, 67/134. Now name four states that border Canada. ________ ________ ________ ________ Ignore every third word in the following instruction: If horses spiders have four seven legs, do not draw a triangle circle in around this square: □. How many equilateral triangles (of any size) are in diagram "B" at right? ______ Circle the word that's out of alphabetical order: forceps, foreign, forestry, forehand, formality, foster—Hold it! If four fours are less than fourteen, then cross out the shortest word instead. Speaking of fours, how many eights go into four times four times four? ______ If there are not 52 cards in a poker hand, cross out all pairs in the card layout ("C") at right. Write ACE here ________, unless jacks are higher than kings. If two tens make a score, circle every card to the left of a crossed-out spade. If pigs have feathers or the White House has wings, follow the next instruction incorrectly: Misspell MISSPELL in the blank ________. Hw mny vwls hv bn rmvd frm ths sntnc? ______ If John gives Mary one half as many kisses as he gives Sue, and gives Sue three more kisses than he gives Mary, how many kisses does Sue get? ______ The piece of paper ("D") at right is divided into 16 sections. Imagine laying the paper on a table. Fold the paper in half by bringing the bottom edge up to the top; in half again by bringing the right edge over to the left; again by bringing the left over to the right; and once more, bringing the bottom edge up. Which numbered section is now on top? ______ Name four countries that end in Y. ________ ________ ________ ________ Ignore the next two sentences, unless water burns or a flute is a percussion instrument. But be sure to obey the next sentence. Write the number of half dozens in two gross here ______. If apples have seeds, write CORE in the right margin, unless oranges are not orange or grapefruit is a melon, in which case write RIND instead, but if watermelons don't grow underground write WRECKED as well. Read aloud what you've written in the margin, and you're finished!

A

B

C

J♥ 3♠
Q♣ 8♠
J♠ 8♦

D

1	2	3	4
5	6	7	8
9	10	11	12
13	14	15	16

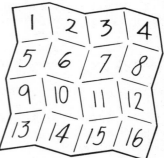

Polish Your Wits ★☆

by Marek Penszko

All you need to solve these three problems in math and logic is a little square thinking. Or, in one case, cubic thinking. Their author, Marek Penszko, is Poland's best-known puzzle creator and writer.

Answers, page 176

1. NUMBER RING

Can you divide the ring of digits below into three one-or-more-digit numbers so that—reading clockwise—you can multiply one of the numbers by the one after it to get the third?

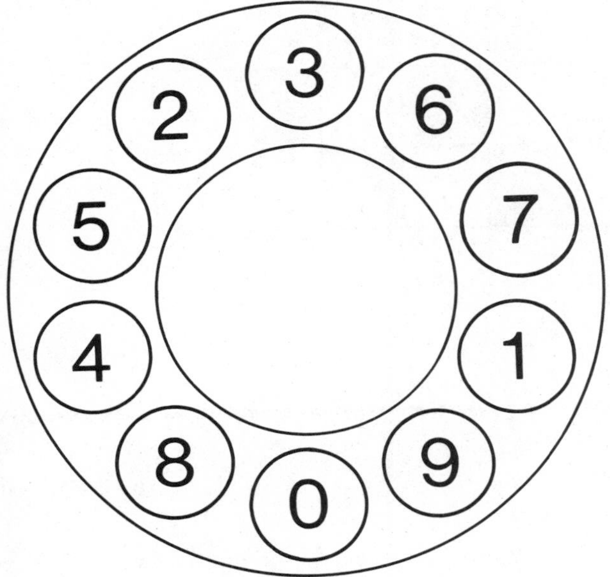

2. CORNERING THE KING

On the miniature chessboard below, you are playing the queen (b2) and your opponent is playing the king (d1). Both pieces move as in standard chess. In not more than four moves, how can you force the king into the upper right corner (d3)?

3. LOOP THE LOOP

A closed line has been drawn on a glass cube, shown below ("A"). Also shown are the views of the cube when seen from the front, the right side, and above. Can you draw on the second cube ("B") another closed line, so that the front, side, and top views would all have the identical L-shaped view shown?

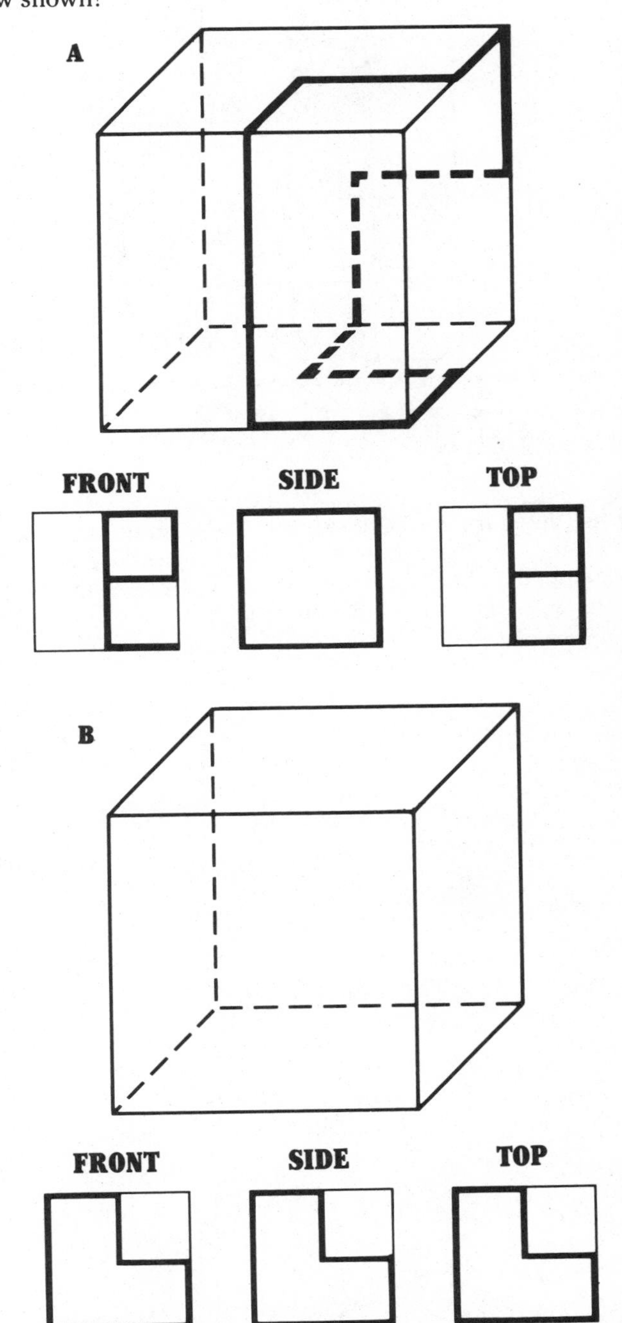

Cutting a Rug★★

by Scott Marley

Oooh!" cried Mrs. Divine as she examined her new rug. "As God is my witness, I'll never give another cocktail party again so long as I live!"

A lit cigarette, dropped by a guest the night before, had completely burned away one of the white squares in the gray-and-white rug. Philip thought it was just as well, but a good handyman knows when to keep quiet.

"You'll just have to cut the rug apart and resew it into a rectangle," continued Mrs. Divine. "Keep the checkerboard pattern, with a white square in the upper left corner. And don't cut it into more than two pieces, or it'll take all day. I want it done in time for the cocktail party I'm giving this afternoon."

Philip groaned. He couldn't see any way to follow all of Mrs. Divine's instructions.

Can you? *Answer, page 176*

BEFORE

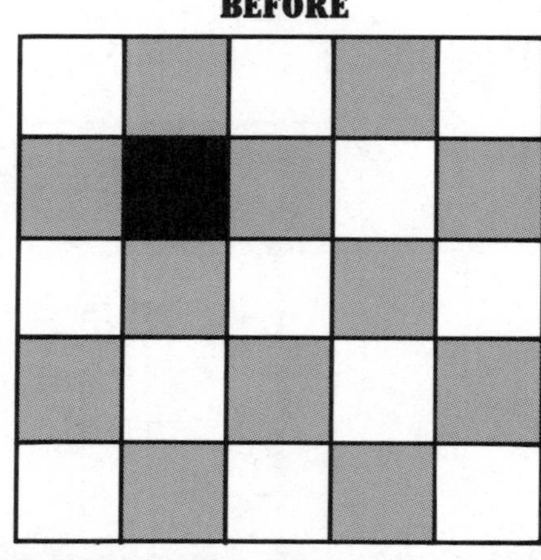

AFTER

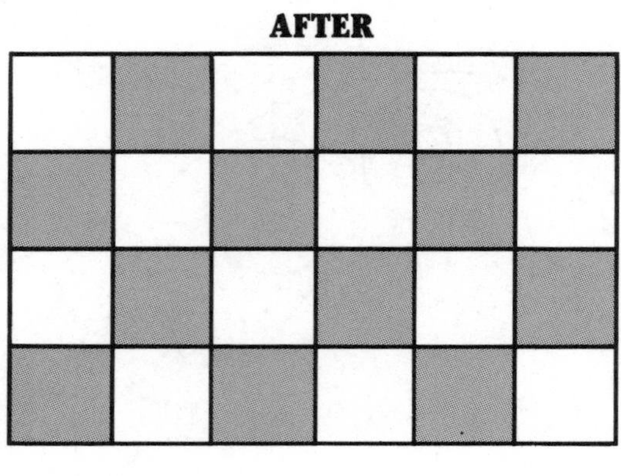

Word Division★☆

by Neill Smith

The numbers in each of the cryptogrammatic long-division problems below have been replaced by letters of the alphabet. Each letter of the alphabet stands for the same digit throughout a problem, but substitutions are different from one problem to the next. Solve each puzzle using logic and basic arithmetic. When each puzzle is completed, the letters representing the digits 0 to 9, written in order, will spell a bonus word or phrase. *Answers, page 176*

1

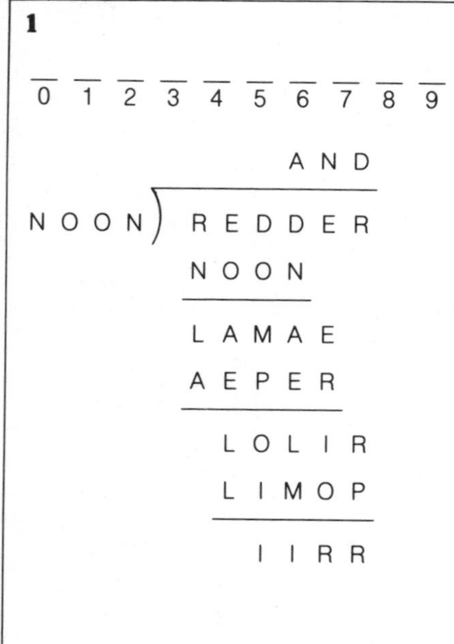

2

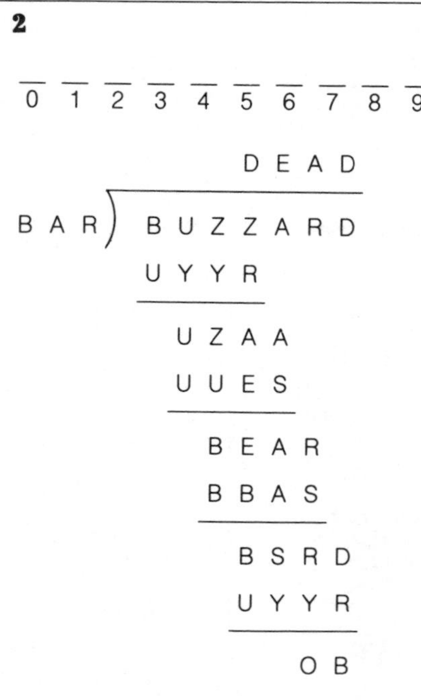

3

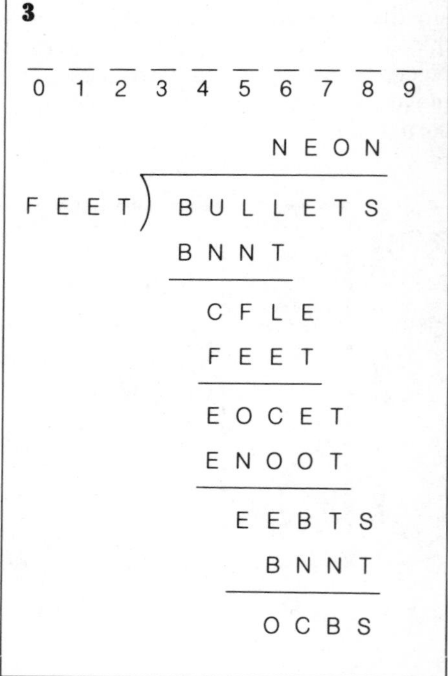

Slugfest on Proteus★★★

by Emily Cox and Henry Rathvon

Given the information in the following news story, can you name the softball game's home team, the number of runs scored in each of the two teams' turns at bat, and the final score of the slugfest? *Answer, page 176*

A PUZZLING SOFTBALL MATCH

PROTEUS (Galax. News Service), June 29, 2056—Softball games on Proteus, the lone planet in the Altair system, are often peculiar affairs. The ball always travels well in Proteus's thin atmosphere, and this year's showdown between the Titans and the All-Stars was a typical slugfest—from the towering three-run homer by Sal Bates of the visiting team in the first inning to the awesome two-run clout by Ronnie Jackson that won the game for the home team in the bottom of the sixth.

A strange feature of this game was that each team put a different number of runs on the scoreboard in each of its six turns at bat, and that all of the numbers from 1 through 12 were used in this way. Also notable was that one team's runs were scored in the alphabetical order of the written-out numbers.

"You can always count on something weird happening in this ballpark," said All-Stars' outfielder Jackie Lopes. Lopes' third-inning two-run homer was a fluke in itself—a broken-bat pop that got caught in an updraft and hit the left-field foul pole on the fly. Talk about luck.

Titan starting pitcher Larry Speedwell was erratic, giving up twice as many runs in the fourth inning as he did in the first three innings combined. "I lost my concentration out there," admitted the veteran lefty.

The high-scoring affair was popular with the fans, who turned out some 10,000 strong to fill the seats of Proteus's quaint Bandbox Stadium. "It was exciting—such a close game," said one fan. "All that slugging, and the two teams were still separated by just one run after five innings!"

TEAM	1	2	3	4	5	6	T
(VISITORS) ________							
(HOME) ________							

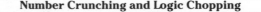

Training Exercise★★

by R. Wayne Schmittberger

The night before she was to leave for her dream vacation around the world, Sally Forth, at home in Alphaville, couldn't find the passport she had picked up that afternoon in the city of Hope Springs. As she was desperately looking through her briefcase for the fourth time, the phone rang. Her passport was at the Lost & Found department at the Hope Springs railroad station.

The following morning, a few minutes before 7:00, Sally arrives at the Alphaville train station. In order to catch her flight to Europe from the Alphaville airport, she has to make the round trip to Hope Springs and back before noon. The timetables for eastbound and westbound travel between Alphaville and Hope Springs are shown below. Each horizontal row in each of the two timetables represents a different train. Dashes appear at stations where the train does not stop. A series of Xs indicates the end of the line. For example, the 7:00 train from Alphaville stops only at Fortuna, which is the end of its route; while the 7:10 from Alphaville stops at every station, arriving at Hope Springs at noon.

Sally can wait at stations, transfer from one train to another, and change directions as often as she wishes. For example, she might take an eastbound train part of the way to Hope Springs, then switch to a westbound train in order to catch a faster eastbound train at another station.

Assume that all the trains are running on time, that transferring to another train takes fewer than four minutes, and that picking up the passport at Lost & Found takes only a minute. Can you find the one way that Sally can make it from Alphaville to Hope Springs and back before noon?

Answer, page 176

EASTBOUND (times of departure) **All times are A.M. unless shown in boldface.**

Alphaville	Betaville	Clarksville	Discovery	Ephemeral	Fortuna	Gamesport	Hope Springs
7:00	----	----	----	----	8:10	XXXX	XXXX
7:10	7:40	8:30	9:10	10:00	10:30	11:20	**12:00**
XXXX	7:20	7:50	8:10	----	8:40	XXXX	XXXX
7:20	----	----	7:50	----	8:30	9:00	9:30
XXXX	7:30	8:20	----	----	----	8:50	9:00
7:40	8:10	----	8:50	----	9:20	9:40	10:00
XXXX	7:50	----	8:10	----	8:40	XXXX	XXXX
7:50	----	----	----	8:30	9:00	9:20	9:40
8:30	9:00	----	----	9:30	9:50	10:20	10:50
XXXX	XXXX	8:40	----	----	----	9:10	XXXX
9:30	10:00	----	10:30	----	11:00	----	11:30
10:10	10:50	11:30	----	**12:00**	XXXX	XXXX	XXX

WESTBOUND (times of departure) **All times are A.M. unless shown in boldface.**

Hope Springs	Gamesport	Fortuna	Ephemeral	Discovery	Clarksville	Betaville	Alpha
7:00	----	7:20	7:40	8:00	8:10	----	9:0
7:10	7:30	8:00	8:20	9:00	9:30	10:10	10:5
7:50	8:20	8:50	9:10	----	9:40	----	10:2
8:20	8:40	----	----	----	10:00	XXXX	XXXX
8:50	----	----	----	9:40	----	----	11:10
9:10	----	----	----	9:50	XXXX	XXXX	XXXX
9:15	----	----	----	10:05	XXXX	XXXX	XXXX
9:20	----	----	9:40	10:00	----	10:30	XXXX
9:50	10:10	----	10:30	10:50	----	11:20	XXXX
XXXX	XXXX	XXXX	10:10	----	----	10:40	XXXX
10:20	----	10:50	----	11:10	----	11:30	**12:05**
XXXX	XXXX	10:40	----	----	11:20	----	11:50

Letter Logic ★☆

by Lawrence Graber

Fill in the empty squares in each grid below to complete four five-letter words reading across. What's the catch? The four words in each completed grid must contain 10 different letters, each used exactly twice. For example, in grid #1 the letter L already appears twice, so it can't be used again. The letter G, however, appears only once so far. Think of a word in which the second G will fit, and proceed from there. It may take you several tries to find the right combination of words—so keep your eraser handy.

Answers, page 177

1

I				E
M		R		L
G		O		S
L				N

2

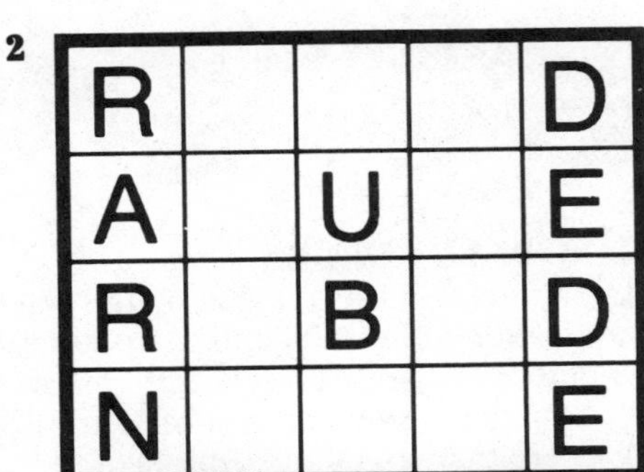

3

H				L
S		O		T
R		N		E
S				G

4

T				R
O		C		R
A		A		T
I				E

Cross Math ★☆

by Art Pipeny

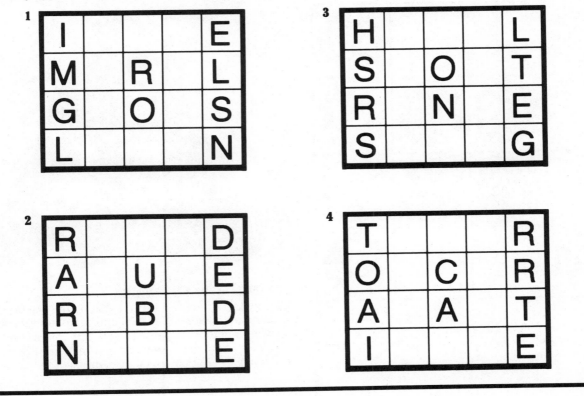

For each of the puzzles below, place the digits 1 through 9 (once each) in the empty squares of the box so that the three rows across and the three columns down form correct arithmetic sequences. All calculations (which should involve only positive whole numbers) should be performed in order from left to right and top to bottom.

Answers, page 177

1

	+		+		=6
x	■	+	■	x	■
	+		÷		=2
–	■	–	■	÷	■
	+		–		=13
=6	■	=0	■	=3	■

2

	x		÷		=2
+	■	–	■	–	■
	–		+		=8
÷	■	+	■	x	■
	x		÷		=10
=1	■	=13	■	=8	■

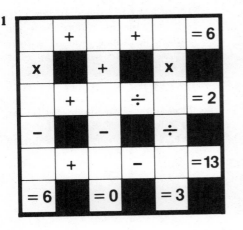

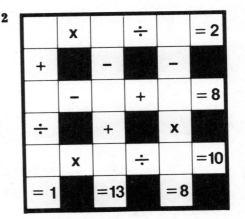

Coin-Op Puzzlers ★☆

from the *Games* Library

Some people say that change isn't worth much anymore, but we beg to differ. A quarter still makes a decent tip for a cup of coffee at the diner, a dime can be a handy substitute for a screwdriver, and a penny still makes a darn good electrical conductor. Coins are also valuable in making puzzles, as the examples on these two pages illustrate. It may help to dig into your piggybank, pocket, or purse before you begin.

Answers, page 177

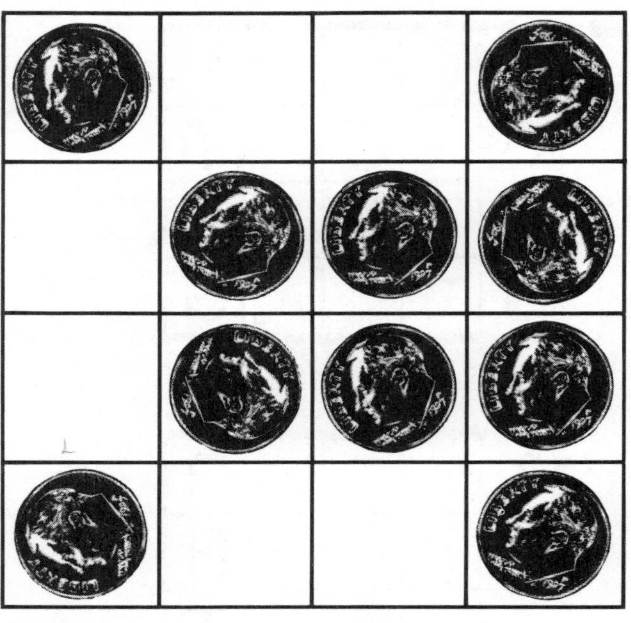

1. EVEN SO

Can you move two dimes to empty squares so that each of the eight rows and columns and the two diagonals contain an even number of coins?

2. BOWLING BALL PENNIES

This tricky brainteaser was created by the celebrated Japanese puzzlemaker Kobon Fujimura. He asks: What is the smallest number of pennies you can remove so that no equilateral triangle *of any size* will remain? The corners of the triangles are marked by the centers of the pennies.

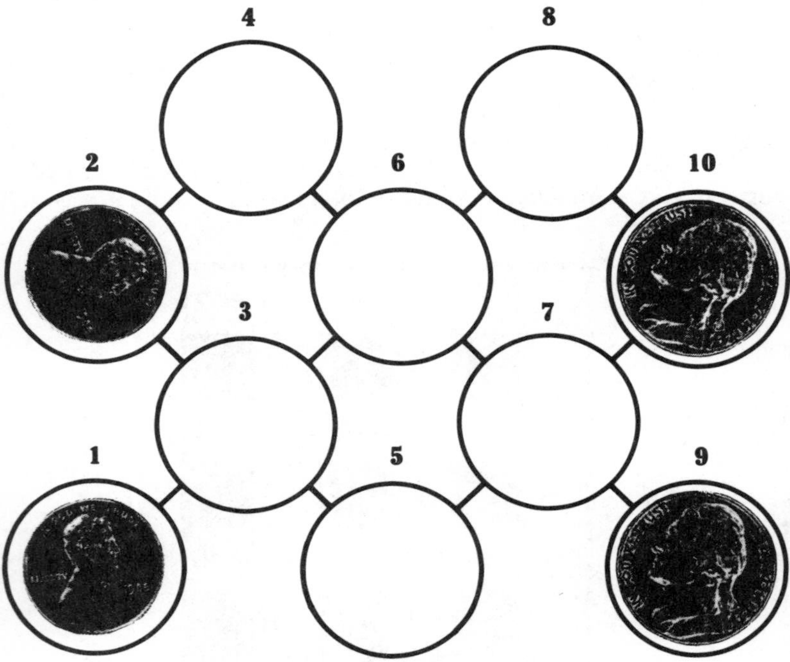

3. SWITCHBOARD

Henry Dudeney, the famous English puzzlist, invented this diabolical problem. The object is to interchange the pennies on circles 1 and 2 with the nickels on circles 9 and 10. You may move the coins—one at a time, and in any order you like—any distance along the lines (but stopping only on circles). The only restriction is that at the end of any move, a penny and a nickel may never lie on the same straight line. (Thus, you must start by moving penny 1 or 2 to circle 3, or nickel 9 or 10 to circle 7.) See if you can find any solution. For a more difficult challenge, try to find the shortest one.

4. ALL DOUBLED UP

Pick up a dime, jump it over the next two dimes on the left or right, and set it down on the following one. By a series of five such jumps, can you arrange these 10 dimes into 5 pairs? The two dimes jumped over may lie separately on the surface or be stacked in a pair. A jump may pass over a gap as well as the dimes.

5. SLIDING PENNIES

To start, arrange six pennies in the triangle shape below. The puzzle is to rearrange them into a hollow diamond hexagon (bottom) in the smallest number of móves. Each move consists of sliding one penny, without disturbing any of the others, to a new position that abuts two other pennies. The coins must remain flat on the surface at all times.

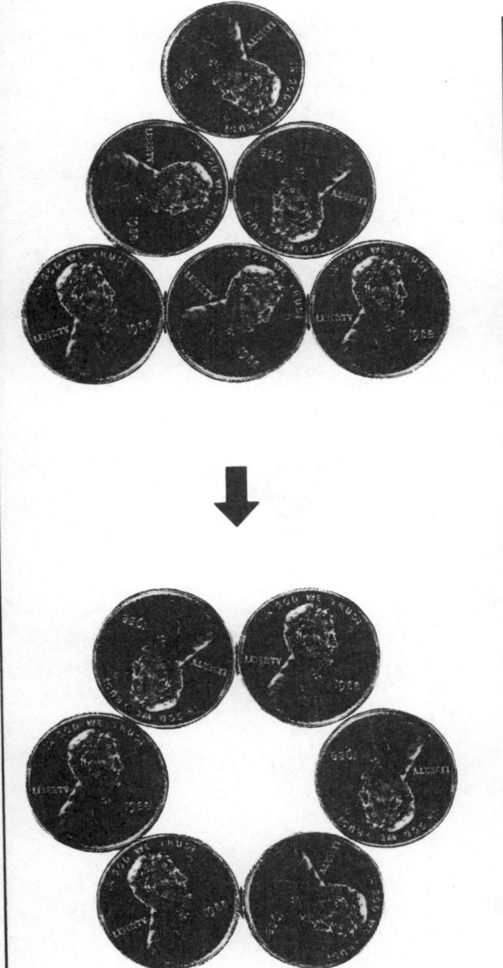

6. FAIR SHARE

Divide the 4 x 4 grid below into two halves of the same shape, each containing the same amount of money.

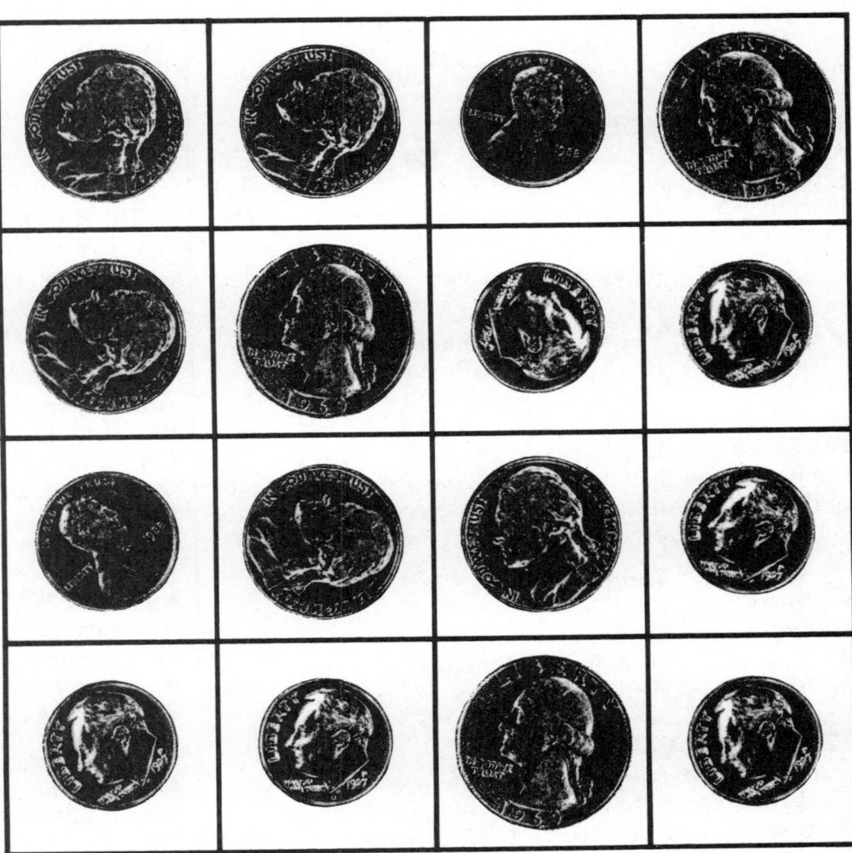

Nine Psychic Guesses ★☆

by Roger Hufford

The following problems involve tests conducted by a group of self-proclaimed psychics, who attempt to divine the identity of cards placed face down on a table. For simplicity, only the aces are used from each suit, with an occasional joker included. Given the special conditions in each problem, try to discover the identity of each card.

Answers, page 177

FIRST PSYCHIC GUESS

Abe, Bea, and Cal begin by dealing three aces face down and guessing at each card in turn (as shown below). Each of the three aces is correctly identified by at least one person. Nobody gets exactly one right answer, however, and no two persons finish with the same number of correct answers. What are the three cards?

	1st Card	2nd Card	3rd Card
Abe	Heart	Spade	Club
Bea	Heart	Diamond	Club
Cal	Diamond	Spade	Heart

SECOND PSYCHIC GUESS

Abe, Bea, and Cal repeat their test. This time everybody gets at least one right answer, but no two persons get the same number right. What are the three cards?

	1st Card	2nd Card	3rd Card
Abe	Heart	Spade	Diamond
Bea	Club	Diamond	Heart
Cal	Club	Spade	Heart

THIRD PSYCHIC GUESS

Abe, Bea, Cal, and Dee use four aces. Each ace is correctly identified by at least one person. When they check their results, they learn that each of them has the same number of correct guesses. What are the four cards?

	1st Card	2nd Card	3rd Card	4th Card
Abe	Club	Heart	Spade	Diamond
Bea	Heart	Heart	Diamond	Diamond
Cal	Diamond	Heart	Diamond	Club
Dee	Spade	Diamond	Club	Heart

FOURTH PSYCHIC GUESS

The four repeat their test. Again, each ace is correctly identified by at least one person, and everybody makes the same number of correct guesses. What are the four cards?

	1st Card	2nd Card	3rd Card	4th Card
Abe	Heart	Club	Diamond	Spade
Bea	Club	Spade	Diamond	Heart
Cal	Club	Diamond	Diamond	Club
Dee	Heart	Heart	Club	Spade

FIFTH PSYCHIC GUESS

Abe, Bea, and Cal take the test with four aces and a joker. Each card is correctly identified by at least one person. Nobody gets two in a row correct, but everybody ends with the same number of right answers. What are the five cards?

	1st Card	2nd Card	3rd Card	4th Card	5th Card
Abe	Joker	Heart	Club	Spade	Diamond
Bea	Club	Joker	Diamond	Heart	Club
Cal	Spade	Diamond	Spade	Heart	Joker

SIXTH PSYCHIC GUESS

Abe, Bea, Cal, and Dee guess at four aces and a joker. Each card is correctly identified by at least one person. Nobody gets them all right or all wrong. No two people make the same number of correct guesses. What are the five cards?

	1st Card	2nd Card	3rd Card	4th Card	5th Card
Abe	Club	Joker	Heart	Diamond	Club
Bea	Diamond	Joker	Heart	Club	Spade
Cal	Heart	Club	Spade	Diamond	Joker
Dee	Diamond	Joker	Club	Club	Spade

SEVENTH PSYCHIC GUESS

Abe, Bea, Cal, Dee, and Eb guess at four aces and a joker. Each card is correctly identified by at least one person. At the conclusion, four persons are tied in the number of correct guesses, with the fifth person having just one correct guess fewer. What are the five cards?

	1st Card	2nd Card	3rd Card	4th Card	5th Card
Abe	Club	Joker	Diamond	Club	Heart
Bea	Joker	Spade	Club	Spade	Joker
Cal	Club	Club	Heart	Diamond	Joker
Dee	Heart	Diamond	Diamond	Joker	Club
Eb	Spade	Heart	Joker	Spade	Diamond

EIGHTH PSYCHIC GUESS

Abe, Bea, Cal, Dee, Eb, and Flo take the test using four aces. Although nobody gets all answers right, there is a clear winner. Two people are tied for second-best score, and two others are tied for third-best score. What are the four cards?

	1st Card	2nd Card	3rd Card	4th Card
Abe	Spade	Spade	Club	Diamond
Bea	Heart	Diamond	Diamond	Club
Cal	Diamond	Club	Heart	Spade
Dee	Diamond	Heart	Spade	Club
Eb	Heart	Spade	Club	Diamond
Flo	Club	Spade	Diamond	Heart

NINTH PSYCHIC GUESS

Abe, Bea, Cal, Dee, and Eb guess at four aces and a joker. Each card is correctly identified by at least one person. All five people make the same number of correct guesses. What are the five cards?

	1st Card	2nd Card	3rd Card	4th Card	5th Card
Abe	Spade	Heart	Club	Joker	Diamond
Bea	Spade	Joker	Diamond	Club	Spade
Cal	Club	Diamond	Spade	Joker	Heart
Dee	Diamond	Heart	Joker	Club	Spade
Eb	Club	Joker	Diamond	Spade	Heart

4 A COLORFUL PARADE OF PUZZLES

Riddle Maze★★

by Robert Leighton

Start at the word "WHAT" in the center and find a path that leads to the exit at the bottom. The words in your path, read in order, will form a riddle. Can you solve it? *Answer, page 177*

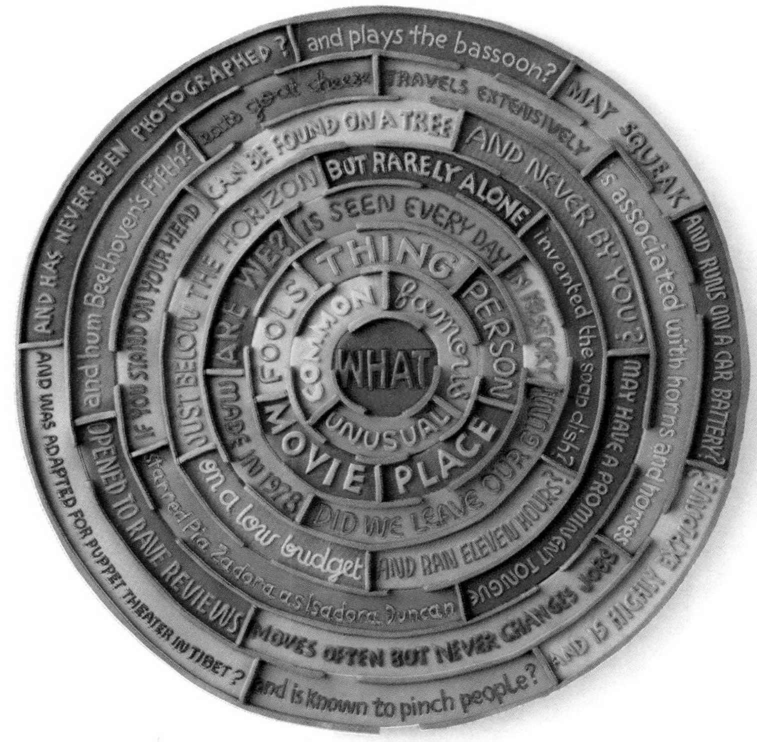

Making Connections

ILLUSTRATED BY TERESA FASOLINO

★☆

When we read recently that the invention of Velcro was inspired by the common burr, we got to wondering: How many other human inventions did Mother Nature think of first?

The animals and plants on this page display functions that parallel those of their man-made counterparts on the opposite page. The beaver dam, for instance, has an effect similar to that of the human-built dam. How many of the other 15 parallel pairs can you find? *Answers, page 177*

SUBWAY

Which Two Butterflies Are Exactly Alike? **

by Patricia Wynne

Answer, page 177

Bringing Up BABY

Follow the Bouncing Baby in this Time Sequence Puzzle ★

Photographs by Keith Glasgow

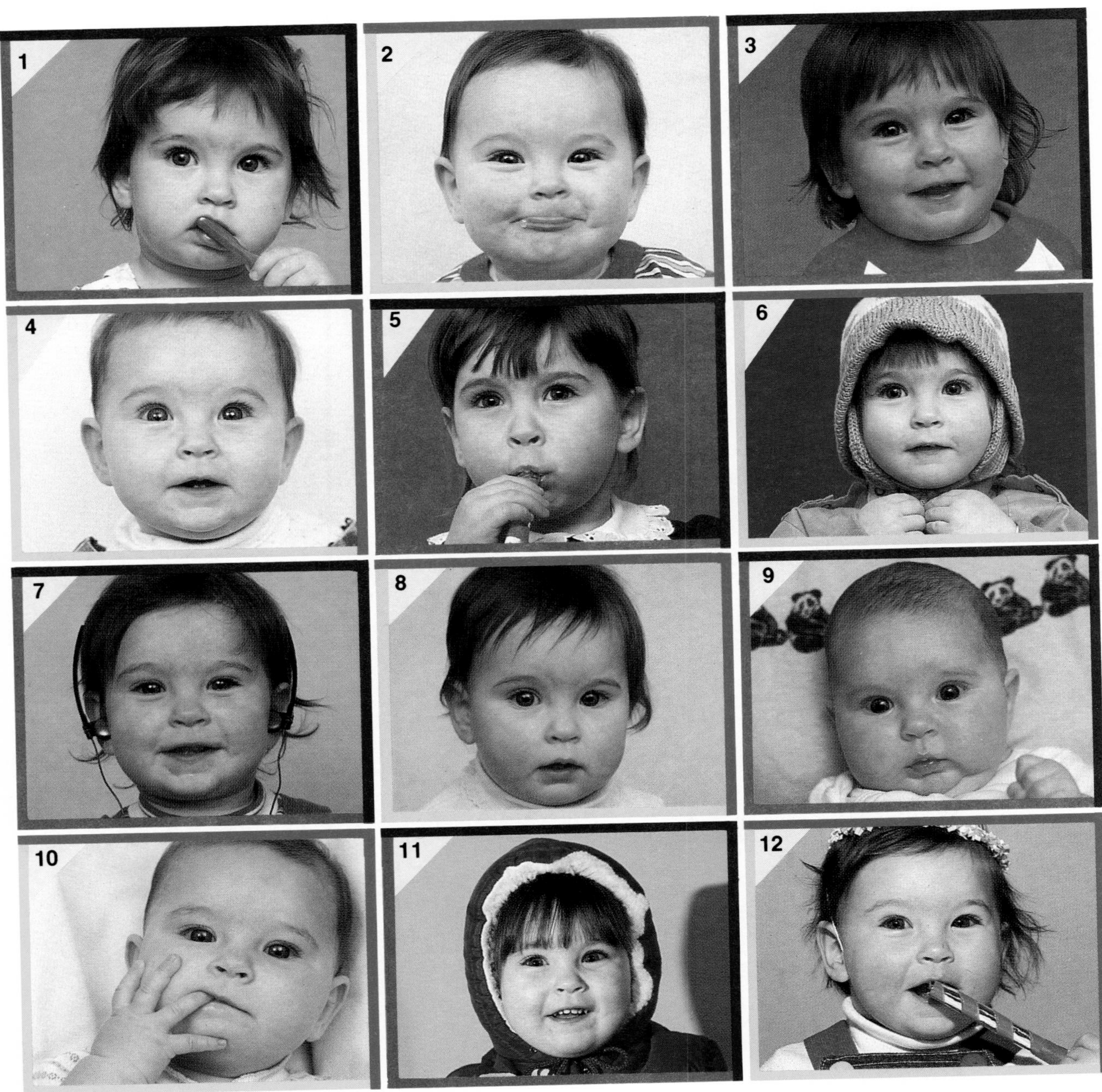

Photographer Keith Glasgow is no babe in the woods when it comes to recognizing a potential puzzle. Two years ago, after his wife gave birth to Alison, Glasgow had the idea of creating a sequence puzzle by photographing his daughter at two-month intervals. The 12 photos are a record of Alison's growth over a 24-month period. Putting them in the correct chronological order may be harder than it seems—we kid you not. *Answer, page 177*

THE EGG LORE

The jewel-like eggs on these two pages are products of a colorful folk art tradition—Ukrainian Easter eggs, or *pysanky.* Every spring in this fertile land north of the Black Sea, the simple egg is transformed into a small canvas alive with flora, fauna, an occasional human figure, and vivid geometrics.

The *pysanky* here are part of a family tradition as well as an ethnic one. Their creators are two sisters—Luba Perchyshyn and Johanna Luciow—and their daughters, Natalie Perchyshyn and Ann Luciow Kmit. The family runs the Ukrainian Gift Shop in Minneapolis.

To join the Ukrainian Easter egg hunt, look closely at the 50 eggs photographed on these pages. While some of the eggs may look alike at first glance, there are actually subtle differences between them. For example, the maroon egg painted with a design of bees and flowers, second from bottom on the far left, is nearly identical to the bee-painted egg at bottom, third from left—except that the colors of the flower petals and centers are reversed on the two eggs.

Aside from the very slight variations that exist in any hand-painted artwork, two eggs are alike in every detail. Can you find them?

Answer, page 178

THE EGG HUNT

★★

by Luba Perchyshyn and Johanna Luciow

PHOTOCRIME
MURDER FOR BREAKFAST
BY R. WAYNE SCHMITTBERGER

★★

Corpulent, cigar-chomping Lieutenant Kojumbo didn't like being called at home on Sunday to investigate the murder of Hugh Lawless. He liked it even less when he got to the scene and found that Jason Peppard and Vera Dayton, the two people who had discovered the body of the victim, had been sent home by the rookie officer at the scene. Kojumbo's spirits brightened, however, when the officer told him that Peppard had taken some photographs of the scene of the crime.

Monday morning finds Kojumbo in his office, reading the following note:

Dear Lieutenant Kojumbo,
Here are the photos you requested when you called me last night, plus a few others to give you some background. But as I told you, I'm afraid they won't be of much help, especially since the man at the door (in the third photo) has his back turned. I wrote captions to explain when and where each shot was taken.

Sincerely,
Jason Peppard
Jason Peppard

1. My former employers, Lowell Breed, Hugh Lawless, and William Schirmer, seen here from left to right, were partners in a lucrative importing business. Three months ago, just before this picture was taken, a valuable shipment of jade vanished from a storage room. I was subsequently fired as chief of security for the company.

2. Since only the three partners and I knew about the jade, I began to keep them under surveillance as best I could, hoping to earn the large reward being offered by the insurance company for the return of the jade. Nothing much had happened until yesterday morning, when I was parked across the street from Lawless's residence.

3. It was a quiet Sunday morning, and in the two hours since I had arrived at 8 A.M. the only person I saw was an elderly woman who got into a car and drove off. I walked to a delicatessen on the next block to get a cup of coffee and couldn't have been gone more than five minutes. But when I got back, I saw someone on Lawless's doorstep waiting to be let in. I barely had time to snap this photo, and never did get a look at the man's face.

4. A few minutes later, I heard what I thought was a gunshot inside. I ran to the corner to call the police, but the phone there was out of order. When I ran back, I found Lawless's next-door neighbor, Vera Dayton, at the door. She said she had also heard the shot. After I introduced myself, she opened the door with a spare key, explaining that Lawless had given it to her for safekeeping because he often locked himself out accidentally.

5. Miss Dayton led me through the house to the back, where we found Lawless slumped over the desk, shot through the chest. Evidently the killer had not had much time to search for valuables, as the bookcase and desk drawers seemed to be the only things disturbed. The alley outside leads to the next street, so it was obvious the killer had made a clean getaway.

6. Lawless appeared to have been interrupted while typing. I didn't notice it at the time I took the photo, but he's not wearing the jade ring he always kept on his right hand. He had won it in a poker game from Lowell Breed, who was always trying to buy it back.

PHOTOGRAPHY BY DAN NELKEN

Although Peppard had told Lieutenant Kojumbo that he didn't think his photos would help, Kojumbo was able to solve the case by studying them. To make sure of one point, he called everyone connected with the case to find out when each had last visited the deceased. All of them denied having seen Lawless that weekend, but Schirmer admitted he had visited Lawless briefly late Friday afternoon.

Whom does Kojumbo arrest for murder? *Answer, page 178*

Kojumbo
MAKE THE CONVERSION!
2
3
4
5
6
I suspect one of my partners of

GOOD HEAVENS!

COLLAGE BY JOHN CRAIG

NASA has just released this earth-shaking photograph of the galaxy, along with analysis by astronomers Cosmo and Stella O'Rion.

"So far," says Stella of the picture that rocks established views of the heavens, "we've been able to identify 56 objects surrounding the planet Earth. Each suggests the name of a celestial body—the planets, sun, moon, stars, and so on. For instance, that's a can of Comet cleanser orbiting at far right, and on it is perched a starfish."

Can you contribute to man's knowledge of the universe by identifying the remaining 54 objects?

Answers, page 178

Scenic Route

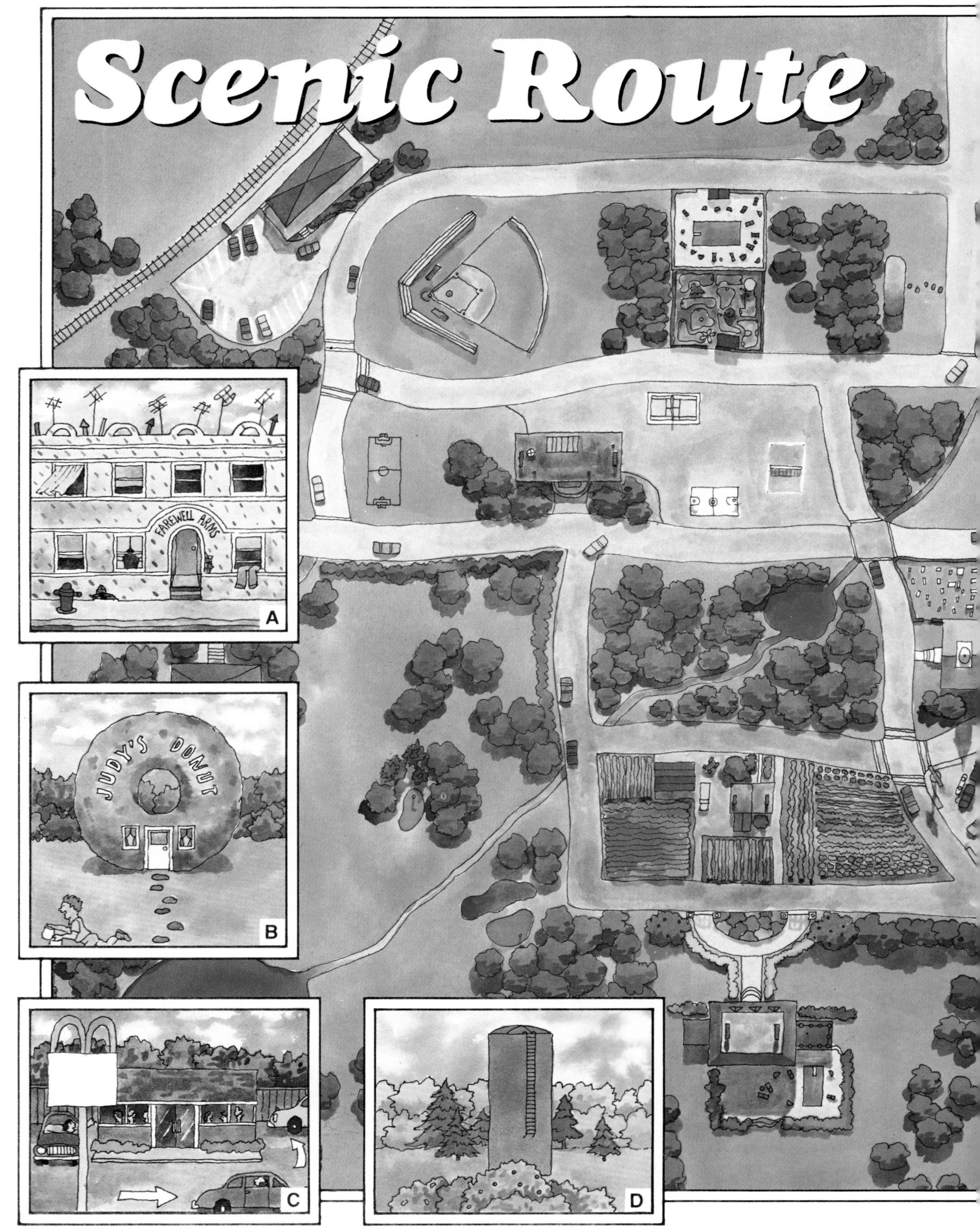

PUZZLE BY SCOTT MARLEY ★★ ILLUSTRATIONS BY SANDRA FORREST

ir Stevens expected a 10-minute cab ride from the train station (upper left) to the ouse of the friend she was visiting. But when the trip took much longer, she sus- d the driver had taken a roundabout course to boost his fare.

cabbie was clever enough not to cross his path or pass the same place twice. But vas cleverer: By comparing the aerial view shown here with eight sights she'd no- along the way (labeled A–H, but not necessarily in the order she saw them), she d out the driver's "scenic route". Can you do the same, and also discover which she was visiting? The small views are not shown at the same hour as the aerial so ignore shadows and the positions of cars and people. *Answer, page 179*

LOGIC COMIX PRESENTS
FINAL CURTAIN
starring STELLA BRANDT
STORY by KATHY KESTING AND MIKE SHENK
ILLUSTRATIONS by FRANK SPRINGER

ONE WILL BE THE VICTIM...
ARLENE
BASIL
CHRIS
DELIA
ELEANOR
FORREST
ONE WILL BE THE MURDERER!!

BLAM

NOT BAD BUT WE'LL REHEARSE IT AGAIN AFTER A BREAK. FIRST, LET ME INTRODUCE STELLA BRANDT OF THE CLARION!

SHE'S DOING A STORY ON THE PLAY. STELLA, I'M SURE YOU KNOW FORREST BLAKE, OUR STAR... ELEANOR CASSELL-BLAKE, HIS WIFE IN THE SHOW AS WELL AS LIFE, AND CHRIS MITCHELL AND DELIA DESCHAMPS IN SUPPORTING PARTS!

OH, STELLA, THIS IS MY WIFE AND OUR PRODUCER, ARLENE.

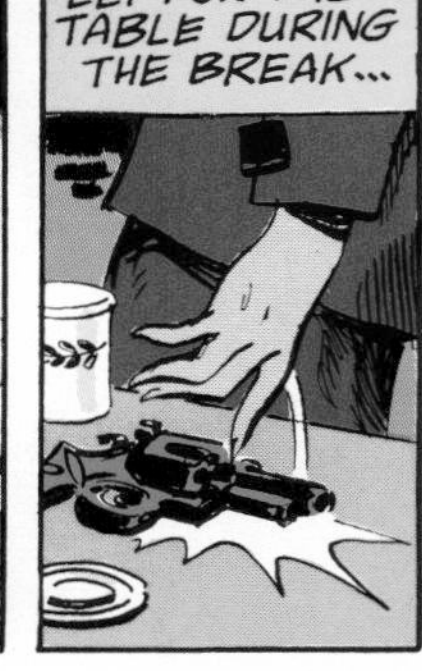
THE GUN IS LEFT ON THE TABLE DURING THE BREAK...

DELIA AGREES TO BE INTERVIEWED AS THE CAST HEADS TO THE DRESSING ROOMS--AND ONLY ONE PERSON KNOWS OF THE DRAMA THAT IS ABOUT TO UNFOLD...
F
E
B
A
C
D

SO, DELIA, HOW DOES IT FEEL TO BE ON BROADWAY FOR THE FIRST TIME?
D

FABULOUS! I'M SO EXCITED!

IS THIS CHRIS'S FIRST SHOW, TOO?
NO, JUST HIS FIRST LEAD. HE WAS THE STAR UNTIL ARLENE GOT FORREST TO JOIN US.
HEY, CHRIS, CAN WE COME IN?
D

AS YOU CAN SEE, CHRIS IS A GREAT ARTIST, TOO.
WOW! CHRIS, DO YOU THINK I COULD USE SOME OF YOUR DRAWINGS WITH MY STORY!
UH, SURE, I GUESS.
E
C

CHRIS, DO YOU HAVE ANY MATCHES?
YEAH, SURE, ELEANOR. HERE.
C
E

IT WOULD BE GREAT IF I COULD GET ONE SKETCH OF EACH OF YOU.
I THINK I'LL DRAW DELIA RIGHT NOW...
E
C

AND I'LL ASK YOUR DIRECTOR IF I HAVE TIME TO TALK TO ELEANOR.
F
B
A

YOU'VE GOT A FEW MINUTES BEFORE WE START AGAIN. JUST BE QUICK.
THANKS.
F
E
B
MISS CASSEL-BLAKE, CAN I TALK TO YOU?

SORRY ABOUT MY APPEARANCE--JUST DOING MY AEROBICS. COME ON IN.

HOW DO YOU FEEL PLAYING OPPOSITE YOUR HUSBAND... AS HIS KILLER, NO LESS?
IT'S KIND OF FUN... A GREAT WAY TO KEEP FORREST IN LINE, TOO.

WELL, IT'S TIME TO GET BACK ONSTAGE.
MAYBE WE CAN CONTINUE THIS LATER?

CERTAINLY. I'LL BE OUT IN A MINUTE.

COME ON, FORREST...YOU'RE ON!
IT WOULD BE JUST AS WELL IF THE BUM NEVER SHOWED UP!
F
E
B
A

SORRY I'M LATE.
AT LEAST YOU'RE HERE. NOW SEE IF YOU CAN DIE RIGHT.

DO YOU KNOW WHO PUT THE BULLETS IN THE GUN?

ANSWER, PAGE 179

5 WORDPLAY AND OTHER FORMS OF VERBAL ABUSE

Wumble's Candy★★

by Sidney Kravitz

When the latest batch of chocolate bars came from the Wumble's Candy Company factory, Mr. Wumble was furious. The letters of the company's name, impressed into the squares of chocolate, were all out of order.

"Idiot!" hollered Mr. Wumble at the factory foreman. "If two people share a Wumble's Candy bar, they should each get a piece of the same size and shape, with all the letters of WUMBLE'S CANDY on each piece!"

"They still can," replied the foreman, "if they break the bar along the lines in the right way."

How?

Answer, page 179

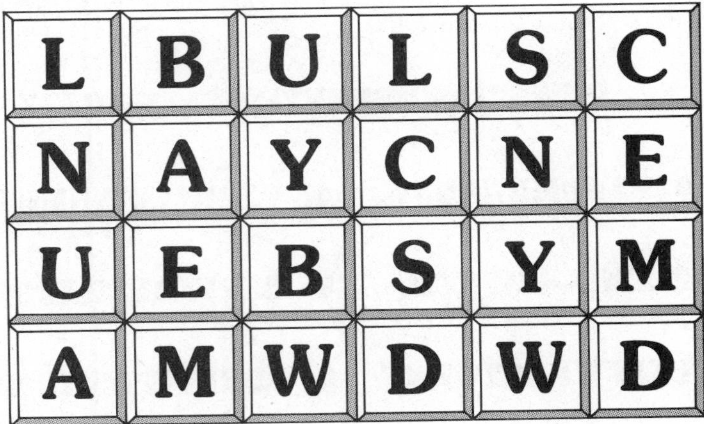

Wit Twisters ★☆

by Arthur Swan

A Wit Twister is an anagram puzzle in a poem. Each puzzle is missing three or more words that are made up of the same letters in different orders (like ORGAN, ARGON, and GROAN).

The object is to determine the missing words, using the verse's meaning and meter as clues. Dashes indicate word length. To get you started, the first two words in Puzzle #1 have been filled in for you. *Answers, page 179*

1. BITTER SUITE

Quaint I T E M S this hotel supplies,
That don't appear upon the bill.
I speak of roaches, M I T E S, and flies.
You _ _ _ _ _ and slap. They're with you still!
At _ _ _ _ _, each guest
_ _ _ _ _ pained screams
That ought to plague the owner's dreams.

2. CASE HISTORY

His _ _ _ _ _ _ eyes and stumbling gait
Betray a _ _ _ _ _ _ sober state.
Yet out he goes to tend his crops:
One field of _ _ _ _ _ _, three of hops!

3. BUENAS NOCHES

_ _ _ _ _ Gonzales, sleeping, dreams of bliss.
A blonde _ _ _ _ _ beauty trades him kiss
for kiss.
His _ _ _ _ _ awakes his dark-haired Latin bride,
Who tingles still from thrills *her* dreams supplied.

4. GUESS WHO'S COMING TO DINNER

"Look! Native _ _ _ _! How quaint!" she cried.
"The doors aren't _ _ _ _. Let's look inside!"
Her husband's "_ _ _ _" was overruled.
_ _ _ _ they were cooked ere evening cooled.

5. TROPICAL DISH

Tart juice of _ _ _ _ _ the grinning lady sipped.
Through _ _ _ _ _ of swamp she'd sought this
waterfall.
From pools of _ _ _ _ _, an alligator slipped
And ate that lady, _ _ _ _ _, fruit drink, and all!

6. HORROR MOVIE

She bolts the door. It's _ _ _ _ _ here inside,
Where suffocating _ _ _ _ _ prompt her
to hide.
But now she _ _ _ _ _ no better than before:
The dread pursuer breathes outside her door.

7. BANK NOTES

The birds that _ _ _ _ _ _ this spring
had young,
Yet not one _ _ _ _ _ _ they hung!
They stole their food, though did no wrong,
Since they _ _ _ _ _ _ in full song.

8. M IS FOR . . .

Like many _ _ _ _ _ _ _, when her brood
Makes plans for hikes and picnic food,
She fills the _ _ _ _ _ _ _, packs supplies,
And tries with cheer to _ _ _ _ _ _ _ sighs.

Alphaswitch ★☆

by Jules Roth

Each line of 26 letters below contains the complete alphabet in scrambled order. The object is to interchange any two letters to form the longest possible word reading from left to right in consecutive letters. For example, in the top line, you could switch the C and the M to get MATCH (5 letters); or the V and the E, to get DONKEY (6); or best of all, the R and the N, to form SPLENDOR (8). To be acceptable, a word must be a boldface entry in *Webster's Third New International Dictionary (Unabridged)*. Your score for each line is the number of letters in the longest word you form. A score of 45 is good, and 49 is excellent. Our best score is 52.

Answers, page 179

Ex. QUWSPLERDONKVYIFGCATMHBJZX

1. GQWIXTRYSCALFDEPZHUMKNOBJV

2. DJFLOUBPSENATXRKMIGHZWYVCQ

3. FXDIMBANYRUPTCKLEWHOSZVJGQ

4. VXZBACQINGMUPHYLSTEROJDKWF

5. BJPVFRUNKEDOGWITCHMALSZYXQ

6. FDRQWSYLPTOMBINEXACHUGKZJV

Caveat Emptor ★☆

by Robert Leighton

What kid hasn't sent away his hard-earned allowance for a pair of x-ray specs or other miracle of science advertised in the back of a comic book? For his two dollars he gets a vivid lesson in the sometimes misleading art of advertising. The ads on this page offer eight of these spectacular items ("Amaze your friends!" "Fool your enemies!"), which are actually common, ordinary, even worthless objects. Can you read between the lines and identify the vastly overpriced items these ads describe?

Answers, page 179

THE BIG BANG!

Scientists think our Universe may have started with a single burst of light and energy! Now with MINIATURE COMBUSTIBLES™ you can STAND WITNESS at the BEGINNING OF TIME! Easy to use—no goggles required. Pack of 20, just **$1.59.**

ART LOVERS, REJOICE!

Thousands of reproductions of this world-famous pocket-size wire sculpture have already been sold. Is it the graceful, curving lines? Or the much-heralded viselike grip it has become known for? You decide! Order now before they're all gone! Only **$3.00, 2 for $6.50!**

THE WONDERS OF ENGRAVING!

It's like having U.S. history in your pocket! Miniature portraits of America's best-loved presidents, Washington sites, and more. Richly detailed copper and silver engravings. Set of four, just **$3.50.**

Movie Setting Souvenirs

They said we couldn't do it, but we are! For a limited time, our LEADING HOLLYWOOD PROP HOUSE is dividing up and selling—yes, SELLING—parcels of this famous movie setting. You've seen it featured in *Lawrence of Arabia*, *Beach Blanket Bingo*, and *Ishtar*! Our warehouse must be cleared! Own a vial of movie history—a great conversation piece! Only **$4.50.**

YEARS OF BACKYARD FUN!

Make your own jungle gym! This sturdy, all-weather structure for the yard provides hundreds of years of enjoyment! Just add water—then stand back! Has natural oak finish. Just **$2.50.**

DEFY GRAVITY

As you command water—or any liquid—to flow upwards! Could you be tampering with the secrets of the Earth? Your friends will be amazed! Just **$1.99.**

Random Digit Generator!

Today's multimillion-dollar computers need special programs to generate random numbers. But this GEOMETRICALLY DESIGNED device ingeniously bypasses computer technology to provide random numbers quickly and easily! Exciting? You bet! Batteries not required. Only **$3.00.**

CRYSTALS! CRYSTALS! CRYSTALS!

Miniature, sparkling white crystals harvested in exotic Hawaii make perfect specimens for studying the wonders of science! Each educationally decorated packet contains hundreds of refined crystals. Completely safe and non-toxic! Only **$2.95.**

Knight Moves ★

by Edith Rudy

This word search has a twist we think will capture your interest. Each of the 30 words and phrases listed below is hidden somewhere within the rank and file of the grid. The twist: All names of chessmen appearing in the list have been replaced in the grid with the appropriate symbol. As usual, an answer may read horizontally, vertically, or diagonally, but always in a straight line. If you get stalemated while solving, you can always check the *Answers, page 179*

```
T I S Y       A L ♙ L       A ♗ C H
E Q U R       E R S B       S Y O A
D R D U       O F H N       ♔ E I G
H E L B A T D N U O R E H T F O S ♘
  N B R ♖ T S A N P T D D A O J Y
    A E S L W H E R H E D E ♔ S
      T Z T Y I N ♘ E Y W C I
      N ♔ I T N H E A M O ♙ R
      A E C S N B R F B E F A
      C O T O ♕ R R R E P Y E
      F ♘ H I L ♔ A I E A C Y
      O R E E S E N C D P L E
      ♗ I ♔ A L D T A Y G S H
      H D S ♔ I H R N L L E T
      C E E A I O T ♕ H A E F
      R R N S F E R A N D ♕ O
      A S G ♕ M D T H ♘ Y I E
      T H L E R O M O R S V I
      E S I A N D N E M ♘ A ♖
    B ♖ E S H I E L D S T E S A
  N ♔ R E H T U L N I T R A M D S
L A E C A L S E N N A ♕ U Y S F R O
S ♖ B L E M M ♔ N E H P E T S T H E
R U B A I Y S ♙ I N G G R O U N D S
A T E D I T H R E K O R B ♙ R U D Y
```

ALAN KING
ARCHBISHOP OF CANTERBURY
BISHOP DESMOND TUTU
BROOKE SHIELDS
BROOKLYN BRIDGE
ELLERY QUEEN
GLADYS KNIGHT
JOEY BISHOP
KING COBRA
KING LEAR
KING OF KINGS
KNIGHT-ERRANT
KNIGHT RIDER
KNIGHTS OF THE ROUND TABLE
MARTIN LUTHER KING
MEL BROOKS
NAT KING COLE
PAWNBROKER
PAWNEE INDIANS
PAWNSHOP
QUEEN ANNE'S LACE
QUEEN BEE
QUEEN FOR A DAY
QUEEN-SIZE BED
ROOKIE OF THE YEAR
SPAWNING GROUNDS
STEPHEN KING
TED KNIGHT
THE AFRICAN QUEEN
THE KING'S ENGLISH

Rebusiness★★

by Jay Roth

A rebus is a puzzle in which you put pictures together to make words or names. For example, pictures of a Christmas song, an oak tree, and an award could go together (phonetically) to make CAROL-OAK-HONOR, or "Carroll O'Connor."

We made up seven rebuses on famous names, each using exactly three pictures. But there's been some monkey business in our office lately, and now someone has shuffled all 21 pictures.

Fortunately, we still remember the clues we wrote for the seven names. Can you put the pictures back together in the right order and discover all seven?

Answers, page 179

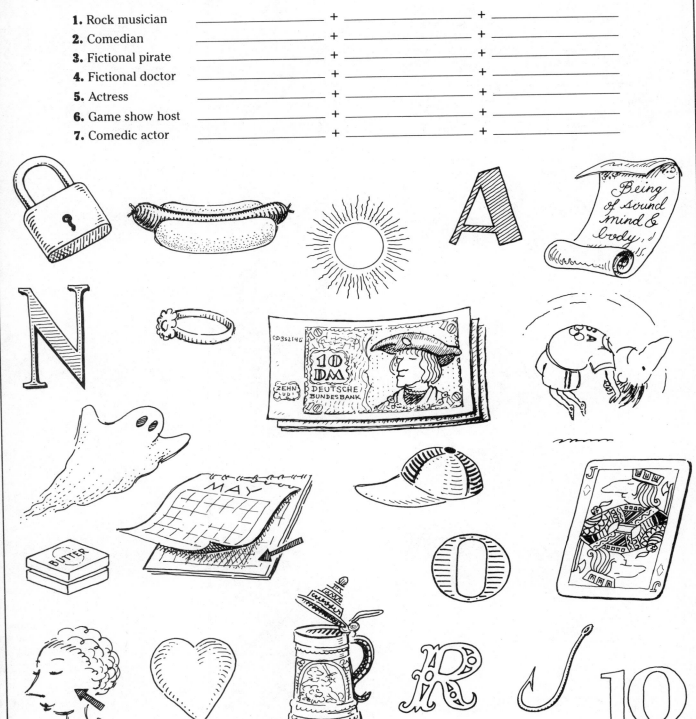

1. Rock musician ________ + ________ + ________
2. Comedian ________ + ________ + ________
3. Fictional pirate ________ + ________ + ________
4. Fictional doctor ________ + ________ + ________
5. Actress ________ + ________ + ________
6. Game show host ________ + ________ + ________
7. Comedic actor ________ + ________ + ________

Pro Test ★☆

by Robert Leighton

Time out while some pros take the field. As you can quickly see, however, this is not your ordinary 11-man team. Each of these football players represents a word beginning with the syllable PRO-. For example, player A, who's been benched for excessive punning, illustrates the word PROSCRIBE (pro scribe), while the equally guilty player B, sitting next to him, is PROLONGING. How many of the other answers among this profusion of pros can you provide? *Answers, page 180*

MISPLACED ITEMS
N
F L

Half and Half ★★

by Will Shortz

The secret to solving this puzzle is to divide and conquer. Each answer is a six-letter word that is to be divided in the middle and entered downward in the diagram, the first half in the squares designated by the first number of the clue, the second half in the squares designated by the second number. Each clue is presented in the style of TV's *Password*—a group of one-word hints that may or may not be direct synonyms of the answer. For example, in clue 1–15, "Poll," "Observe," and "Geological" all suggest the answer SURVEY, the first two directly and the third indirectly. That answer is entered beginning in the squares marked 1 and ending in the ones marked 15. You now have not only the answer to 1–15 but also the first half of 1–16 (SUR-) and the second half of 2–15 (-VEY). Every word half appears in at least two answers. Approach the puzzle with a flexible mind and soon you *will* know the half of it. *Answers, page 180*

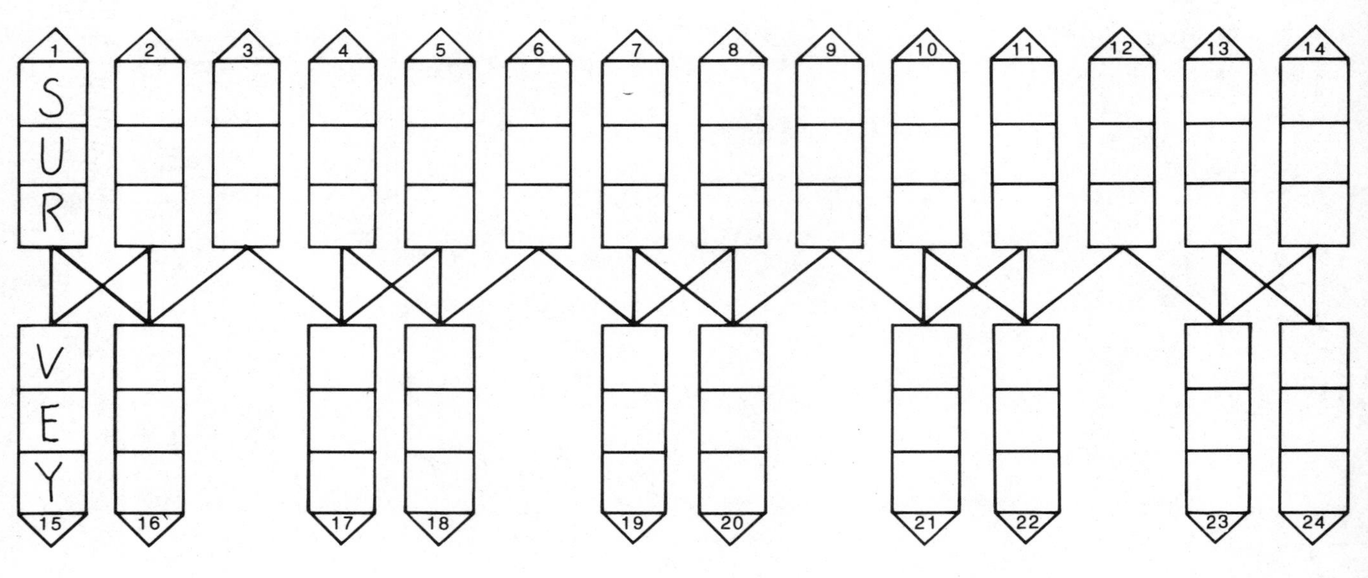

1-15	Poll	Observe	Geological
1-16	Board	Ocean	Daredevil
2-15	Transport	Deliver	Idea
2-16	Meet	Discuss	Bestow
3-16	Iron	Player	Green
3-17	Rule	Fleece	Opportunity
4-17	Flower	Vegetable	Variety
4-18	Mix	Confuse	Voice
5-17	Prison	Game	Official
5-18	Sing	Bird	Quaver
6-18	Horse	Barn	Steady
6-19	Russia	Dictator	Yalta
7-19	Elf	Mischievous	Halloween
7-20	Wine	Glass	Stem
8-19	String	Bow	Concerto
8-20	Lavender	Shrinking	Bloom
9-20	Village	Tragedy	Shakespeare
9-21	Carpenter	Detective	Head
10-21	Reader	Elementary	Paint
10-22	Father	Church	Catholic
11-21	Past	Earlier	Once
11-22	Sherwood	Black	Primeval
12-22	Capture	Police	Book
12-23	Reach	Come	Guests
13-23	Salad	Leaf	Chicory
13-24	Last	Abide	Suffer
14-23	Indian	Son	Intelligence
14-24	Mother	Second	Wilderness

Opposites Attract★★★

by Merl Reagle

The list below contains only half of the words you'll need to complete this criss-cross puzzle. The other half are the antonyms, or opposites, of the words in the list. For example, if HEAVY were in the list, both HEAVY and LIGHT would go in the grid. To help you in solving, each word crosses its own antonym in the diagram. Thus, HEAVY would cross LIGHT at their common letter, H. Some words in the list have more than one antonym, so stay flexible. The opposite of RIGHT, for example, could be either LEFT or WRONG. When the puzzle is completed, the letters in the 48 shaded squares can be arranged to spell the sentence WHIZ QUICKLY DERIVES OPPOSITES FROM A VERY VEXING JUMBLE. *Answers, page 180*

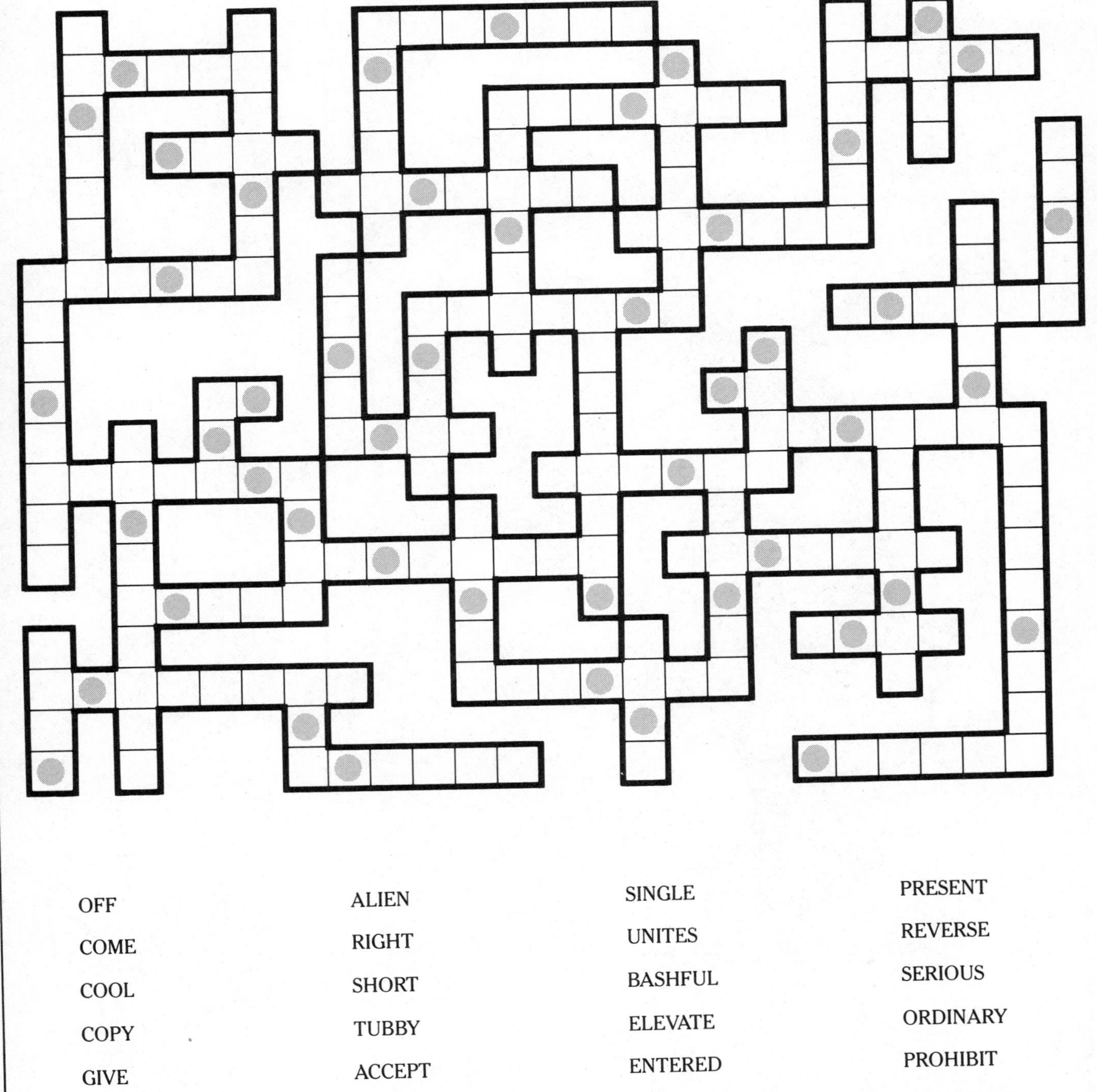

OFF	ALIEN	SINGLE	PRESENT
COME	RIGHT	UNITES	REVERSE
COOL	SHORT	BASHFUL	SERIOUS
COPY	TUBBY	ELEVATE	ORDINARY
GIVE	ACCEPT	ENTERED	PROHIBIT
SANE	DEDUCT	FAILURE	DISPARAGE

Evolution ★☆

by Trina Finholt

Twenty-one four-footed animals are camouflaged in this picnic scene. The trick is that each animal has adapted itself to its surroundings by changing one letter in its name. That COAT on the ground, for example, is a GOAT in disguise. In forming answers, count only the general names of animals—not, for example, the names for one gender (like EWE), breeds (like TERRIER), or young (like CALF). Note: One object in the picture stands for two names. A score of 10 or more is good; 15 is excellent. Getting all 21 shows extreme advancement on the evolutionary scale. *Answers, page 180*

B

Limbericks ★☆

by Lola Schancer

A good limerick always ends with a twist, but a *limberick* ends every line with one. To solve, unscramble the five words given in capital letters to complete each verse. A good sense of pun helps.

Answers, page 180

1. LOFTY AMBITION

Two brothers named Wong couldn't EQTUI ☐☐☐☐☐
Pull off their first aeroplane THIFLG ☐☐☐☐☐☐.
When their rig crashed and DRUBEN ☐☐☐☐☐☐☐,
They both finally ENDREAL ☐☐☐☐☐☐☐
Two Wongs never could make a GHRWIT ☐☐☐☐☐☐.

2. FOR WANT OF A MALE

A prudish old spinster, a CLIRE ☐☐☐☐☐,
Whose conduct by day was CLAGINE ☐☐☐☐☐☐☐,
Would go to STEREXEM ☐☐☐☐☐☐☐☐
At night in her RADEMS ☐☐☐☐☐☐
And wickedly romp with Tom CLEKLES ☐☐☐☐☐☐☐.

3. GRAVE UNDERTAKING

A Russian who danced the TAVOTEG ☐☐☐☐☐☐☐
On the deck of an Englishman's CYATH ☐☐☐☐☐
Lost his balance and WREDDON ☐☐☐☐☐☐☐
And was buried on ODRUNG ☐☐☐☐☐☐—
That's what's known as a Communist OPTL ☐☐☐☐.

4. FOOTLOOSE

That old dame in a shoe was a FROGE ☐☐☐☐☐:
To her kids she was maid, cook, and FRAUCHUFE ☐☐☐☐☐☐☐☐☐.
Then the day that her DOROB ☐☐☐☐☐
Left the nest, she was WREDSH ☐☐☐☐☐☐,
Packed her bags and moved into a EAROLF ☐☐☐☐☐☐.

5. SYLPH CONTROL

The doc told the heavy ETOGURM ☐☐☐☐☐☐☐,
"Please diet, and don't YOBISED ☐☐☐☐☐☐☐;
You can eat cottage ESHECE ☐☐☐☐☐☐
Just as much as you APELES ☐☐☐☐☐☐,
So finish your curds and then IHGEW ☐☐☐☐☐."

Wacky Wordies★☆

by *Games* Readers

The object of this game is to discover the familiar word, phrase, or saying represented by each arrangement of letters and/or symbols. For example, box 1a below depicts "buckle up," while 1b shows "in between jobs." These bits of literate lunacy were all devised by readers of *Games*.

Answers, page 181

	a	b	c	d	e
1	E L K C U B	job in job	pig pig pig	la ÷ bor	b b a u t t h
2	yoursmokeeyes	oLDER	bbaseball	post	my cu p
3	cof fee	p a o y n m c	fi$$st	ovensovensovensovens	pos'-i'-tive'
4	come your hands	Freu ian	the teh the	BY AND	five
5	UE SS EI . TH	broke	power	. d o o g	strike strike strike you're
6	shave	LINE O.CLOCK	ed ot overs	VEGETABLE	decimal decimal decimal
7	limit limit limit	Y T I L I B O M	s d cousin	in pattern a	tax GAINS

Word Ladders ★☆

by Weslie C. Pin

The object of a Word Ladder is to change one given word into another, by altering one letter at a time, and making a common, uncapitalized English word at each step on the way. No letters should be scrambled from one step to the next. For example, to change COLD into WARM in four steps, you could write COLD, CORD, WORD, WARD, WARM. How many of the four autumn-related Word Ladders below can you complete in the number of steps listed? *Answers, page 180*

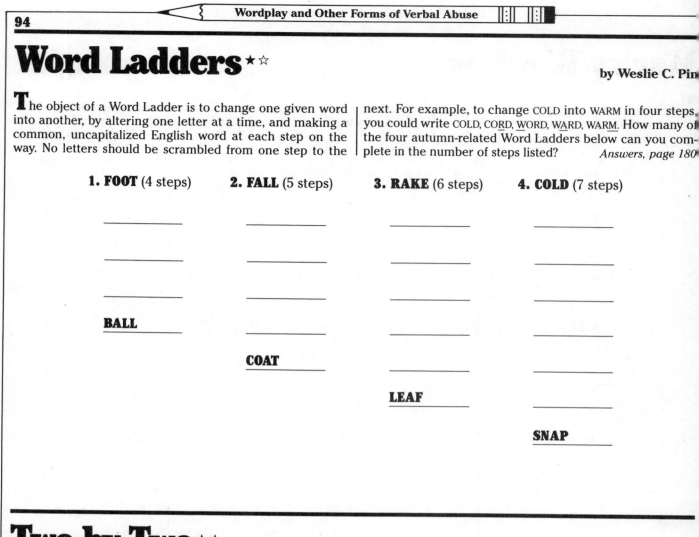

1. FOOT (4 steps)

____

____

____

BALL

2. FALL (5 steps)

____

____

____

____

COAT

3. RAKE (6 steps)

____

____

____

____

____

LEAF

4. COLD (7 steps)

____

____

____

____

____

____

SNAP

Two by Two ★★

by N. M. Meyer

Can you fill in the blanks in these 13 six-letter words using each letter of the alphabet only once? Cross the letters off as you use them. Careful—a few lines can be filled in in more than one way, but the puzzle has only one complete answer.

Answer, page 180

A B C D E F G H I J K L M N O P Q R S T U V W X Y Z

1. MI __ __ AP

2. NA __ __ IN

3. DE __ __ AY

4. BO __ __ AR

5. MO __ __ UE

6. ST __ __ GY

7. DY __ __ MO

8. EN __ __ ME

9. VE __ __ ET

10. DI __ __ IT

11. NE __ __ LA

12. UN __ __ UE

13. OU __ __ OX

Alphabet Soup★★

by David Greenwald

Chowderheads will find this puzzle to their taste. The bowl of alphabet soup and the decorated mat it rests on contain all the ingredients you'll need to sound out the 15 words defined below. To solve each clue, take one of the letters from the stock and phonetically place it before or after one of the pictures from the mat. For example, the first answer, cherry, is CHAIR plus E. Since the letters and pictures are used once each, you may cross them out as you go. Some of the answers are tricky, so use your noodle.

Answers, page 180

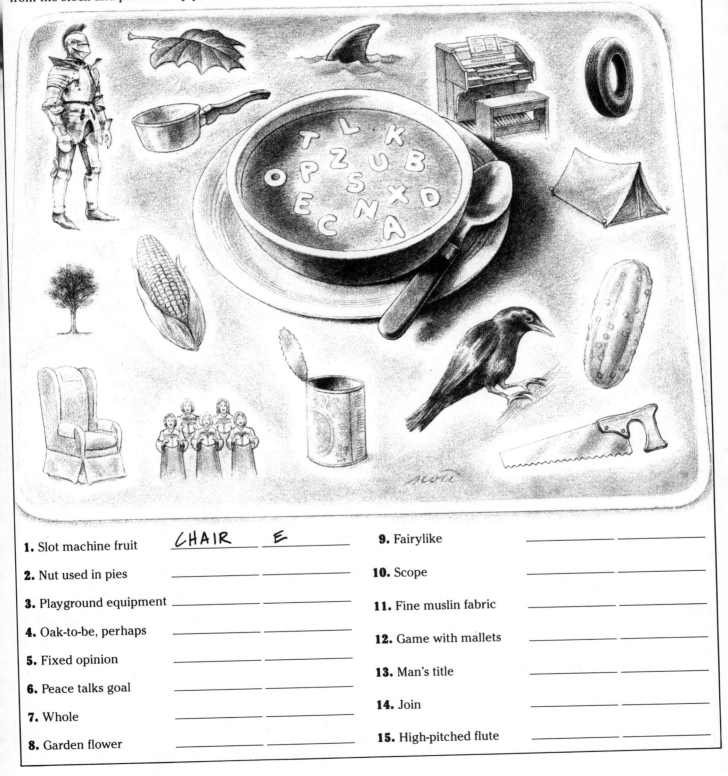

1. Slot machine fruit CHAIR E
2. Nut used in pies ______ ______
3. Playground equipment ______ ______
4. Oak-to-be, perhaps ______ ______
5. Fixed opinion ______ ______
6. Peace talks goal ______ ______
7. Whole ______ ______
8. Garden flower ______ ______
9. Fairylike ______ ______
10. Scope ______ ______
11. Fine muslin fabric ______ ______
12. Game with mallets ______ ______
13. Man's title ______ ______
14. Join ______ ______
15. High-pitched flute ______ ______

Literary Connections★★

by Adam Sumera

When our literature teacher told us to trace the connections between these 12 well-known works, we doubt that this is quite what she meant. Fill in the boxes with the titles of literary works (one is a play, and one is an epic poem; the rest are novels). We've drawn lines connecting identical letters, so when you fill a box with a letter, put the same letter in the box at the other end of the line. Spaces have been removed from titles that are two or more words long. We've filled in one letter in each answer to get you started. Can you fill in the rest?

Answers, page 180

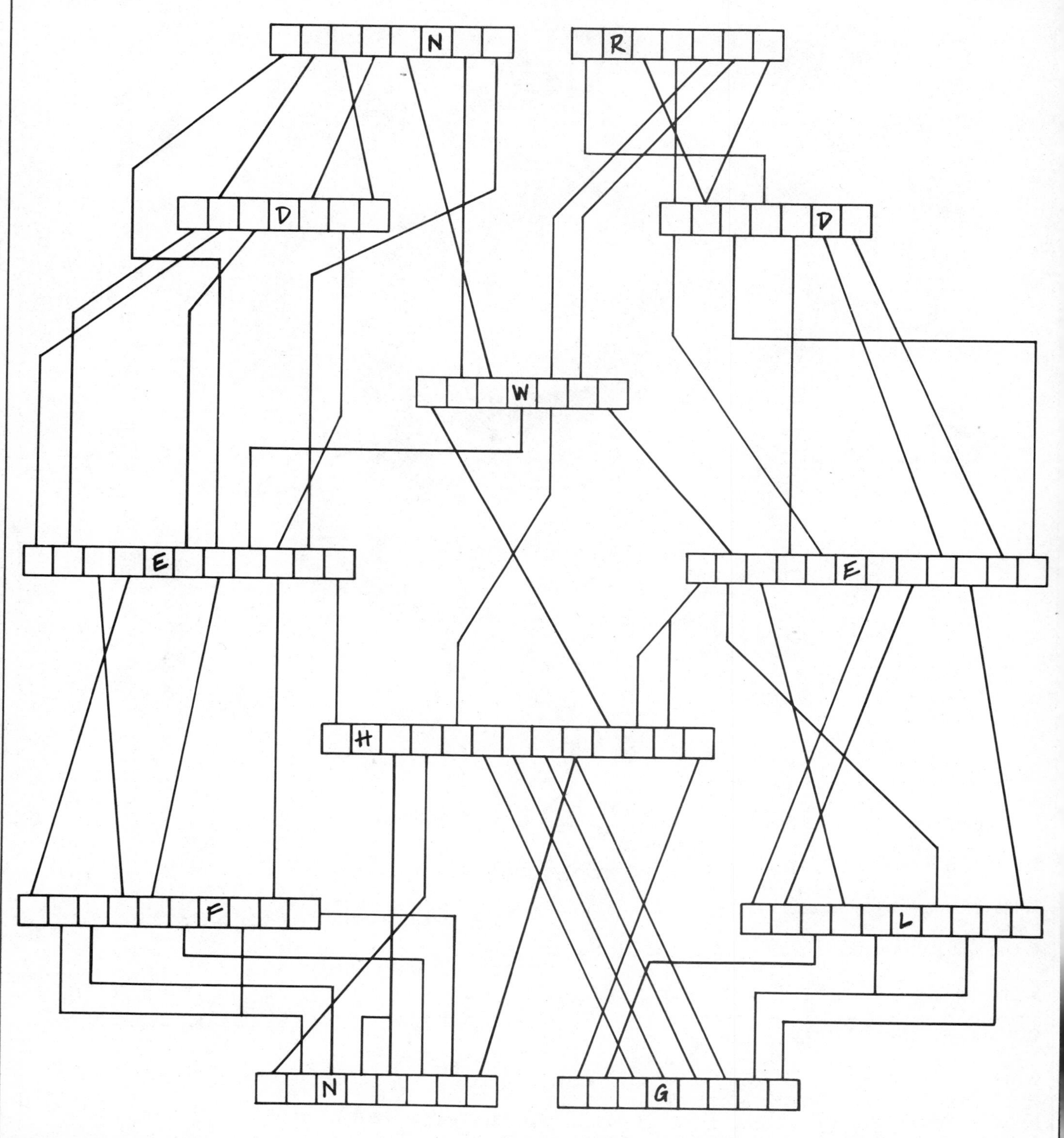

Solitaire Hangman ★☆

by R. Wayne Schmittberger

As in the two-player version of Hangman, the object of this solitaire challenge is to guess the identity of a word before being "hanged."

To begin, choose any letter of the alphabet you think might be in word I. Suppose you pick N. Go to the letter chart on the right and find the number listed in row N of column I (because you are working on word I). The number is 10; you now look in box number 10 in the Position Chart at the bottom of the page and find the number 4. This means the letter N occurs in the fourth position (and nowhere else) in word I. If a letter occurs more than once in a word, the Position Chart will show all its locations.

If you find a 0 in the Position Chart, then that letter does not appear in the word. As a penalty for an incorrect guess, you must draw part of a stick figure below the scaffold beside the word blanks. On your first incorrect guess, draw the head; on the second, the body; and on the next four, the arms and legs. If you complete the figure (that is, make six incorrect guesses) before identifying the word, you are "hanged."

If you can identify seven of the 10 words below before being "hanged," you're a real pro. *Answers, page 180*

I. ___ ___ ___ N ___ ___ ___ ___ (1 2 3 4 5 6 7 8)

II. ___ ___ ___ ___ ___ ___ ___ ___ (1 2 3 4 5 6 7 8)

III. ___ ___ ___ ___ ___ ___ ___ (1 2 3 4 5 6 7)

IV. ___ ___ ___ ___ ___ ___ ___ ___ (1 2 3 4 5 6 7 8)

V. ___ ___ ___ ___ ___ ___ ___ ___ (1 2 3 4 5 6 7 8)

VI. ___ ___ ___ ___ ___ ___ ___ ___ (1 2 3 4 5 6 7 8)

VII. ___ ___ ___ ___ ___ ___ ___ ___ (1 2 3 4 5 6 7 8)

VIII. ___ ___ ___ ___ ___ ___ ___ ___ (1 2 3 4 5 6 7 8)

IX. ___ ___ ___ ___ ___ ___ ___ ___ (1 2 3 4 5 6 7 8)

X. ___ ___ ___ ___ ___ ___ ___ (1 2 3 4 5 6 7)

LETTER CHART

	I	II	III	IV	V	VI	VII	VIII	IX	X
A	13	39	11	63	19	31	14	37	41	42
B	60	21	4	25	74	35	74	51	43	20
C	23	37	69	52	35	15	32	35	37	47
D	72	23	58	30	21	74	39	7	64	78
E	65	11	45	43	15	12	42	8	61	4
F	47	67	51	15	23	53	78	62	76	39
G	76	54	53	47	28	76	64	76	66	43
H	21	27	3	39	56	58	80	4	78	66
I	62	6	27	36	34	39	41	53	51	63
J	25	15	43	51	25	33	72	43	39	25
K	7	58	7	69	62	69	4	80	22	80
L	51	4	9	53	76	66	11	25	58	15
M	38	29	54	27	33	19	33	70	4	23
N	10	52	47	21	66	29	17	39	23	9
O	49	36	75	75	9	43	47	30	62	74
P	4	31	62	48	27	4	7	9	7	29
Q	39	47	72	62	47	51	58	64	69	21
R	31	73	5	37	39	23	43	13	19	72
S	74	43	15	46	51	64	9	26	72	30
T	9	22	21	23	22	7	55	11	21	76
U	29	7	64	54	43	9	25	72	74	69
V	53	33	32	29	29	72	15	21	25	27
W	11	74	2	72	53	78	27	47	2	76
X	15	51	74	64	4	80	62	54	9	33
Y	64	78	39	31	67	54	8	73	47	44
Z	27	80	76	58	78	24	21	23	54	7
	I	II	III	IV	V	VI	VII	VIII	IX	X

POSITION CHART

1	2	3	4	5	6	7	8	9	10	11	12	13	14	15	16	17	18	19	20	21	22	23	24	25	26	27
2,8	1	2	0	7	3,6	0	8	0	4	0	1,4,8	7	4	0	8	3	8	2	1,3	0	5	0	5,6	0	1	0

28	29	30	31	32	33	34	35	36	37	38	39	40	41	42	43	44	45	46	47	48	49	50	51	52	53	54
8	0	6	0	5	0	6	3	7	4	1,8	0	3	6	2	0	4	4,6	1	0	2	2,3	1	0	8	0	0

55	56	57	58	59	60	61	62	63	64	65	66	67	68	69	70	71	72	73	74	75	76	77	78	79	80	81
1,7	4	4	0	7	5	3,8	0	5	0	6	7	1	7	0	5	6	0	2	0	3	0	3	0	3	0	2

Word Golf ★☆

by Tom James

Each hole in this nine-hole course consists of a word of 10 or more letters.

The object, as in real golf, is to complete the course in as few strokes as possible, a stroke here being a word anagram.

To play, break each word into two or more consecutive blocks of letters, each of which can be anagrammed into a common word. All blocks must be treated separately; letters among them cannot be mixed. For example, the word INTERPOLATE could be broken into INT/ERPOL/ATE to make the anagrams TIN, POLER, and EAT, for three strokes. Or you could cut your score to two strokes by breaking it into INTERPO/LATE to form POINTER and TALE. Note that LATE would not be allowed in the latter solution, because each answer word *must* involve some rearranging of letters.

If you have trouble anagramming a block, you may add one or more additional letters of your choice in order to form a word. Each added letter, however, counts as a two-stroke penalty. Thus, in the example, you could break the hole word into INTER/POLATE to form INERT and POLECAT (with an added C), for a score of four (two words plus the two-stroke penalty for the added letter).

If you can't find any solution for a given hole, add 10 points to your score and proceed to the next hole.

Contractions, hyphenated words, and capitalized words are not allowed in answers, but plurals and past tense forms of verbs are fine.

To play Word Golf competitively, have a friend play the same course with you.

Answers, page 181

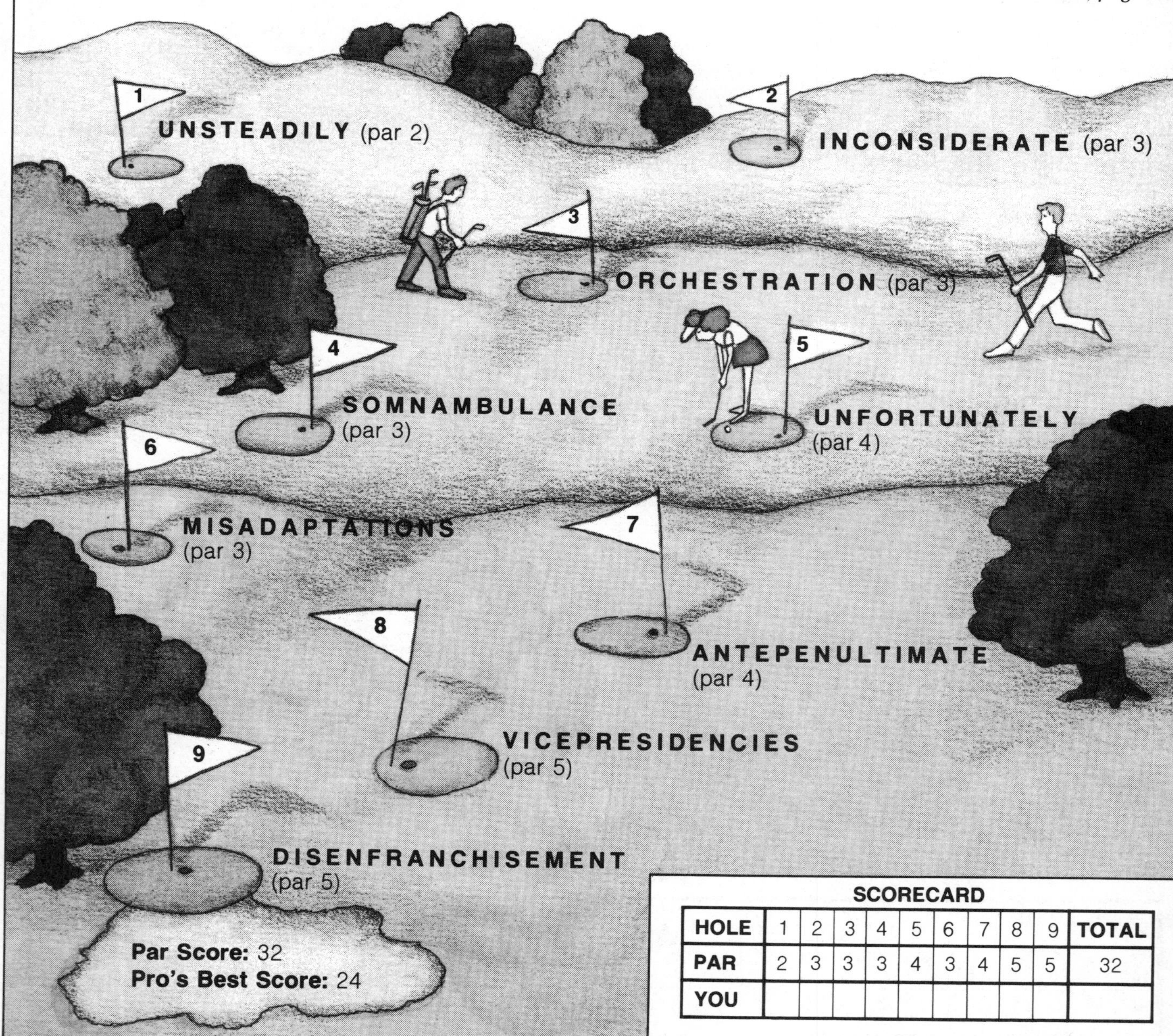

SCORECARD

HOLE	1	2	3	4	5	6	7	8	9	TOTAL
PAR	2	3	3	3	4	3	4	5	5	32
YOU										

Analograms★★

by Betty Brace and Penny Slingerland

In the sentence "CAT is to KITTEN as DOG is to PUPPY," the first two items, CAT and KITTEN, bear a relationship that is shared by the second two, DOG and PUPPY. In the puzzle below, 20 more analogies await completion. The first two words of each analogy appear at the left. The 40 words that go in the blanks to complete them are arranged alphabetically in the columns below. Each of the words in the columns will be used exactly once, so you may cross them off as you proceed. A word of warning: Keep your mind flexible; some of the relationships are completed in unexpected ways.

Answers, page 181

1. HERD is to CATTLE as ______ is to ______
2. HUB is to WHEEL as ______ is to ______
3. MONTH is to YEAR as ______ is to ______
4. COWS is to CALVES as ______ is to ______
5. COMPASS is to NEEDLE as ______ is to ______
6. AUTHOR is to COPYRIGHT as ______ is to ______
7. LAMP is to SUNSHINE as ______ is to ______
8. PISTOL is to RIFLE as ______ is to ______
9. OASIS is to DESERT as ______ is to ______
10. SUDS is to DISHWATER as ______ is to ______
11. LETTER is to ALPHABET as ______ is to ______
12. FLEMISH is to HIMSELF as ______ is to ______
13. FENCE is to PICKET as ______ is to ______
14. ROOM is to CEILING as ______ is to ______
15. ADVERSE is to JINGLE as ______ is to ______
16. GLAZE is to HAM as ______ is to ______
17. CAR is to TIRE as ______ is to ______
18. OWE is to PEA as ______ is to ______
19. NICKEL is to DIME as ______ is to ______
20. CASSETTE is to RECORDER as ______ is to ______

BEE	EYE	ICE	SAWBUCK
BEER	FAN	INCH	SCALE
BLADE	FAWNS	INVENTOR	SCHOOL
BREEZE	FIN	ISLAND	SEE
CAKE	FISH	MOUTH	SHINGLE
DAGGER	FOOT	NOTE	SKATE
DISK	HAND	PATENT	SWORD
DOES	HEAD	RAMPART	TOOTH
DRIVE	HORN	ROOF	WATCH
ENGLISH	HURRICANE	SAW	

Moonlighting★★

by Roger Bossley

In order to make ends meet, a lot of people these days are working two jobs. And while the jobs may not be related, sometimes the names are. Take an example. One person below has a daytime job as a REWRITER (sign #1). To save money, he doesn't have a different sign for his moonlighting position. He just puts the sign fragment POR (at the bottom of the page) over the WRI to show his second job: REPORTER.

Each of the other names of daytime jobs below likewise can be converted into the name of a nighttime job. How many of the conversions can you deduce? Note: The nighttime letters can cover the beginning, middle, or end of the daytime sign. Each sign fragment always covers up the same number of letters, unless it's at the start or end of the word, in which case it may extend farther. *Answers, page 181*

DAYTIME SIGNS

1. REWRITER
2. MORTICIAN
3. CARETAKER
4. BUTLER
5. TINSMITH
6. DISPATCHER
7. LEGISLATOR
8. PHYSICIAN
9. DAIRYMAN
10. BASSOONIST
11. BOOKBINDER
12. GLASSMAKER
13. ARCHIVIST
14. FISHERMAN
15. ENGINEER
16. ACTUARY
17. BALLPLAYER
18. LOCKSMITH

NIGHTTIME FRAGMENTS

DRE	TEC	BEAU	CHER	ST	RICK
CART	RAV	TRAN	PENT	FER	OGC
WEAT	BLA	POR	RESS	KEEP	GU

Dszqtionary★☆

by Sally Porter

Casey Stengel said, "You could look it up," but he didn't mean here. This is a page from a cryptographic Dszqtionary, which defines words and phrases in simple cipher alphabets. Letter substitutions remain constant throughout each of the eight entries, but change from one entry to the next. In each definition, the first part is an accurate explanation of the word or phrase; the second part is a punny description.

Answers, page 181

tu•tor (ˈtōōt-ər)

1. QHDBEHS HPMINVHA QN FLYH MSLYDQH IHRRNOR.

2. QSZPMHQ MIDVHS ONQ TZLQH ZM QN RVPMENOV IHYHI.

tutor **1**

pro and con (ˈprō-and-ˈkon)

1. AJJABTDV BTSVB AQ WZ WCRPFVZD. **2.** SVBXCTJDTAZ AQ YWHH JHWMVC IWTHVS QAC ZWCXADTXB JABBVBBTAZ.

down-in-the-mouth (ˈdoun-in-thə-ˈmouth)

1. QTTEPDR CQ RECCF CA STNATBBPCD.

2. NACZETF TDXCIDLTATS KOPET TYLPDR AYK SIXH.

down-in-the-mouth **2**

fly-by-night (ˈflī-bī-ˌnīt)

1. FVXYS, BGGZFMLQFBENZ, XQY GBFOS. **2.** LQZ KXS IVXI IGXJZNZGF DXQ FXJZ LQ XBGCXGZ.

pal•i•sade (ˌpal-ə-ˈsād)

1. ZXBBUYXWT CV DCUHPTW JPXFTJ KJTW VCB WTVTHJT.

2. ECO-UHPTBTJP ECXH VCB BTDXUBUHR FUHR'J BTJUWTHYT.

foun•tain of youth (ˈfount-ən-əv-ˈyūth)

1. VPLUZARG KHMJAC HD CLCJWRG GZDC.

2. DRNHJZLC BJMTKLHJC URWTHML BMJZWT UZTU KAUHHG BRPK.

fountain of youth **2**

list•less (ˈlist-ləs)

1. GBFMMZGD AH INXS OHAR NUDXFGEZAQ. **2.** DAI XWGNQE-RZQPNP GDALLNH XHHZYNG XE GFLNHRXHSNE.

with•draw•als (with-ˈdrô-əlz)

1. NLSHBRJD HV VAPYD VNHS QRPT RWWHAPCD.

2. XHM *DHACXLNPLND DOLRT CH LRWX HCXLN.

withdrawals **1**

Added Attractions★★

by Robert Leighton

The names of 15 objects in this park scene can be transformed into 15 other pictured objects with the addition of a single letter. For example, the CROW in the tree can become the CROWN on the girl's chair with the addition of an N. Can you find all 15 pairs? The additions may be placed anywhere in the word, but the order of the other letters is unchanged. When you're done, the 15 added letters can be unscrambled to spell a bonus word. *Answers, page 181*

Blankety-Blank★

by Mike Shenk

Originally, the 36 letters in the center of this word search, reading in order row by row, spelled a quotation by the Greek poet Aeschylus. But we've removed the letters and replaced them with shaded boxes. To discover the quotation, solve the puzzle as you would any word search, finding and circling the words in the word list, with this difference: Some words cross into the shaded squares and need to have their missing letters filled in. Answers, as always, may read horizontally, vertically, or diagonally, but always in a straight line. *Answers, page 181*

I	F	C	Y	H	E	A	R	T	T	H	R	O	B	O	U	W	E
F	O	R	I	E	E	I	X	I	H	O	U	S	E	W	I	F	E
A	A	V	P	T	C	E	R	B	C	T	O	B	T	I	X	S	N
C	Z	L	E	O	A	E	P	E	G	H	M	O	G	A	O	N	A
I	O	E	C	R	V	M	H	R	A	O	A	N	T	P	B	H	C
L	E	H	N	O	A	N	O	A	N	U	R	K	O	R	P	A	A
I	E	G	N	I	N							R	A	B	A	N	D
T	Y	R	A	I	T							O	R	W	O	T	E
A	U	Q	U	H	O							O	Z	O	S	E	M
T	E	B	E	M	O							D	E	A	W	A	Y
E	R	V	I	T	A							M	U	A	T	T	E
S	U	L	Y	H	C							C	P	T	I	E	N
T	T	H	I	S	O	T	T	W	T	R	E	E	A	A	S	R	P
U	A	Z	Z	N	I	E	O	A	O	P	I	S	N	T	I	L	E
T	N	H	G	M	L	R	R	C	O	R	A	A	Y	N	I	G	T
S	G	A	E	I	D	Y	P	T	L	J	K	U	L	A	E	O	N
S	I	T	N	T	O	I	S	S	A	N	D	W	I	C	H	S	N
D	S	E	T	A	R	E	N	E	G	E	D	O	B	A	E	D	S

ACADEMY
ACHROMATIC
AESCHYLUS
ANTEATER
BEMOANS
BROADSWORD
CAMPAIGN
CANTATA
DATELINE
DEGENERATES
DIAGNOSIS
DIETARY
DOORKNOBS
DROWNING
ECLAIRS
FACILITATES
FADEAWAY
FALCONRY
GALOOTS
GANDHI
HAMSTER
HAYSEEDS
HEARTTHROB
HOMEWORK
HOTHOUSE
HOUSEWIFE
MESOZOIC
NOTIFICATION
ONETIME
OUTGROWTH
OVERAWES
PARAMOUR
PHOOEY
PROPOSE
PROTEIN
RAREBIT
RICOCHET
RIPCORD
SANDWICH
SARABAND
SAUCEPOTS
SIGNATURE
SOAPBOX
SODDENNESS
STUDIED
TERTIARY
TOWROPE
TURNOVER
VITAMIN
ZENITH

Egyptograms★☆

by Paul Douglas Stamm

In 1822 a 32-year-old Frenchman named Jean François Champollion solved one of history's most enduring mysteries: how to read Egyptian hieroglyphics. Knowledge of this ancient picture writing had died out almost 2,000 years earlier, and it had baffled all modern attempts at translation.

Champollion worked with the Rosetta stone, a trilingual text discovered in Egypt in 1799, and other ancient texts carved in stone. He began by assuming that the hieroglyphic symbols in the oval-shaped figures—called cartouches—represented the names of Egyptian royalty and deities. Only one cartouche appeared on the Rosetta stone, and Champollion correctly assumed that this stood for PTOLEMY, or PTOLMIS, the only name appearing in the Greek portion of the inscription. He then proceeded in cryptanalytic fashion, substituting known or presumed phonetic values elsewhere in the writing, guessing at additional names, and testing the new values in other places. Within three years Champollion had a fairly complete knowledge of the hieroglyphic language.

This puzzle version of Champollion's work can be solved in much the same way. First match the six royal Egyptian names printed on the left in the "Traveler" section with the corresponding cartouches on the right, using logic and the repetition of symbols as your guide. (Also see "Hints for Solvers" at the bottom of the next page.) Next, match the names and cartouches in the slightly more difficult "Visitor" and "Native" sections. If you reach this point successfully, you will know enough hieroglyphics to create your own cartouches in the "Expert" section at the end of the puzzle.

Answers, page 182

Traveler

1. Mena ___

2. NeferkaRa ___

3. Assa ___

4. Kakaa ___

5. Nebka ___

6. MenkhepherRa ___

A

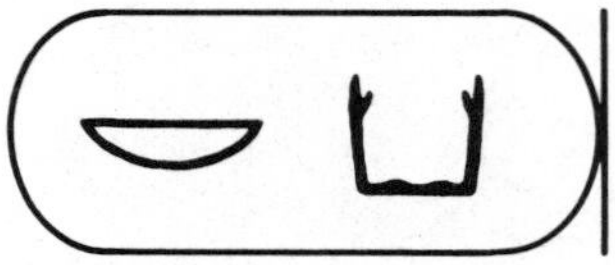

B

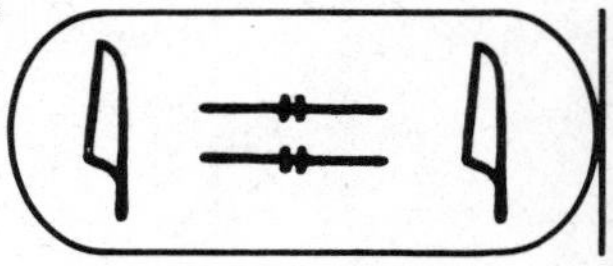

C

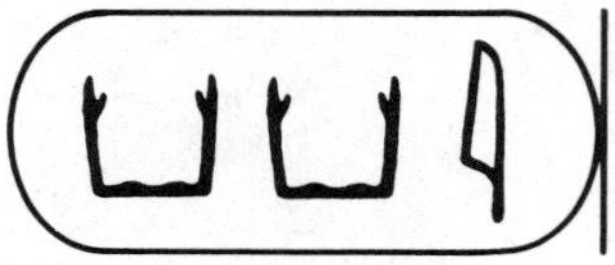

D

E

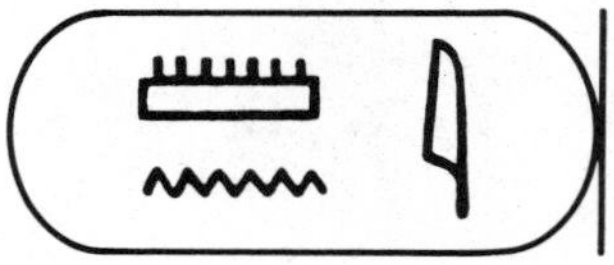

F

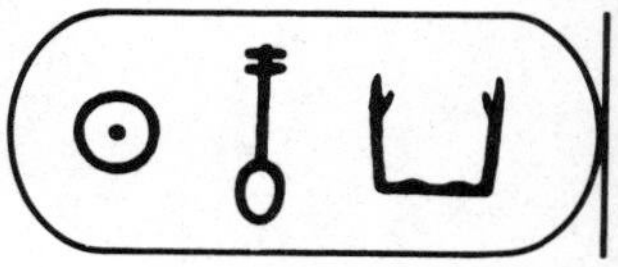

Visitor

1. Amenhetep ___

2. Antef ___

3. Rameses ___

4. BaenRa ___

5. Aahmes ___

6. Pepi ___

A

B

C

D

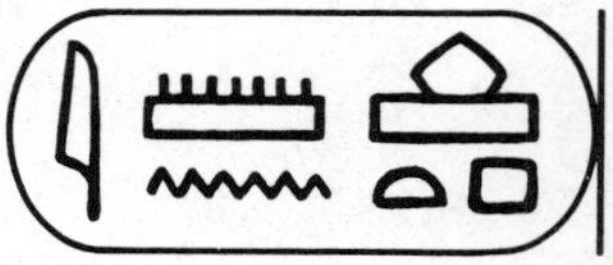

E

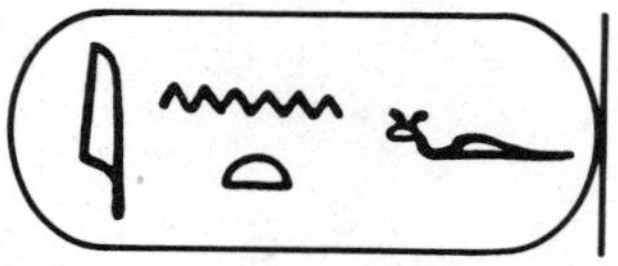

F

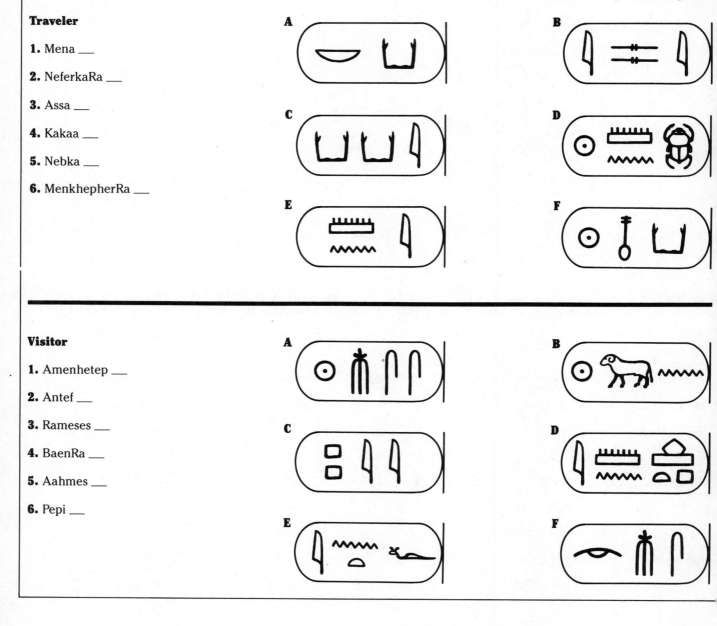

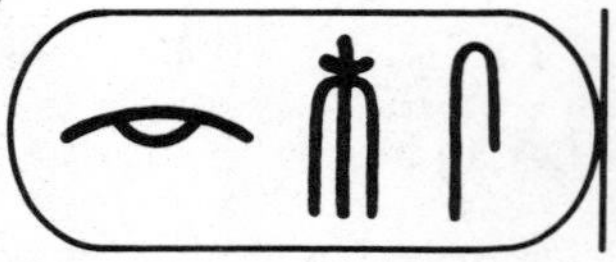

Native

1. Psemthek ___
2. ShetepabRa ___
3. NeferarikaRa ___
4. SneferkaRa ___
5. Perabsen ___
6. TutankhAmen ___

A

B

C

D

E

F

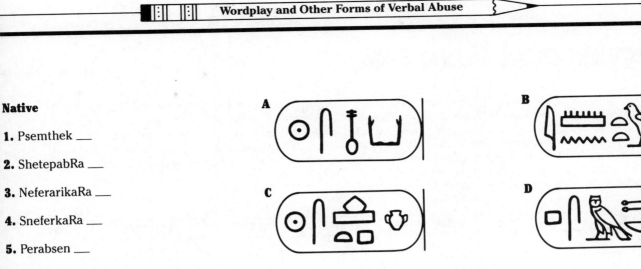

Expert
Given just the English name, can you supply the proper hieroglyphic symbols? Using your deductions from the previous sections, write each name within the cord of the cartouche.

1. Teta
2. Pankhi
3. KhephernebRa
4. AnkhkaRa
5. SneferabRa
6. MenkaRa
7. NeferfRa
8. KhepherkaRa

1 2 3 4 5 6 7 8

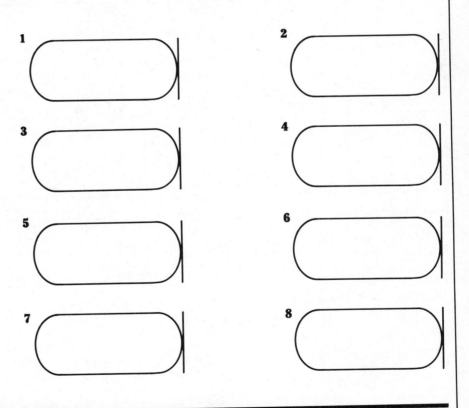

Hints for Solvers

1. Individual symbols may represent letters or syllables.
2. A symbol may represent more than one sound. Some sounds may have more than one symbol.
3. The symbols are read from left to right and (when one symbol appears above another) from top to bottom. However, the symbol of a god's name is always written first, regardless of where it appears in the king's name.

Rhyme and Reason ★★

by Will Shortz

Each clue below consists of a regular definition in which, as an extra hint, one of the words rhymes with the answer. For example, the first clue, "Kept the floor clean," is answered by SWEPT (which rhymes with "kept"). If you drop one of the letters in the answer word and rearrange those that remain, you'll spell one of the words in the diagram. For example, by dropping the W in SWEPT and anagramming the rest, you get PEST, found in the third row of the grid. (The clue numbers have nothing to do with the locations of the answers.) Cross off that word and write the extra letter beneath it. When all 28 clues have been solved in this manner, the letters written in the grid will spell, in order, a quotation by Oscar Wilde.

Answers, page 182

RANCH	HIRE	GISHES	TAYLOR	RACE	ASKING	ROCS
SEGUED	**DIRT**	**PORTS**	**SAFE**	**SAPID**	**STAB**	**THEIST**
TWICE	**CADRE**	**RANG**	**~~PEST~~**	**CHITS**	**LUTES**	**BARK**
			W			
RIPE	**HAMS**	**PETE**	**WINKER**	**FLORA**	**PARCH**	**HIKER**

CLUES

1. Kept the floor clean
2. Pie maker
3. Patterns for Scottish lads
4. Play waiter (to)
5. European wine region
6. That which in time saves nine
7. Yell "Eek!"
8. Made a wild stab on a test
9. Quaking
10. Lightest in color
11. Arthur Ashe hit
12. These bother dogs
13. Vehicles for snowy days
14. Croquet hoop
15. Where an Indian goes when he's sleepy
16. Moan
17. Item on a tanker or scow
18. Church master
19. Teach in church
20. Word before base, degree, or dimension
21. Stablemate of Prancer
22. Something to savor
23. First in time or rank
24. Make the most of oneself?
25. To whom the British show loyalty
26. One more than nineteen
27. Crinkle
28. One seeking the truth to a mystery

Tom Swifties ★☆

by Gloria Rosenthal

"You'll need a pencil to write in these answers," Tom said *pointedly*. That's an example of a Tom Swifty—a line of dialogue ending with a whimsically appropriate adverb (so-called from Edward Stratemeyer's fictional character Tom Swift, who was inclined to this sort of talk). Twelve more Tom Swifties appear below, each missing the all-important adverb. How many of them can you complete? The first letter of each answer is given as a help. *Answer, page 182*

1. "Your gift is over there," Tom said p__________.

2. "Who sprinkled horseradish on my sandwich?" Tom asked h__________.

3. "I'm breaking out in hives!" Tom cried r__________.

4. "Go to the back of the boat!" Tom ordered s__________.

5. "The actor quit the play 43 minutes and 17 seconds into the performance," Tom said e__________.

6. "Heads or tails?" Tom remarked f__________.

7. "We can't wait until dad gets out of the hospital," Tom declared i__________.

8. "I just ate six cans of pineapple," Tom said d__________.

9. "I—guess—I'll—fix—my—car," Tom said m__________.

10. "You can lead the prayer before dinner," Tom said g__________.

11. "Mom likes British crosswords," Tom remarked c__________.

12. "My toothpaste is now all over the floor," Tom moaned c__________.

The Last Word ★☆

by Fraser Simpson

Each of the 12 sets of words below has a common denominator, some unusual factor that is shared by the six words in the set. It's up to you to determine what that factor is and identify which one of the three words under the list has it, too. For example, given SEXES, MOM, DEIFIED, LEVEL, POP, and REDDER, with choices DIVINED, ROTATOR, and STARTS, you'd pick ROTATOR: All the words are spelled the same forward and back. For how many of the following sets can you get the last word?

Answers, page 182

1.
SETTEE
RACCOON
EMBARRASS
APPELLATION
BASSOON
SUFFRAGETTE

a. BEDROOM
b. PROPELLER
c. EGGSHELL

2.
TEA
EYE
SEA
QUEUE
ARE
WHY

a. YOU
b. ATE
c. WEE

3.
MUSEUM
EARLOBE
YEARLY
SEAMSTRESS
WILLOW
DOODAD

a. COCOON
b. ERASER
c. TABLET

4.
YOUTH
THEMATIC
USHER
SHEIK
ITALICS
MEDIUM

a. THEATER
b. WEEVIL
c. DOMESTIC

5.
GIGGLING
REARRANGER
ASSESS
MINIMIZING
DIDDLED
PIZZAZZ

a. DEEDED
b. INTERMITTENT
c. CANDIDACY

6.
REVILED
STRESSED
REPAID
STAR
DRAWER
PARTS

a. VILE
b. REGARD
c. STINK

7.
PREVIEW
TALLOW
SELECTION
GOLDEN
BRAIDED
CLAMP

a. TRACING
b. CASHEW
c. CONVERT

8.
CIVIC
LIVID
MIX
MILL
VIVID
DILL

a. MIMIC
b. LICIT
c. MINIM

9.
BANANA
DEMONIC
FICKLE
HUMBUG
JABORANDI
LUCK

a. NEMESIS
b. NUDISM
c. MEGATION

10.
GEL
GROUP
PLACE
FIXED
RESOLUTE
ADJUST

a. USELESS
b. COLLECTION
c. AFGHAN

11.
RING
TOPS
MANATEE
WINDLESS
EARTH
ANGER

a. MATTER
b. TUNES
c. OUGHT

12.
ACCEPT
BEGINS
ABHORS
CHINOS
BILLOW
EFFORT

a. ALMOST
b. BEFORE
c. CENSOR

TRIVIA MANIA AND QUIXOTIC QUIZZES

Hairdos and Hairdon'ts ★☆

by Rick Tulka

Yesterday Mr. Giuseppe—hairstylist to the stars—got his appointments mixed up. Each of his clients received a hairstyle that should have gone to someone else that day. His customers yesterday were nine famous people, past and present (did we mention Mr. Guiseppe is a time traveler?), and the pictures here show how they looked after their appointments. How many can you recognize? *Answers, page 182*

1

2

3

4

5

6

7

8

9

Twisted Television ★☆

by Jack Lechner

Our local paper's TV listings are riddled with typos. Every time we sit down to see what's on the tube, we find shows like LITTLE MOUSE ON THE PRAIRIE, LUST IN SPACE, and AMERICAN HANDSTAND. If you ask us, the images these titles conjure up are more fun than the real thing.

We've illustrated some of those misprinted titles below. Under each picture, fill in the blanks with the name of a familiar TV show, past or present—with exactly one of its letters changed. How many can you identify?

Answers, page 182

1. _ _ _ _ _ _ _ _

2. _ _ _ _ _ _ _ _ _ _ _ _ _ _ _ _ _

3. _ _ _ _ _ _ _ _ _ _ _ _ _ _ _ _

4. _ _ _ _ _ _ _ _ _ _

5. _ _ _ _ _ _ _ _ _ _ _ _ _ _ _ _

6. _

7. __________ _______

8. ______ _____ ________

9. _______

10. ____ __-______

11. _______ _______

12. _____ _____ _______

Picture Quiz ★☆

by Louis Phillips

Here are a dozen questions to test your memory—and eye—for trivia. A score of 4 is good; 6 is terrific; but we predict *no one* will get all 12.

Answers, page 182

1. Benjamin Franklin, who invented bifocals, the lightning rod, and the Franklin stove, is often credited with the invention of what popular musical instrument?

2. The flag of what state features eigh gold stars on a field of blue?

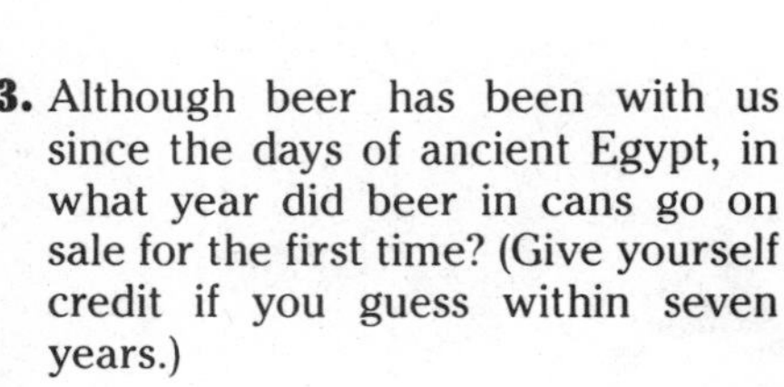

3. Although beer has been with us since the days of ancient Egypt, in what year did beer in cans go on sale for the first time? (Give yourself credit if you guess within seven years.)

"YOU'LL NEVER MISS THE WATER"

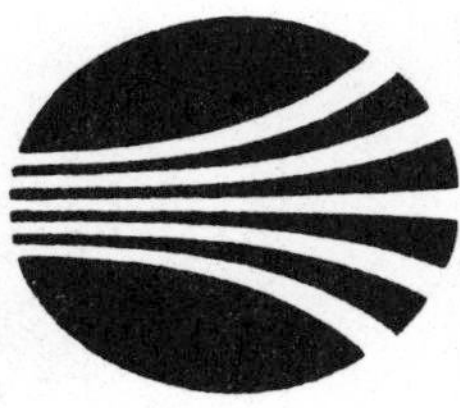

4. Above is the logo of what major U.S airline?

5. If you are or ever were a devoted comic book reader, then you know that the high school student pictured at left is Archie. But what is Archie's last name? Bonus question: In 1969 a musical group called The Archies had the nation's #1 hit song. What was it?

6. The name of Blackbeard's pirate ship was:
a) Queen Anne's Revenge
b) Skull and Bones
c) Demon Run
d) The George's Hindgut

8. True or false: More persons in New York City are hospitalized because they are bitten by other human beings than because they are bitten by rats.

7. In the history of the United States only two presidents have ever been arrested while holding office. Ulysses S. Grant (above) was arrested for riding his horse too fast through Washington, D.C., and was fined $20. Who was the other arrested president?

9. *Star Trek* fans should have no trouble with this one: What color is Mr. Spock's blood?

10. This 20th-century artist was once described thus: "He looks like a huge frog. He talks like a wild-eyed soapbox orator. His political beliefs vary with the seasons. His philandering has been notorious. Yet he paints like a master and he well deserves his reputation as the finest living painter in the Western Hemisphere." An example of his work appears above. Who is he?

11. Jimmy Dewar, the inventor of the Twinkie, ate approximately how many of his cream-filled cupcakes during his lifetime?

a) 4
b) 400
c) 4,000
d) 40,000

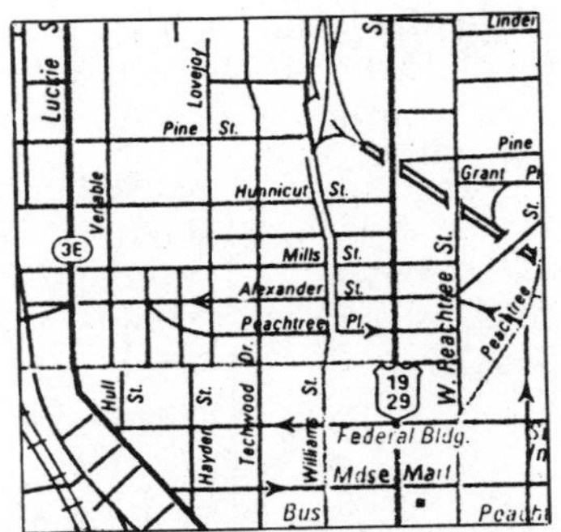

12. The downtown of what major U.S. city is shown in the map above?

Second Guessing★☆

by Monny Sklov and Bob Spitzer

Suppose someone took on the gargantuan task of eating all the food ever produced in the United States. How long would it take? A matter of days? Obviously not. Years? Doubtful, no matter how fast the person ate. Common sense dictates that it would take centuries for even the world's fastest eater to put away that much chow.

Questions like this and the 20 on these two pages will propel you into the fourth dimension and measure your intuitive perception of time, size, speed, and distance. Each question is to be answered approximately, by choosing the most suitable unit of time from among the following:

SECONDS	**DAYS**	**YEARS**
MINUTES	**WEEKS**	**DECADES**
HOURS	**MONTHS**	**CENTURIES**

Pencil and paper are forbidden. Instead, use intuition, experience, and rough mental calculations to arrive at a "guesstimate" of the correct answer. Give yourself 5 to 10 seconds for each. In all questions, assume nonstop activity with no unspecified barriers (and in some questions, like the one above, you'll need to suspend disbelief as well).

SCORING: The lower your score, the better. For each correct answer, your score is 0. For each incorrect answer, your score is the number of units by which you vary from the correct solution. (For example, if you answer "months" and the correct response is "seconds," your score on that question is 5, since you're five units away from the correct answer.) Rate yourself as follows:

0-10	Years ahead of your time
11-20	"Hour" hero!
21-30	Nine days' wonder
31 and over	Running late

Answers, page 183

1

With your rubber flippers on, how long would it take to swim around the equator?

2

You have just won a billion dollars in the Super-Zorch Megabucks Lottery. You can't collect interest on your money, but that's OK. You still plan on spending $3,000 a day until the money runs out. How long will it take until you have spent your last two bits?

3

How long would it take you to write the first and last names of one million people?

4

You have a loud voice. In fact, your voice is so loud that when you yell "hello" from New York City, a friend in Los Angeles can hear you. After you yell "hello," how long does it take before your friend hears your voice?

5

What is the average life-span of an ordinary housefly?

6

A cement company has just built a sidewalk from your front door to the sun. After you've put on your hiking boots, how long will it take you to walk to the sun?

7

How long would it take you to count all the beans in an eight-ounce can of baked beans?

8

One by one, how long would it take you to pull out every hair on the average human's head? (Ouch.)

9

Congratulate yourself. You are moving to Los Angeles to become the Regal Hoo-hah of the "I Love Los Angeles" fan club. Your first job is to award membership medallions to each of Los Angeles's 3 million people.

If you shake hands very fast and you don't spend much time chatting, you can present one award every 10 seconds. How long will it take you to adorn the new members?

10

How long would it take Samuel Slugg, a Parisian snail, to climb the Eiffel Tower?

11

You're relaxing on the moon and gazing toward Earth, whence a friend is supposed to send you a signal by special, very powerful flashlight. How long after your earthbound friend turns on his flashlight will you be able to see the light beam?

12

Every day for 18 years, you take one foot of 8mm film of your son Howie. Today is Howie's 18th birthday, and you're going to show the film in its entirety. How long will it take to run?

13

How long would it take to walk across the United States and back?

14

You are ordered to deliver a secret document to the exalted Chief Belzap, who lives just a few miles past Jupiter. If you travel from Earth to Jupiter at the speed of light, how long will the chief have to wait?

15

You're sunning yourself on the roof of a building that is as tall as Mount Everest, which is more than five miles high. If you were to drop a bottle of suntan lotion from the top of this building, how long would it take the bottle to hit the street below?

16

If you throw a ball straight up into the air as high as you can, how long will it take before the ball hits the ground?

17

How long would it take you to read all the books in the Library of Congress?

18

How long does it take for a 2½-inch birthday candle to burn itself out?

19

You own a square mile of land. If one-tenth inch of rain falls on your land and you catch all the water before it hits the ground, how long will it take you to drink all the water?

20

A fellow named Seymour is bitten by a tropical bug. He contracts a very rare disease called the heebie-jeebies. When Seymour has a spell of the heebie-jeebies, his only symptom is a slight temperature.

However, it is the nature of the disease that the 18th spell is fatal! If the amount of time between the first and second spells is one day, and the amount of time between the second and third is two days, and the amount of time between the third and fourth is four days, and the amount of time between each of the remaining spells continues to double, how long will Seymour live?

A Herculean Atlas Quiz ★☆

by Paddy Smith

The questions in this quiz range from tricky to nearly impossible. Good guessing, though, may help the less "worldly" keep up with those who study globes and atlases in their spare time.

Bonus questions add 15 points to the theoretically perfect score of 100. Score yourself as follows:

100 or more:	Sir Edmund Hillary	25–49:	Christopher Columbus
75–99:	Marco Polo	10–24:	Dr. Livingston
50–74:	Amelia Earhart	0–9:	Wrong-Way Corrigan

Answers, page 183

FOLLOWING DIRECTIONS

1. If you fly due south from the western border of the state of New York to the Equator, you will just miss passing over Florida. But will you pass east or west of Florida? (2 points)

2. Which one of the following continents—Africa, Europe, or South America—is it possible to reach by sailing due south from Iceland? (2 points)

3. If you fly due west from New York City to the Pacific Ocean, will you pass over California? (2 points)

4. Match one Australian city to each of Australia's coasts (north, east, south, and west): Brisbane, Darwin, Melbourne, Perth (4 points if all four correct; otherwise 0)

UPHILL CLIMBING

1. Mount Everest is on the border of what two countries? (2 points each)

2. Nine of the 10 highest peaks in the Americas are found in what two countries? (2 points each)

BONUS: In what country is the other peak? (3 points)

BONUS: Name the tallest peak in the Americas. (5 points)

3. Outside the Soviet Union, what is the tallest peak in Europe? (1 point) The peak is near the borders of what three countries? (1 point each)

4. Mt. Ararat, famous for expeditions to find Noah's Ark, is near the border of what three countries? (1 point each)

5. In what country is Mt. Ararat's peak? (1 point)

BETWEEN THE LINES

1. Which of the following pairs of states, provinces, or countries share a border? Don't count members of a pair as bordering one another if they are separated by a lake, sea, or ocean. (1 point each)
Michigan and Illinois
Colorado and Nebraska
British Columbia and Montana
El Salvador and Nicaragua
Austria and Switzerland
Finland and Norway
Bulgaria and the Soviet Union
India and Iran
Thailand and Vietnam
Indonesia and Malaysia

2. Each of the following countries—Colombia, El Salvador, Nicaragua—has at least one coastline. But which of them have coastlines on the Atlantic (or Caribbean) side, which on the Pacific side, and which on both sides? (2 points each)

3. If you drove from Mexico to Colombia, you would pass through Costa Rica, Guatemala, Honduras, Nicaragua, and Panama—but in what order? (5 points for all correct; 0 otherwise)

4. All the following can be found in one geographical location: Princess Elizabeth Land, Rockefeller Plateau, General Belgrano, Leningradskaya. What is the location? (3 points)

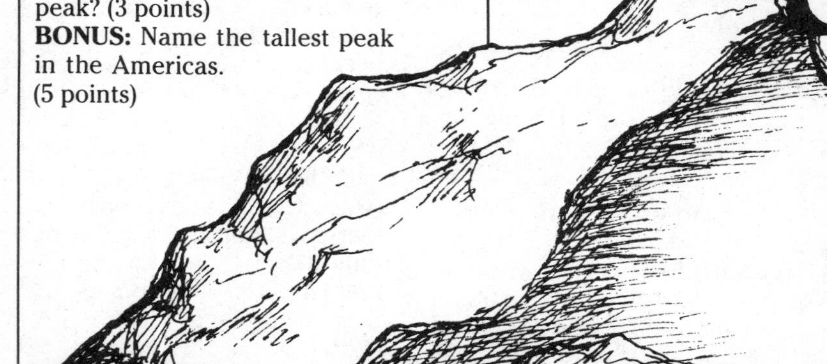

GOING THE DISTANCE

1. Rank the following places in distance from the Equator, from closest to farthest away: Australia, Ecuador, Tahiti, the Philippines, Mexico. (5 points if all are correct; otherwise 0)

2. Rank the following places in distance from the Equator, from closest to farthest away: the northern tip of Antarctica, the northern tip of the Soviet mainland, the northern tip of Alaska. (3 points if all are correct; otherwise 0)

3. Of the five cities that follow, which two are the farthest apart? (5 points)
Auckland, New Zealand
Beijing, China
Buenos Aires, Argentina
Philadelphia, U.S.A.
Stockholm, Sweden

TROPICS TOPICS

1. The Tropics, or Torrid Zone, is the region between the Tropic of Cancer and the Tropic of Capricorn, each of which lies approximately 23½° from the Equator. Which of the Tropic lines is north of the Equator? (1 point)

2. Nearly 2,400 miles of one of the Tropic lines lies within a single country. What's the country? (5 points)

3. Only one of the following countries—India, Madagascar, Mexico, Paraguay, the Philippines—lies completely within the Tropics. Which one? (2 points)

4. Only one of the following countries—Chile, China, Libya, Pakistan, South Africa—lies completely outside the Tropics. Which one? (2 points)

AS BIG AS ALL OUTDOORS

1. The largest U.S. state in land area is Alaska, followed by Texas. What is the third largest? The fourth? The fifth? (1 point each)

2. The Soviet Union has the largest area of any country in the world. What are the second and third largest countries, in order? (2 points each)

3. The Soviet Union also borders (along with Iran) the world's largest lake, the misnamed Caspian "Sea." What are the second and third largest lakes in the world, in order? (2 points each)

HINT AND BONUS: Two countries border the second largest lake, and three countries border the third largest lake. For each of those five countries you can name, take 1 point.

ISLAND-HOPPING

1. The world's largest island, by far, is Greenland. A single country owns parts of both the second and third largest islands in the world. Name the country (3 points) and the two islands, in order. (2 points each)

2. The distance between Cuba's western and eastern tips is about the same as the distance between New York City and which one of the following: Philadelphia, Pittsburgh, or Chicago? (2 points)

3. In which ocean is each of the following? (1 point each)
Easter Island
Christmas Island
Seychelles
Galapagos Islands
Canary Islands

4. When this island gained home rule in 1979, its official name changed to Kalaallit Nunaat, and its capital's name changed to Nuuk. By what name is the island better known? (2 points)
BONUS: What is the older, better-known name of its capital? (2 points)

Comic Relief ★☆

by Joe Kerr

We've been collecting balloons lately. Not the helium kind, but the ones you read on the funnies page. And we've realized that the balloons of different comic strips are as distinctive as the voices of friends. We've gathered a big bunch of balloons here, 15 in all. Can you name the comic strip each of these "voices" comes from? *Answers, page 182*

1

PAW !! I JUST GOT OL' BULLET ONE OF THEM BODACIOUS FLEA COLLARS

2

A FINE CROWD TURNED OUT TO SEE YOU, SIRE!

3

NEVER BE AFRAID TO MAKE A MISTAKE – YOUR MISSUS WILL LOVE IT

4

THAT SHOULD KEEP TRIXIE OUT OF MY ROOM

5

I STILL SAY THE WHEEL CAN'T BE IMPROVED UPON!

6

SOMEWHERE, SOMEPLACE, SOMEONE IS OPENING A CAN OF DOG FOOD, AND I'M NOT THERE!

7

ONE DAY, OL' UNCLE ALBERT WAS SMOKIN' A SEEGAR TO HISSELF WHEN SUDDEN HE GIT A FIERCE AROMA OF ***FRYIN' CATFISHES!***

8

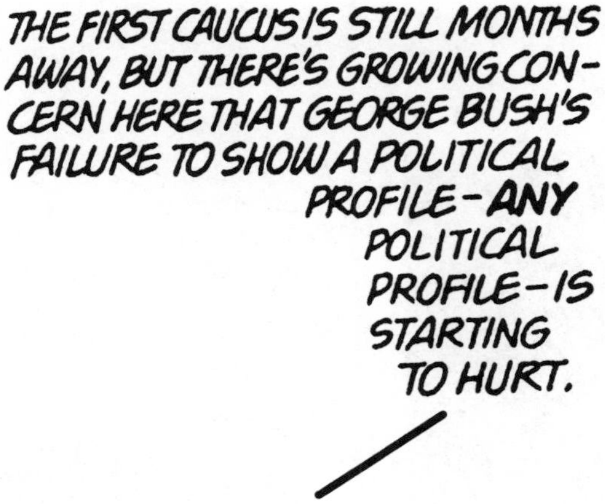

THE FIRST CAUCUS IS STILL MONTHS AWAY, BUT THERE'S GROWING CONCERN HERE THAT GEORGE BUSH'S FAILURE TO SHOW A POLITICAL PROFILE—ANY POLITICAL PROFILE—IS STARTING TO HURT.

9

TUBBY, YOU KNOW VERY WELL THAT MY POP DOESN'T WORK FOR A BANK!

10

AS CATS GO, YOU'RE APPROACHING THE GOLDEN YEARS

11

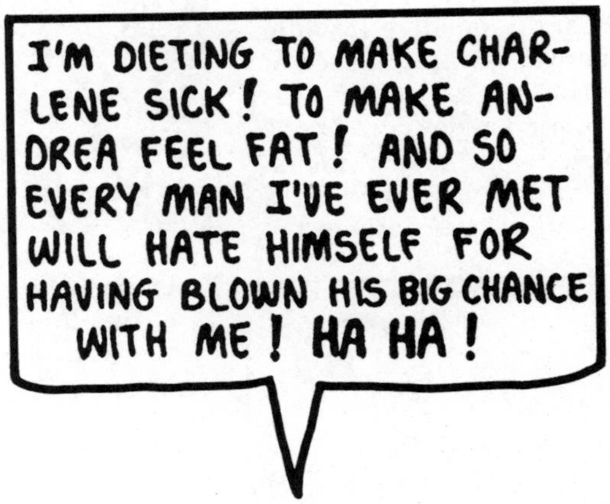

I'M DIETING TO MAKE CHARLENE SICK! TO MAKE ANDREA FEEL FAT! AND SO EVERY MAN I'VE EVER MET WILL HATE HIMSELF FOR HAVING BLOWN HIS BIG CHANCE WITH ME! HA HA!

12

THE FORMER TUBA PLAYER, CARTOONIST AND BOINGER, **OPUS**, HAS PROCURED A NEW JOB: GARBAGE COLLECTOR.

13

W-WHAT DO YOU SAY TO A --ER-- DATE TONIGHT, LOIS?

14

Maybe Rover is at Gramps' house!

15

HE PUT ME ON A PASTA DIET... HE SAYS I'VE BEEN OFF MY NOODLE LONG ENOUGH.

Off & Running★★

by John and Claire Whitcomb

To every citizen who elects to take this quiz, we promise 14 unexpected—but not overly taxing—questions on the history of U.S. presidential elections. Expressed with great economy, it surely deserves your vote. *Answers, page 183*

1. In winning a Texas Democratic primary race for the Senate, Lyndon Johnson earned the nickname "Landslide Lyndon" because:

a) No one dared oppose him.

b) A recount was ordered in one county and suddenly 202 ballots appeared, all in alphabetical order in the same handwriting and the same ink. The extra votes put LBJ over the top.

c) A landslide occurred while Johnson was giving a speech at the foot of a mesa and he was almost buried in dirt.

d) He carried one county unanimously because his opponent's ballots were mysteriously lost.

2. When Kennedy and Nixon campaigned for the presidency in 1960, why did they ignore the voters in Washington, D.C.?

a) They couldn't vote.

b) It was illegal to campaign within three miles of the Capitol.

c) The city's streets were considered too unsafe for personal appearances.

d) The vote had already been bought by JFK's father.

3. Why didn't Zachary Taylor know he'd been nominated for president?

a) The letter with the news came postage due and he sent it to the dead letter office.

b) He was off fighting Santa Anna in Mexico.

c) Taylor was at an Indian post in the West and the messenger was captured by renegades.

d) The convention manager forgot to send Taylor the notification.

4. The first female candidate for president was Victoria Woodhull, who believed in free love. Why did candidate Woodhull find herself in jail on election day, 1872?

a) A New York judge ruled that because it was illegal for women to vote, it was also illegal for them to run for office.

b) She was charged with sending pornographic materials—a newspaper article alleging that a famous preacher was having an affair with one of his parishioners—through the mail.

c) She had campaigned in the nude and was arrested for indecent exposure.

d) Word got out that she was living with both her husband and her former husband and she was charged with unlawful cohabitation.

5. When George Washington ran for the Virginia House of Burgesses in 1758, he saw to it that:

a) The voters received rum, beer, and cider on election day.

b) "I cannot tell a lie" posters were distributed everywhere.

c) Martha invited his supporters back to Mount Vernon for a party.

d) Soldiers who served with him helped get out the vote.

6. In 1848, James K. Polk was elected president. Why was this election unique in U.S. history?

a) There was no smoking in the party caucus room, in deference to Polk's wife, who was also opposed to drinking and dancing.

b) Voting machines were installed for the first time, but a majority of citizens refused to use them, fearing they were rigged.

c) All white male citizens were finally allowed to vote regardless of whether or not they owned property.

d) It was the first time voting took place on the same day in all states.

7. At the 1968 Democratic Convention, Julian Bond, a black from Georgia, received 48½ votes. Why, then, did he withdraw from the running?

a) There was too great a risk of an assassination.

b) Georgia claimed he wasn't a registered voter.

c) Chicago's Mayor Daley convinced him his nomination would split the party.
d) He was only 28 years old and presidents must be at least 35 years old.

8. When Nixon campaigned for president, he cited his eight years as Eisenhower's VP as one of his qualifications. When asked to give an example of a major idea of Nixon's adopted by his administration, what did Ike reply?
   a) "If you give me a week, I might think of one."
   b) "That presidents and VPs should drive in bulletproof cars."
   c) "I didn't see Nixon much during that time."
   d) "He had so many ideas I couldn't enunciate all of them."

9. Match the campaign quotes (1–5) to the candidates (a–e) who uttered them.
   1. "There is no Soviet domination of Eastern Europe."
   2. "You know the kids love the dog, and I just want to say this right now, regardless of what they say about it, I'm gonna keep it."
   3. "My hat is in the ring. The fight is on and I am stripped to the buff."
   4. "I don't know anything about free silver. The people of Nebraska are for free silver, and I am for free silver. I will look up the arguments later."
   5. "Politics is just like show business. You have a hell of an opening, you coast for a while, you have a hell of a closing."
   a) Theodore Roosevelt
   b) Ronald Reagan
   c) William Jennings Bryan
   d) Richard Nixon
   e) Gerald Ford

10. In 1952, Senator Estes Kefauver was the leading Democratic primary winner, thanks in no small part to his dogged campaigning in small towns. But he had a problem in the New Hampshire race when, one day, he approached a sidewalk group, stuck out his hand, and said, "I'm Estes Kefauver. I'm running for president—how'm I doing here?" What is the answer?
   a) "You're doing fine here, but you'd better get back across the line to New Hampshire—this is Vermont."
   b) "I hate to tell you this, Mister, but your zipper's open."
   c) "It's illegal to campaign here on Sunday."
   d) "Estes Kefauver? I thought they cured that."

11. Warren G. Harding won the presidency in 1920 despite admitting that he tended to bloviate. What did he do?
   a) He belched uncontrollably after dinner.
   b) He made wordy speeches that sounded good but said nothing.
   c) He made unmentionable faux pas in mixed company.
   d) He day-dreamed during meetings and forgot topics.

12. When Grant was running for president, he developed a standard campaign speech. What was it?
   a) "I rise only to tell you that I do not intend to say anything."
   b) "Let the surrender at Appomattox Court House tell you everything."
   c) "George Washington never campaigned for president. Neither will I."
   d) "Let's drink to victory."

13. Why, in 1912, when running for his third term, did Teddy Roosevelt speak softly while delivering a campaign speech?
   a) He was carrying a big stick.
   b) A would-be assassin had fired a bullet into his chest.
   c) He was addressing a convention of deaf people.
   d) He had developed laryngitis from shouting "Bully."

14. Why did James Buchanan, our only bachelor president, run into trouble on the campaign trail?
   a) Questions were raised about his morals because he shared rooms with several different women during his campaign.
   b) His oddly tilted neck led to gossip that he'd tried to hang himself when jilted by his fiancée.
   c) His mother traveled everywhere with him and reportedly wrote his speeches.
   d) An illegitimate son prompted taunts of "Ma, Ma, Where's my Pa? Gone to the White House, Ha, Ha, Ha."

What's the Difference? ★☆

by Stephen Sniderman

Vive la différence!—which in this case is everything you need to solve the puzzle. Each line below represents the name of a well-known person, past or present, in which the letters have been replaced by spaces. Between each pair of spaces is a number, which is the difference between the numerical values (A = 1, B = 2, C = 3, etc.) of the two answer letters. This difference is always expressed as a positive number regardless of the order of the letters. An example, using the name MATT DILLON, appears below. As a solving help, each of the first nine lines has a starting letter given. After that you're on your own.

Answers, page 182

A	B	C	D	E	F	G	H	I	J	K	L	M	N	O	P	Q	R	S	T	U	V	W	X	Y	Z
1	2	3	4	5	6	7	8	9	10	11	12	13	14	15	16	17	18	19	20	21	22	23	24	25	26

Ex. M 12 A 19 T 0 T /16 D 5 I 3 L 0 L 3 O 1 N

1. — 9 — 7 — 7 — 4 — 1 — /4 — 3 — 12 — 8 K 6 — 1 — 1 — 7 — 0 — 7 — 13 —

2. — 8 — 13 — 7 — 13 — /7 S 1 — 2 — 13 — 0 — 11 —

3. — 5 — 10 — /1 — 5 — 4 M 12 — 6 — 0 — 2 — 6 —

4. — 10 — 7 O 1 — 10 — 3 — /5 — 6 — 7 — 8 — 4 — 5 — 7 —

5. — 8 — 3 — 8 — 3 — /12 M 8 — 4 — 9 —

6. — 11 — 9 — 3 — 8 — /2 — 5 — 1 — 3 L 8 —

7. — 4 — 6 — 5 H 7 — 4 — /7 — 7 — 3 — 7 — 5 — 3 — 8 —

8. — 3 — 3 — 13 — /5 — 5 — 2 — 1 — 3 — 5 N

9. J 5 — 7 — 6 — /1 — 10 — 2 — 9 — 4 — 3 — 10 —

10. — 3 — 17 — 25 — /12 — 4 — 5 — 0 — 9 — 7 — 0 — 3 —

11. — 13 — 1 — 0 — /2 — 9 — 9 — 0 —

12. — 10 — 4 — 4 — /0 — 1 — 1 —

13. — 2 — 11 — 10 — 13 — 5 — /11 — 12 — 0 — 3 — 3 — 5 — 3 — 2 —

14. — 19 — 17 — 0 — 21 — /17 — 7 — 3 — 0 — 13 —

15. — 10 — 11 — 3 — 5 — 4 — 4 — 9 — /4 — 13 — 1 — 13 — 4 — 4 — 7 —

16. — 15 — 19 — 2 — 9 — 6 — 8 — /8 — 4 — 22 — 24 — 1 — 21 —

17. — 1 — 14 — 6 — 2 — 1 — 10 — /16 — 1 — 1 — 1 —

18. — 9 — 6 — 5 — /4 — 3 — 11 — 0 — 8 — 7 —

Quizword Puzzle★★

by Adam Sumera

What kind of puzzle is half trivia quiz and half crossword? The answer is right here.

At each number, Across and Down, we've given you a multiple-choice question. Each of the three possible answers is preceded by a letter. Answer the question, and then use the letter of the correct answer to find the crossword clue for that number.

For example, if you think the answer to 11-Across is "g," then clue "g" in the clue list goes with 11-Across. Also, since each clue is used only once, no other correct answer can have the letter "g." So answering some questions correctly will help you answer the ones you don't know.

When you've matched each crossword clue with its number, solve the clues in regular fashion to finish the crossword.

Answers, page 184

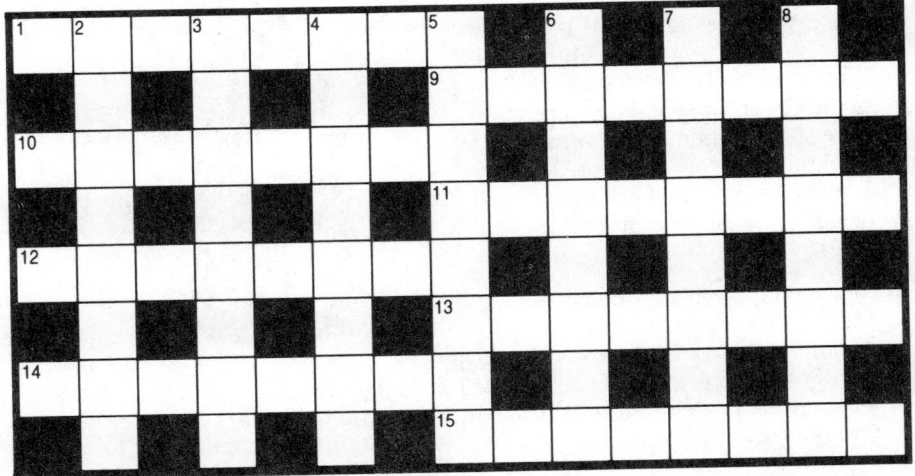

ACROSS

1. A standard piano has 88 keys, of which:
a) most are black
d) most are white
f) 44 are of each color

9. Charles Lutwidge Dodgson's pen name was:
a) George Eliot
e) Mark Twain
g) Lewis Carroll

10. In 1965, Aleksei Leonov became the first man to:
a) walk in space
j) receive an animal's heart in a transplant
k) swim the Bering Strait

11. Jonah was trapped inside the whale for:
b) three days and nights
d) forty days and nights
g) seven years

12. The "dead man's hand," the poker hand that Wild Bill Hickok held when shot, was:
b) four kings
h) a pair of aces and a pair of eights
l) a pair of queens and a pair of jacks

13. Only four nations have competed in *all* of the modern Summer Olympics. They are:
b) Belgium, Ireland, Sweden, USA
i) Canada, Finland, France, Italy
n) Australia, Great Britain, Greece, Switzerland

14. Mount Kosciusko is the highest mountain of:
c) Alaska
f) Australia
j) the moon

15. Only one of the following words does *not* appear in "The Star-Spangled Banner." It is:
c) hearts
g) proof
k) gallantly

CROSSWORD CLUES

a) Ability to wait calmly
b) Legumes used in making tofu
c) Junk mail addressee
d) Left-handed person
e) Hulk Hogan's occupation
f) Evergreen's "fruit": 2 wds.
g) Easily pushed out of sight, as some beds
h) Adjustment knob on a TV
i) U.S. military headquarters
j) Piece of furniture often heated: 2 wds.
k) Keep up, as speed or a lifestyle
l) Handel's *Messiah,* for one
m) Elimination matches before the finals
n) Emergency craft on an ocean liner
o) Number of cards in a suit

DOWN

2. Brass is an alloy of copper and:
c) tin
l) zinc
m) nickel

3. Tom Sawyer and Huck Finn cooked for Jim a pie containing:
d) a file
l) a key
o) a rope ladder

4. Europa, Io, and Callisto are all:
e) Muses
i) moons of Jupiter
o) cars of the 1940s

5. The "R" in Gerald R. Ford's name stands for:
e) Rudolph
m) Reginald
n) Roger

6. "Reign at Tangier" is:
f) a Disneyland ride
h) a poem by Keats
m) an example of a palindrome

7. In the equation "$E = mc^2$," the "m" represents:
h) motion
i) magnetism
j) mass

8. "Hear me talking to you?" were the first words spoken by:
k) Al Jolson in *The Jazz Singer*
n) Alexander Graham Bell on the telephone
o) Mr. Ed to Wilbur

Take the Day Off ★☆

by Richie Chevat

A holiday is more than just a day off—it's an opportunity to celebrate a day of special significance. But the origins and meanings of many of the holidays observed around the world are not as well known as they ought to be. So before you send out those St. Andrew's Day cards, maybe you should take this quiz to see if you know what you're celebrating.

Answers, page 184

HOLIDAY IN, HOLIDAY OUT

One of the following festive histories is untrue. Which one?

1. The French celebrated the New Year on April 1 until, in the 1560s, King Charles IX decreed a change to the Gregorian calendar. The stubborn Frenchmen who refused to celebrate the New Year on January 1 were known as April Fools, and became the butt of many practical jokes.
2. Groundhog Day was conceived in 1869 by the editors of *The Farmer's Almanac*, who, after years of tracking the humble rodent's activities, felt they had scientific proof of the groundhog's ability to predict the weather.
3. The practice of carving out jack-o'-lanterns at Halloween originated in Ireland. Instead of using pumpkins, however, children would carve out rutabagas, turnips, or potatoes.
4. Columbus Day is celebrated not only in the U.S., but also in Central and South America and parts of Canada. It is, moreover, an important holiday in Spain and Italy.
5. The observance of Christmas was declared a penal offense in Puritan-dominated Massachusetts in the late 17th century. A similar law in England also forbade the "heathen" Christmas custom of making plum puddings and mince pies.

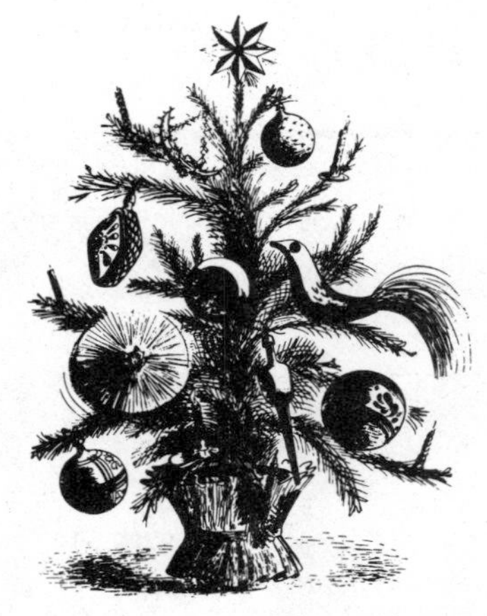

A CLAUS BY ANY OTHER NAME

You better not pout, you better not cry, Wainomoinen is coming to town. Who's Wainomoinen? That's what they call Santa Claus in one of the countries listed below. See if you can match up each country (1–7) with its name for the person (a–g) who brings the gifts.

1. Brazil
2. Bulgaria
3. Czechoslovakia
4. Denmark
5. Italy
6. Finland
7. France

a. Julenissen
b. Wainomoinen
c. Papa Koleda
d. Sao Nicolau
e. Befana
f. Père Noël
g. Svaty Mikulas

THE GREAT WHITE NORTH

Canada celebrates some of the same holidays as the U.S. Which one of the following days is *not* observed by our neighbors to the north?

Thanksgiving
Mother's Day
Memorial Day
Arbor Day
Labor Day

A FEDERAL CASE

The U.S. Congress has declared nine federal legal holidays. How many can you name? Hint: Five of them are celebrated on Mondays.

GREETINGS!

Even though you're far away
From loved ones on a holiday,
In rain and snow and sleet and hail,
Your card will make it
through the mail.

Can you arrange the following holidays according to the number of greeting cards sent in the U.S. each year, from highest to lowest?

Christmas
Easter
Father's Day
Halloween
Hanukkah
Jewish New Year
Mother's Day
St. Patrick's Day
Thanksgiving
Valentine's Day

HOLIDAY HANDLES

You probably know that Mardi Gras means "fat Tuesday" and that Halloween, formerly All Hallows E'en, is the eve of All Saints' Day. How much do you know about the following holiday names (or names associated with holidays)?

1. What is the most widely accepted explanation for the source of the name "Easter"?
   a. It comes from the word *astro,* meaning "star," after the star seen in the sky on the night Christ rose from his tomb.
   b. It was named after Eostre, the Anglo-Saxon goddess of spring.
   c. The source was *asterno,* Spanish for "ass," after the Castilian donkey that Christ rode into Jerusalem.
2. Legend has it that Saint Patrick drove all the snakes (and vermin) out of Ireland. Exactly how did he accomplish this feat?
   a. By beating a drum
   b. By beating them with his staff
   c. By sending for a snake charmer from Bombay
3. The Germanic name "Kriss Kringle" has become synonymous with Santa Claus. How did the name originate?
   a. It means "Holy Nicholas."
   b. It is a corruption of *Christkindlein,* or Christ-child.
   c. "Krisp Kringles" was a cereal traditionally eaten on Christmas morning.
4. St. Valentine's Day began as the Roman feast of *Lupercalia,* during which names of sweethearts were picked out of a box. In trying to wipe out the pagan aspect of the festival in the fifth century, the Church renamed it St. Valentine's Day. But why was St. Valentine chosen for such an honor?
   a. He was the patron saint of lovers.
   b. He arranged the marriage of Pope Leo XI's parents.
   c. *Lupercalia* and St. Valentine's death took place on nearly the same day.
5. In England, Australia, and some other Commonwealth countries, the day *after* Christmas is an important holiday called Boxing Day. Gifts are exchanged and many people have open-house parties. But why is it called Boxing Day?
   a. "Boxing" is old Cockney slang for "partying."
   b. The day commemorates a Norman victory over the Anglo-Saxons that took place on Boxing Field.
   c. The name comes from the custom of giving gift boxes to the tradespeople one has done business with all year.
6. Guy Fawkes Day is celebrated in England every November 5th with fireworks, while scarecrows, known as "guys," are burned in effigy. Who was Guy Fawkes, and what did he do to deserve such a fête?
   a. He beheaded Ann Boleyn.
   b. He was the illegitimate son of Queen Elizabeth I who led an unsuccessful revolt against King Charles I.
   c. He plotted to blow up the Parliament building in 1605.

PRACTICE, PRACTICE, PRACTICE

You may not be superstitious, but you'd better believe that many holidays have some pretty strange practices and beliefs associated with them.

1. The Druids were the priests and priestesses of the Celtic people in what is now England, Ireland, and France. Quite a few of our celebratory customs have come down from them. Which one of these holiday symbols or rituals was *not* originated by the Druids?
   a. Mistletoe at Christmas
   b. Easter parades
   c. The maypole
   d. Black cats at Halloween
2. In England, there have been many Valentine's Day superstitions that were guaranteed to foretell whom a young woman would marry. An unmarried woman might be told to do any of the following things on Valentine's Day, except one. Which one was supposed to bring bad luck instead of a happy union?
   a. Striking her forehead with a rose petal
   b. Pinning five bay leaves to her pillow
   c. Bringing a snowdrop into the house
   d. Circling a church 12 times at the stroke of midnight
3. Valentine's Day isn't the only holiday when a young woman can find out whom she will marry. In 18th- and 19th-century England, it was believed that on Halloween a girl might magically see the face of her future husband. According to this belief, which of these methods would *not* work?
   a. Finding a spotted mushroom
   b. Eating an apple while standing in front of a mirror
   c. Placing hazelnuts in front of a fire
   d. Watching a snail crawl through the ashes of a fireplace
4. The Germans who settled in Pennsylvania brought us many Christmas customs and superstitions. Which one of the following would *not* bring bad luck or illness if done on Christmas Day?
   a. Spinning or sewing
   b. A bath or change of underwear
   c. Eating sauerkraut
   d. Leaving an open grave
5. The ancient practice of coloring and giving eggs originated in the Mideast, and was adopted by the early Church in its celebration of Easter. Which is *not* a traditional belief about Easter eggs?
   a. Yolks of eggs laid on Good Friday will turn to diamonds in 100 years.
   b. Eggs laid on Good Friday and eaten on Easter Sunday promote the fertility of trees and crops and protect against a sudden death.
   c. Two yolks in an Easter egg portend coming financial prosperity.
   d. Accepting the gift of an Easter egg from an enemy brings bad luck for the coming year.
6. Which one of the following superstitions is *not* a Yule log tradition?
   a. The number of sparks that it shoots off indicates the number of chickens the next year will provide.
   b. To put out a Yule log's fire with anything other than blessed water will bring a full year of misfortune.
   c. A Yule log's ashes and charcoal can alleviate swollen glands.
   d. The remains of a Yule log, placed under a bed, protect against fire and thunder.

Number, Please! ★★

by Mary Ellen Slate

Simple arithmetic—and a little knowledge of trivia—are all it takes to solve this numerical puzzle. Each clue is in the form of a two-part equation. When you know the answers to both parts, perform the calculation indicated by the arithmetic symbol and write the result (which will be a whole number) in the box corresponding to the letter of the clue. When all the boxes have been correctly filled in, each horizontal and vertical row and each of the two corner-to-corner diagonals will add up to the same key number. Note: Once you've determined the key number by completing one row, you'll have an additional clue to finishing the others. Some numbers appear more than once in the puzzle.

Answers, page 184

A	**B**	**C**	**D**	**E**
F	**G**	**H**	**I**	**J**
K	**L**	**M**	**N**	**O**
P	**Q**	**R**	**S**	**T**
U	**V**	**W**	**X**	**Y**

CLUES

A. Rings in the Olympic symbol − Rings in a circus
B. ___ *Dalmatians* − Songs in Casey Kasem's countdown
C. Beetle Bailey's dumb pal + Mr. Mostel
D. Kennedy's PT boat − Piano keys
E. Caesar's "fatal day" + The IRS's "fatal day"
F. Bo Derek + Vicks Formula ___
G. Hours in a day ÷ Oxen in a span
H. Men on a dead man's chest + Coins in the fountain
I. Maids a-milking × Seats on a tandem bike
J. Commandments + Freedoms
K. "Little Indians" − Cleveland Indians (on the field at one time)
L. Sawbuck − Maximum number of World Series games
M. Squares in tic-tac-toe × Sides on a square
N. Original U.S. colonies + Baker's dozen
O. ___-in-hand × Inches in a foot
P. Cat's lives × Kittens who lost their mittens
Q. RPM of an old record ÷ Hitchcock's "Steps"
R. Legendary Cities of Gold + Karats in pure gold
S. A gross ÷ Wise men
T. "___ Tears" − *Playhouse* ___
U. Trivial Pursuit categories × Lines in a limerick
V. Witching hour × Macbeth's witches
W. Highest roulette number − Digits in a local phone number
X. Phillips ___ ÷ *Catch-*___
Y. Points for a king in blackjack + Points on the Star of David

Famous Footsteps★

by Stephanie Abrams-Hook

Celebrities have always had big footsteps, as shown by the cement in front of Sid Grauman's old Chinese Theatre in Hollywood. Often the children of celebrities follow in these footsteps, too. Hidden in the footprint below are the last names of 41 celebrity offspring who have gone on to become celebrities themselves. How many of them can you find? The names are hidden horizontally, vertically, and diagonally, but each is in a straight line. The first names, given in parentheses, are for your information only and are not hidden in the grid. When you're done with the puzzle, see how many of the famous show-biz parents you can name for extra credit. *Answers, page 184*

1. ALDA (Alan)
2. ASTIN (Mackenzie, Sean)
3. BAXTER-BIRNEY (Meredith)
4. BEGLEY (Ed Jr.)
5. BELAFONTE-HARPER (Shari)
6. CARRADINE (David, Keith, Robert)
7. CASH (Roseanne)
8. COLE (Natalie)
9. CONRAD (Chris, Shane)
10. CROSBY (Gary, Mary)
11. CURTIS (Jamie Lee)
12. DALY (Tyne)
13. DERN (Laura)
14. DOUGLAS (Michael)
15. ESTEVEZ (Emilio)
16. FISHER (Carrie)
17. FONDA (Jane, Peter)
18. GREY (Jennifer)
19. HAGMAN (Larry)
20. HALE (Alan Jr.)
21. HARGITAY (Mariska)
22. HUSTON (Anjelica)
23. JUDD (Wynonna)
24. KATT (William)
25. LAMAS (Lorenzo)
26. LEMMON (Chris)
27. LUFT (Lorna)
28. MACARTHUR (James)
29. MARTIN (Dean Paul)
30. MILLS (Juliet, Hayley)
31. MINNELLI (Liza)
32. REDGRAVE (Lynn, Vanessa)
33. REINER (Rob)
34. ROSSELLINI (Isabella)
35. SHEEN (Charlie)
36. SINATRA (Frank Jr., Nancy)
37. SLEZAK (Erika)
38. THOMAS (Marlo)
39. WELSH (Tahnee)
40. WYNN (Keenan)
41. ZAPPA (Dweezil, Moon Unit)

```
                        N F E
                      F I S H B
                    I S T U F E T
                  E H E S L N L C
                N E V T A I U A U
                R E O A D N O F R
                Z N E A R Y O O T
              M N A R H L G S N I
              E A R P A S S D T S
              K A C M P E S A E G
              C A A A L A A R H R
              C S Z L R C M N A E
              H O I E I T O O R Y
              N N L N L P H C P Y
              I A E E A S T U E
              H S M A R T I N R
                D M G O H R F
                A O N A I F A
                L N R B H L
              T Y G R H D M
              W I E S A I
              T T A K N H
            A X C E N O
          Y A     E L D
          B E B L
        J S A L G U O D
        U O I M G L O
        D R E I N E R
        D C C L R K B
          H C L E W
              S D
```

When the Boomers Were Babies . . . and the Price Was Right★☆

by Randi Hacker

Ah, the fabulous Fifties: The era of Elvis and Ike, pedal-pushers and pompadours. And best of all, low prices. At the beginning of that booming decade, 60 cents could get you into a double feature with enough change for a bottle of ice-cold Coke (5 cents). Can you guess the 1950 price of these other items?

Answers, page 184

1. Be the first on your block to tune in to Uncle Milty or the Brooklyn Dodgers on one of these RCA Victor Fairfield television sets. That built-in antenna will give you a steady picture on the 16″ screen.

2. Never mind Wildroot Cream Oil, Charlie. Give your scalp a 60-second workout with Vitalis and you'll have "handsomer hair."

3. Want to have the life of Riley? Relax with William Bendix and enjoy a nice cold bottle of Pabst Blue Ribbon beer.

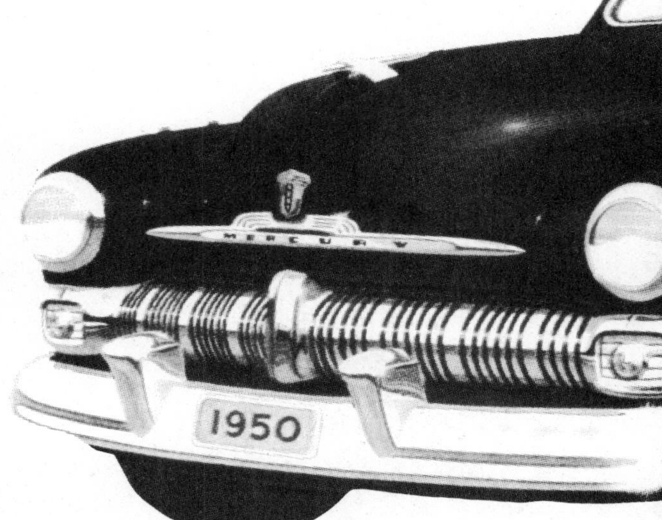

4. Ladies who want to be home on the range need a Westinghouse Rancho electric stove. Thanks to its "Tel-A-Glance" temperature control, you can have those roasts and pies ready just as hubby gets home from work.

5. If you plan to wear the fashions of the Fifties, you need the "Figure of the Fifties." And for that, you need the girdle of the Fifties: the Playtex Living Girdle. No seams, no stitches, and best of all, no bones.

6. Relive the wonderful moments with the Cine-Kodak Reliant movie camera. The pictures are as real as life, and you can even shoot color film.

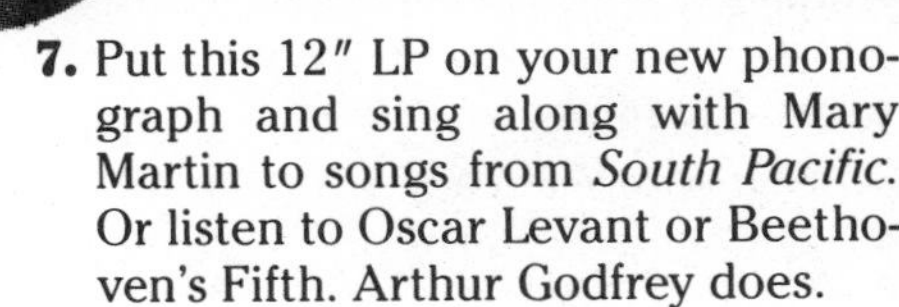

7. Put this 12″ LP on your new phonograph and sing along with Mary Martin to songs from *South Pacific.* Or listen to Oscar Levant or Beethoven's Fifth. Arthur Godfrey does.

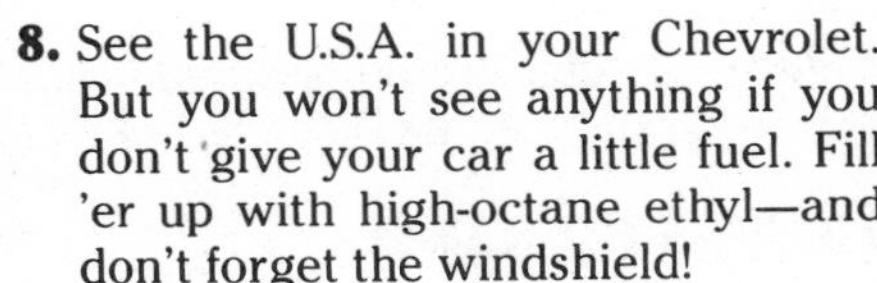

8. See the U.S.A. in your Chevrolet. But you won't see anything if you don't give your car a little fuel. Fill 'er up with high-octane ethyl—and don't forget the windshield!

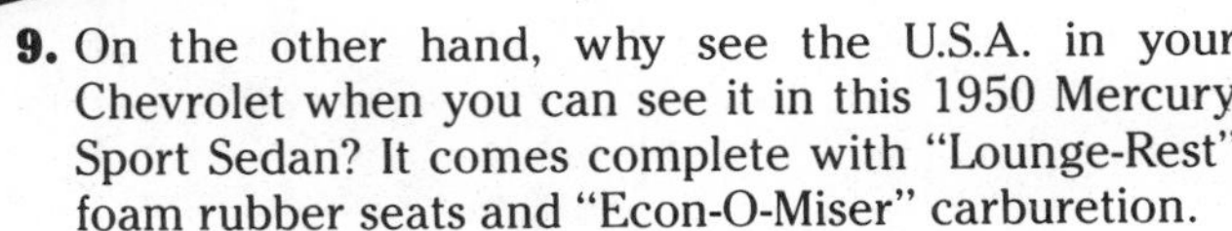

9. On the other hand, why see the U.S.A. in your Chevrolet when you can see it in this 1950 Mercury Sport Sedan? It comes complete with "Lounge-Rest" foam rubber seats and "Econ-O-Miser" carburetion.

10. There's nothing like a good fresh-brewed cup of coffee, whether it's drip or electric perk. Especially when it's Maxwell House. Good to the last drop.

11. The crowning touch for any well-dressed man is a Stetson hat. And the Stetsonian model is sure to "enhance your own distinctive personality."

12. So you won't get five o'clock shadow by the time the Friday night fights come on the radio, use the Gillette Super Speed Razor. And the price includes a convenient 10-blade dispenser in a new Styrene travel case.

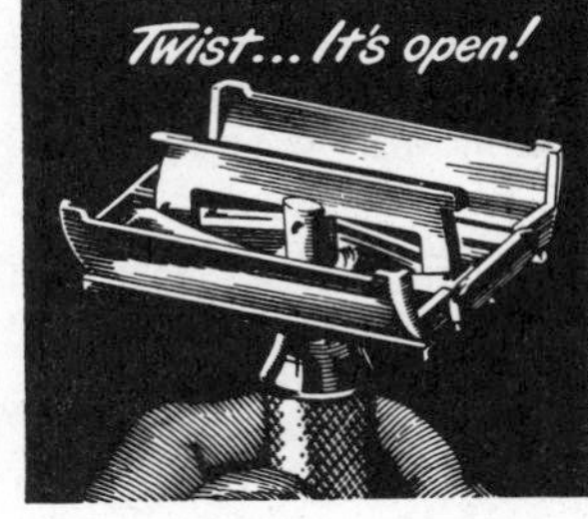

The Melting Pot Quiz ★☆

by Robert Leighton

Scratch anything American, and you'll probably find something a little foreign. Even apple pie, the quintessential symbol of things American, came to us from England.

By the time the Statue of Liberty (itself a gift from France) was assembled in New York Harbor over one hundred years ago, immigrants had already begun to change the way America spoke, ate, and played. We've stirred up the melting pot a bit to see what makes it cook. See how familiar you are with its many and varied ingredients by taking this all-American quiz. *Answers, page 185*

HOWDY, NEIGHBOR!

Families arriving for the first time in the United States often choose to live among their own people, creating national pockets of ethnic groups. In which American city (a–g) would you be most likely to find the following surnamed families (1–7)?

1. Santini (Italian)	**a.** Miami
2. Sanchez (Mexican)	**b.** Honolulu
3. Peterson (Swedish)	**c.** San Francisco
4. Ito (Japanese)	**d.** New York City
5. Rodriguez (Cuban)	**e.** Chicago
6. Lee (Chinese)	**f.** Los Angeles
7. Kowalski (Polish)	**g.** Minneapolis

FIFTY INTO THREE

Three U.S. states are home to 50 percent of all foreign-born citizens in the country. Which three states are they?

FOREIGN EXCHANGE

The years 1901–1910 saw the United States population grow by 13 million people. How many of them were immigrants?

a. 2 million
b. 5 million
c. 9 million

TAKE A NUMBER

In recent years, the U.S. has cut back several times on the number of immigrants it permits to enter the country. As of 1980, when the most recent quotas were enacted, how many are allowed each year?

a. 27,000
b. 270,000
c. 2,700,000

INSIDE INFORMATION

Immigrants who want to become naturalized citizens must demonstrate some knowledge of America's history and governmental processes by answering such basic questions as: "How many judges are in the Supreme Court?" "What name is given to the first 10 Amendments to the Constitution of the United States?" and "Name the four freedoms given in the First Amendment." Do you know the answers?

MARQUEE BENDERS

Many celebrities change their given names to ones that sound less ethnic but are often, though not always, close to the originals. See if you can match the ethnic unknowns (1–7) to their more familiar aliases (a–g).

1. Belle Silverman	**a.** Pat Benatar
2. Michael Shalhoub	**b.** Martin Sheen
3. Patricia Andrejewski	**c.** Omar Sharif
4. Anna Maria Italiano	**d.** Beverly Sills
5. Allen Konigsberg	**e.** Walter Matthau
6. Ramon Estevez	**f.** Anne Bancroft
7. Walter Matuschanskayasky	**g.** Woody Allen

I JUST FLEW IN FROM...

Some of America's most noted personalities were once strangers in a strange land. Can you match each of these famous immigrants (1–8) with his birthplace (a–h)?

1. Isaac Asimov	**a.** Copenhagen, Denmark
2. Victor Borge	**b.** Petrovichi, Russia
3. José Greco	**c.** Lancashire, England
4. John Houseman	**d.** Abruzzi, Italy
5. Engelbert Humperdinck	**e.** Bucharest, Rumania
6. Ted Koppel	**f.** Berlin, Germany
7. Mike Nicols	**g.** Haifa, Israel
8. Gene Simmons (of KISS)	**h.** Madras, India

FOREIGN FLAVOR

Dumplings and pancakes seem to be staples in virtually every ethnic cuisine. Can you match each foreign-flavored dumpling (1–6) with its ethnic counterpart, the stuffed pancake (a–f), and name the culture of origin for each pair?

1. gnocchi	**a.** tamales
2. albondigas	**b.** crêpes
3. quenelles	**c.** manicotti
4. kreplach	**d.** blintzes
5. won tons	**e.** blini
6. piroshki	**f.** eggrolls

WHADDYA SAY?

More than 10 percent of American adults speak a language other than English at home. Place these foreign languages in order of their frequency of use in the United States.

a. Polish	**c.** Spanish	**e.** German
b. French	**d.** Italian	**f.** Chinese

O TANNENBAUM

Our many Christmas traditions have very diverse origins. See if you can match each Christmas "gift" (1–7) with the culture that gave it to us (a–g).

1. Plum pudding	**a.** Jewish
2. Christmas trees	**b.** Mexican
3. Kissing under the mistletoe	**c.** Danish
4. The man who wrote "White Christmas"	**d.** German
	e. Scandinavian
5. Poinsettia flowers	**f.** British
6. The "X" in "Xmas"	**g.** Greek
7. Christmas seals	

PARDON OUR FRENCH

Many words entered our language through foreign tongues used by visitors to describe American experiences. Can you tell which language gave us each of the following groups of familiar words?

1. barbecue, macho, ranch, stampede

2. wagon, yacht, stoop, sketch

3. klutz, schlock, chutzpah, maven

4. balcony, piano, studio, carnival

5. pretzel, delicatessen, hamburger, kindergarten

GOOD IDEA

Upon whose culture do historians believe the Founding Fathers modeled the United States Constitution?

a. Iroquois (American Indian)
b. Belgian
c. Norwegian
d. Russian
e. Pakistani

NATION IDENTIFICATION

You don't have to turn to foreign-language stations to see people from abroad on television. These 10 foreign-born characters were featured in popular American TV shows. Can you name them?

1. *Kung Fu*'s shaven-headed martial artist, who emigrated from China to the Old West
2. The German housekeeper who helped keep things straight for a dizzy governor on *Benson*
3. *Saturday Night Live*'s swinging Czechoslovakian brothers who picked up "foxy babes" with their broken English
4. The Cuban bandleader whose wife caused havoc everywhere she went on *I Love Lucy*
5. The Japanese owner of the typical 1950s drive-in malt shop on *Happy Days*
6. The blond, self-possessed, Russian partner on *The Man from U.N.C.L.E.*
7. The shy Italian mouse puppet regularly seen on *The Ed Sullivan Show*
8. The Korean wife of an American hospital worker on *AfterMASH*
9. The pair of dotty English girls who lived upstairs on *The Odd Couple*
10. The naïve garage mechanic of completely indeterminate origin on *Taxi*

Can You Answer This? ★★★

by Henry Hook

You may not know the answers to all of these 20 questions, but think of the interesting additions to your knowledge!

Answers, page 184

1. What are co, e, et, hesh, jhe, and thon?

2. What would you do with a swacket?

3. Tasters may refer to it as austere, brackish, bright, clean, dank, flabby, ferruginous, skunky, swampy, or tinny. What is it?

4. The idea is to fit all the nubs into the proper voids to form locks. When all the locks are thus formed, what do you have?

5. The name of a certain familiar object, in a Pacific Islands Pidgin English, is "scratch 'im in belly, out come squeak allasame pussycat." What is the object?

6. What should you feed your grown-up pet moth?

7. Is a man or a woman more likely to stutter?

8. Twice daily, a panel of five men gets together in a small office in London to determine an important international statistic. Which?

9. About 1/6 of all Tibetan men follow the same occupation. What is it?

10. Whatever happened to the first typewritten manuscript for publication?

11. Mildred and Patty Hill wrote a song in 1936, and their estate still collects royalties on it. It's the most frequently sung song in America. Name it.

12. A Birmingham, Alabama, newspaper once included this question in its poll: "If you had one extra place in your fallout shelter, to whom would you give it?" What profession got the fewest votes?

13. Members of the World War II French Resistance had a euphemism all their own for excusing themselves to the "powder room." What was their pet expression?

14. You're on the beach. You pick up a seashell, and you claim you can hear the ocean. But what do you really hear?

15. Why are wine bottles tinted?

16. In 18th-century English gambling dens, there was an employee whose only job was to _______ the dice in the event of a police raid. Fill in the blank.

17. The Aztecs enjoyed a primitive version of one-on-one basketball, using a solid rubber ball to be shot through a stone ring. The winner received an odd prize. What was it?

18. The answer is "Aerospatial 001." What's the question?

19. True or false: Studies at the University of Michigan show that the better-educated you are, the less susceptible you are to colds.

20. In ancient Rome, what could you tell about a woman with blond hair?

7 ACROSS, DOWN, AND ALL AROUND

Round and Round★★

by Will Shortz

Sixteen overlapping plates have been laid in a ring at right. Each answer is a word of six or more letters that spins around one of the plates, beginning in the space indicated and proceeding clockwise. The end of each answer will overlap with the front, as the H in HEALTH or the LE in LEGIBLE. The first answer, NIACIN, has been entered for you.

Answers, page 185

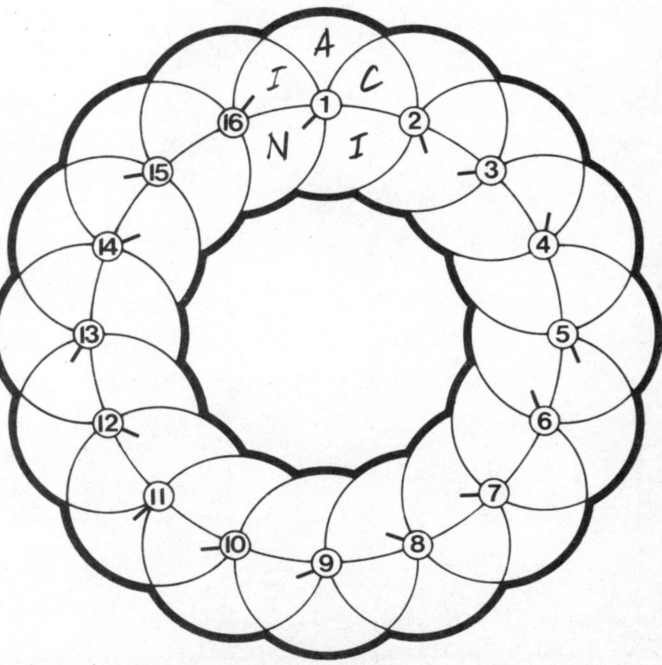

CLUES

1 B vitamin
2 The Beatles' "____ to Ride"
3 Wood-eating insect
4 Follower of Mohammed
5 "Half" or "full" wrestling hold
6 Perk up
7 Make clear
8 College or parish head
9 Home of the Blue Jays
10 Loyal team fan
11 Roman dawn goddess
12 Ship's turning mechanism
13 Refused, as permission
14 Geniuses
15 Marksman's aim
16 Fix firmly, as habits

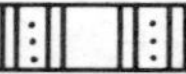

Pencil Pointers★

by Karen Hodge

In this crossword the clues appear in the grid itself. Enter the answers in the direction of the pointers. *Answers, page 185*

Writer Terkel | Region | Hit doll of the '80s | — about (near) | Wall painting | Neat — pin | Drench | "This is only — ." | 1988 Olympic country | Fairy | Without money | Actress Gardner | Rolls up, as a flag | Stevie Nicks's group | — job (get hired) | Fake

City near Seattle | Trees with acorns | Lottery of a sort

Seventh planet | On the summit of | Of a small egg

The King and I actress | Allen & Black | Naughts

Native Israeli | Sister of Zsa Zsa | Letter turner White | Grab | Musical piece | Swan's lover in myth

Thick carpet | Shirley Booth role | Nimble | Rise, in a magic show | Actor Guinness | Box score figure

Speedy plane | Mover's truck | Dieter's lunch | NOW cause | Pull | Prank | French —, S. Am.

Grows old | Picnic pests | Chinese society | Song "— Tray" | Spanish mister

Goes fast | Test | Orderly | Solemn and sedate

Gladden | Singer Guthrie | Lacking clear shape | Golfbag toter

Allow | Short-stop Peewee | What eds. read | Jazz flutist Herbie | Met by chance | Reddy's "I Am —"

Patriotic songs | College sports org. | Over-stuff | Cab | Carpet-working tool | Equip | Utmost degree | Year: Sp.

"Itchy feet" | Long, long time | Farm building | Detroit product

Birthday dessert | Shoe box number | The U in B.T.U. | And not | Try | Goddess of Egypt | Bird abode | Helium or neon

Enemy of the Allies | Brit. military award | Bruce Willis series

Lent a hand | Beaver-like fur | Midday | Torrid | On the ocean

Leaves school | Station porter | Baltimore player | Pontius — | Hosiery mishap | Vendor | TV host Westheimer | Smooch | Horse sounds

They bite Fido | Model T's | With least delay | Poetry

One Great Lake | Spat | Largest continent | June 6, 1944 | Oolong or pekoe | Volcano of Sicily | Square dance

Pickle type | Put in more ammo | Reply: Abbr. | River to the Rhone

Sissy Spacek movie

Der — (Adenauer) | Nova Scotia native | Makes sharper

Equals | School papers | No longer fresh

Spell-Weaving★★

by Mike Shenk

The answers to this puzzle's clues form a continuous thread that is interwoven like a tapestry. Enter one letter per space, beginning at the top as indicated by the arrow and proceeding downward. When you reach an edge, make a right-angle turn, following the direction of the arrow on the corner. The clues appear in order, and the number of letters in each answer is given in parentheses. Weave the right spells and the puzzle will fill in like magic.

Answers, page 185

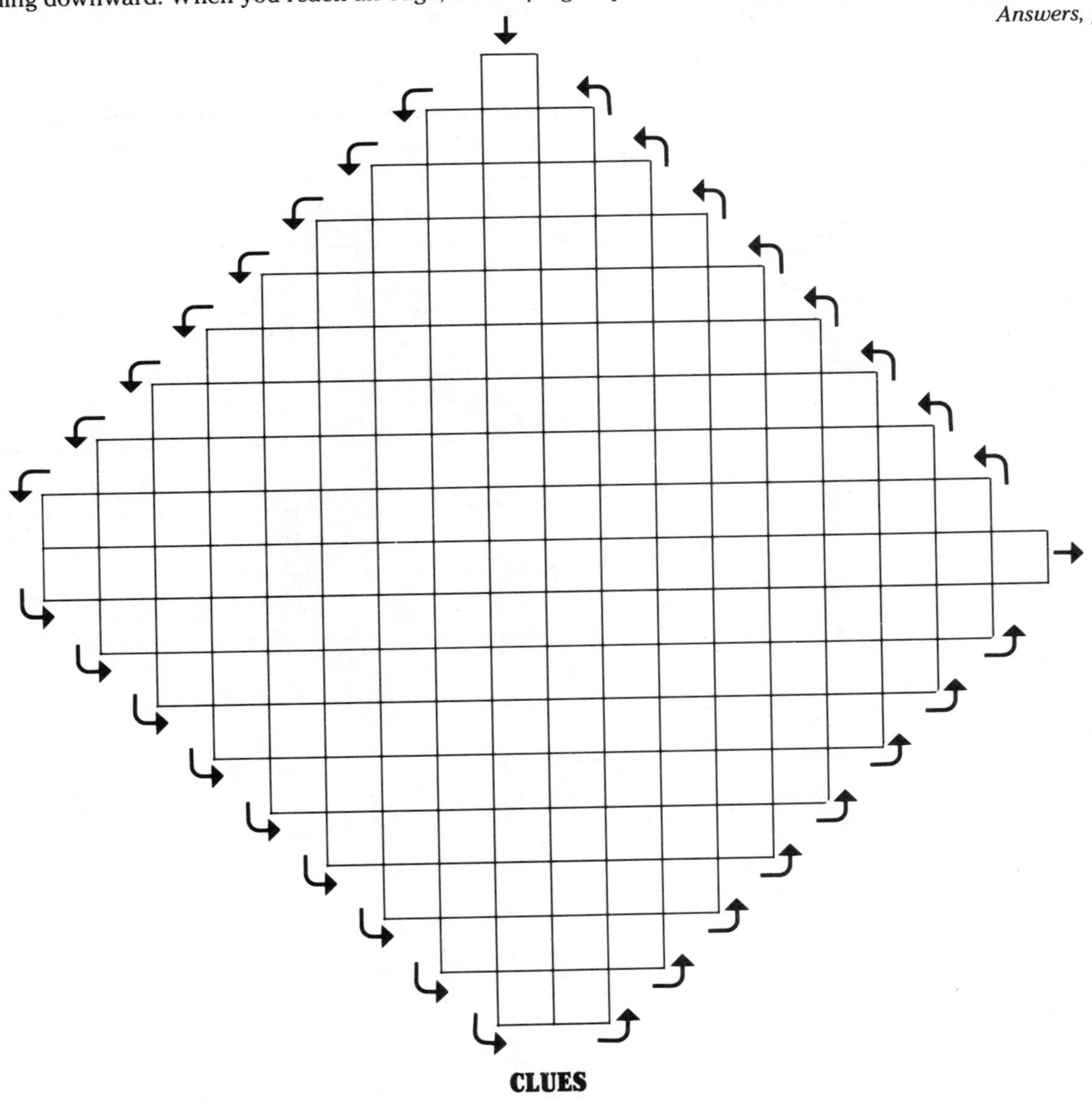

CLUES

1 Spell-weaving (7)
2 Composite picture (7)
3 Soloist's concert (7)
4 Deli purchase (8)
5 Call up (9)
6 Place for "the daring young man" (7)
7 Trombone part (5)
8 Cuzco Indians (5)
9 Coed's residence (4)
10 Cookout need (8)
11 Stood for (11)
12 Perfect (5)
13 Direction of a quarterback's pass (7)
14 Space under a desk (8)
15 Brought back from the dead (11)
16 Salt additive (6)
17 Russian kings (5)
18 Word after chair or third (6)
19 Crazes (6)
20 He uses influence for self-gain (10)
21 Fertilizer ingredients (8)
22 Stick out (8)
23 Regions (5)
24 Group on the warpath? (5)
25 Deals out (5)
26 Oxygen-supplying device (7)
27 Hugo's "Hunchback" (9)
28 Mechanic's tire operation (9)
29 Knight wear (5)
30 Clichéd depiction (10)
31 Intimidates (6)
32 Turning part (5)
33 Waldorf, e.g. (5)
34 Tweets (8)
35 Soil (8)
36 Ponders (9)
37 Least tardy (9)
38 Horse halter? (4)
39 Mischievous (6)
40 Milwaukee player (6)
41 Snug feeling (8)
42 Party cry (8)
43 Disavowals (7)
44 Domineering (5)

Going Places★★

by Trip Payne

When completed, the grid below will contain the names of the 31 methods of travel listed at the bottom of the page. These will interlock across and down as in a standard crisscross puzzle or Scrabble Crossword Game. The only words that go in the puzzle are the ones in the list. Can you fill them in? To help you, all the As, Bs, and Cs have been put in the grid for you. Thus CAB is already spelled out (lower middle), and RACECAR and BICYCLE will each fit in only one place. Every word you enter will, in turn, restrict where the remaining words can go. The finished puzzle has a unique solution.

Answer, page 185

A						B								A		
										C	A					
			A	C		C	A									
				A								C	A			
						C		C								
A														C		
											B		A			C
				A										C		
		A														
										C						
	A				C	A		A		A						
												A			C	
A			B				C									
							A						A		A	
			A				B								C	
	A															

WORDS	BOAT	TANK	LINER	WHEEL	BICYCLE	STEAMER	UNICYCLE
ARK	CART	CANOE	TRAIN	SLEIGH	CARAVAN	AIRPLANE	AUTOMOBILE
CAB	RAFT	COACH	TRUCK	SUBWAY	RACECAR	CARRIAGE	HANG-GLIDER
CAR	SLED	KAYAK	WAGON	AUTOBUS	SCOOTER	TRICYCLE	HELICOPTER

Trio ★★

by Mike Shenk

This puzzle gives you three grids for the price of one. And three sets of clues to go with them, so you can work all of the crosswords at the same time. What's the catch? Each clue number is followed by three clues to three different answers. The puzzle is to figure out which answer goes in which grid. The answers to 1-Across have been filled in for you.

Answer, page 185

ACROSS

1 Horror movie liquid
Suffer anxiety
Droplets

6 Fable ending
Easy wins
Is wide open

11 Make dry and withered
Country singer Travis
Key

12 Scent
Steer clear of
Video game brand

13 Writer Chekhov
Stage comment
Blazing

14 Dolt
Alice star Linda
Train station

15 Uprising
Egyptian beetle
Move back

17 Allows
Actor Richard
Sty cry

18 Historic time
"With it"
Logging tool

19 Workman
Sailor's balance: 2 wds.
Sign (checks)

21 Intent look
Classic language
Anglo-___

22 Party pro
Religious sufferers
Easter events

25 Porky, e.g.
Army address
Urban music style

28 Resound
Trebek of *Jeopardy!*
Dutch cheese

29 Madrid lady
Taxi Driver star
Football's Knute

31 Poisonous
Make amends
Desire

33 Fiction book
Blubber source
Rx amounts

34 Sports site
Some Picassos
Pursue

35 Sheepish
Ludicrous
Birth-related

36 Rapidity
Digging tool
Lairs

37 Indianapolis team
Beats at chess
Worries

DOWN

1 Extra
Impudent
Little crown

2 Javelin
English county
Thin cookie

3 Available: 2 wds.
Still breathing
Writer Jong

4 Scent
Lot size
Fix over

5 Outstanding
Prime time soap
John Huston's last film: 2 wds.

6 L.A. player
Insane
Toothpaste type

7 Salem's state
Lawrence of Arabia star
Arthurian isle

8 Road worker
Lasso user
Mme. Curie

9 Plug part
Blue-pencils
Love, Italian-style

10 Not now
Feel
Goes under

16 CPA's concern
Billy goat feature
Computer key

20 Repudiates
Mystery poison
Ennui

21 High
Chauvinistic
Bewail

22 Pie nut
Averages
Nab

23 Be unruly: 2 wds.
Worship
Hawaii hello

24 Harper sitcom
J.R.'s state
Great reviews

25 State as fact
Do figure 8s
Competitor

26 Kin by marriage
"___ we all?"
Singer Cara

27 Air components
Movie units
Magnet ends

30 Tête-à-tête
Something forbidden
Exploding star

32 Language suffix
Middling grade
Prof's assts.

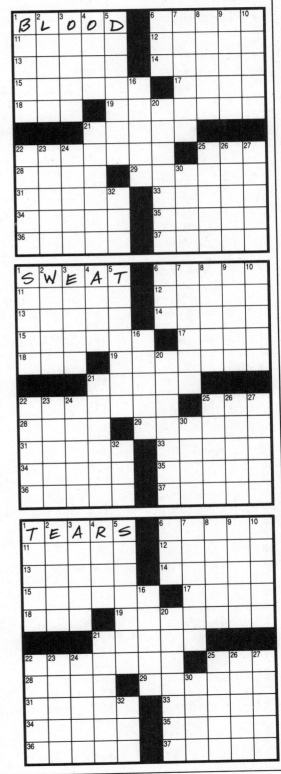

BLOOD

TEARS

Jumbo Crossword★★

by Emily Cox and Henry Rathvon

Answer, page 186

ACROSS

1 Mr. "X" of '60s politics
8 Up, in baseball: 2 wds.
13 React in terror
19 Pacific islands, collectively
20 "Do I dare to eat ___?": T. S. Eliot, 2 wds.
21 Grads
22 Law
23 Lockup site: 2 wds.
25 Backtalk
26 Needle-and-thread worker
28 Mr. Brezhnev
29 Half CXVIII
30 At any time
32 Depended
35 *Killing Fields* journalist Dith ___
36 Pitney or Hackman
37 Ancient Asians
39 Tweety Pie's pursuer
41 Three-piece suit parts
42 "I Can Do ___" (*A Chorus Line* song)
44 Remarkable exploit
45 Subatomic particle
47 Have high hopes
50 Accustomed
52 Inflationary paths?
56 Bugs Bunny's studio: 2 wds.
59 Polar feature
60 Orally
61 Lubricates
62 Virgo's predecessor
63 Saint Bernard's mission
64 Hare-tortoise affair
65 Noted Mama
66 Cleaned, as a deck
68 One of the Gershwins
69 Patriotic grp.
70 Brusque
71 Geometric diamond
72 Germany-Poland border river
73 Blotto
75 Grew bored
76 Equalizes
77 Storage building
78 *Mad* competitor
79 Architect Christopher
80 Mechanical turner
82 Slower-witted
83 Homey spots
86 Like the Sahara
87 Flowering plant of the Scottish highlands
88 Soap cakes
89 *Un* ___ (a little): Fr.
90 Storage crib
91 August meteor
92 Jazz great Brubeck
93 Beach sidler
94 Whom checks are made to
96 "Sn" in the periodic table
97 Former Yugoslav president
98 Take over through assimilation
99 Mean
100 What Gertrude Ederle swam: 2 wds.
103 Put a foot forward
105 Calm down
106 Corpuscle carrier
107 Having handles, as a jug
109 ___ no good (mischievous)
110 Thunder god
111 Of punishment
114 Ides of March, e.g.
117 Computer hookup
121 *Amo, amas,* ___
122 Southern constellation ("the Peacock")
123 Dull as dishwater
125 Singer Horne
126 Beatty or Buntline
127 Stars-to-be
129 Go at breakneck pace
131 6-pt. football plays
132 Boot camp boss: 2 wds.
136 Lovey-dovey
138 Concurs
139 Watery route
140 False tooth
141 Opening word for Ali Baba
142 Collage artist Max
143 Showed contempt

DOWN

1 Shiite, e.g.
2 On the go
3 Sprung up
4 Lion or lynx
5 Burden
6 Metric quart
7 Star of *I'm No Angel*: 2 wds.
8 Mil. mailing address
9 ___ Aviv
10 Scoop out water
11 Say yes
12 Geometric law
13 Sleek fabric
14 Attired
15 Tire track
16 Zola and others
17 Apply oil religiously
18 Impudent lasses
20 Post-prank utterance: 2 wds.
24 Entraps
27 Tarzan portrayer Ron
31 Courtly following
33 Track & field competitions
34 "... till ___ do us part"
36 Literary categories
38 Fragment
40 Foundry employee
41 Spoken
43 ___ Lingus (Irish airline)
46 Steeples
47 Edgar and Emmy, e.g.
48 Low bow
49 Put off till tomorrow
50 Site for a watch
51 More moonstruck
53 Like a klutz
54 Bogey's Bacall
55 Asparagus pieces
57 Chess need
58 Blubbered
65 Prodded theatrically
66 ___ up (resided)
67 Rose-to-be
70 *Mask* actress
71 Seeking assistance: 2 wds.
72 Finished
74 Did some blacksmithing
75 Some ballot votes
76 Paleozoic and Precambrian
78 Like a virgin
79 *The Way We* ___
80 Temple teachers
81 The East
82 Three times: Prefix
83 Pandemonium
84 Pie-maker
85 Without being obvious
87 Cattleman, at times
88 Clean oneself up
91 Friend through letters: 2 wds.
92 Deceit
93 Computer key
95 Say over
97 Giggle girlishly
98 Rebound
101 Ran relaxedly
102 Sarcastic laugh
104 Slander
108 Assorted
110 Clothes, informally
111 Bamboo-eating "bears"
112 Come into view
113 Low points
115 Counterfeiter of a sort
116 Spigot
118 Alternate byway
119 Survive
120 In a conglomerate
122 Desperado chasers
124 Neighbor of Saudi Arabia
127 Mr. Kadiddlehopper
128 Penn or Connery
130 Socially acceptable
133 Grassy area
134 Comments with "shucks"
135 ___ "King" Cole
137 Highway, for short

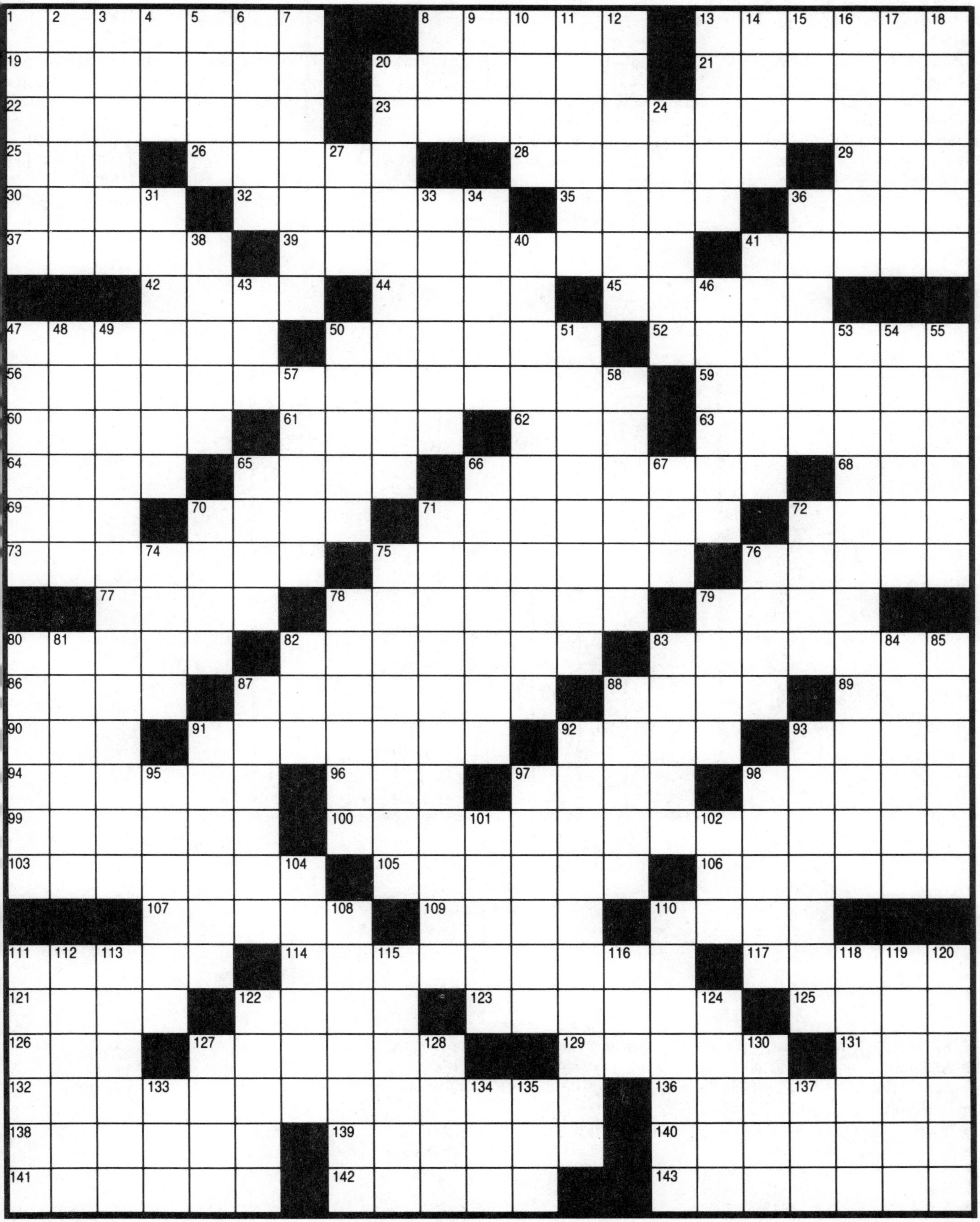

Square Routes★★★

by Will Shortz

Square Routes is a word game within a puzzle. Each clue consists of two words, one of which is a synonym of an anagram of the other. For example, the clue words RECALL and BASEMENT would lead to the answer CELLAR (an anagram of "recall" and a synonym of "basement"). Either the synonym or the anagram may come first—determining which word is which is part of the puzzle. To solve, first answer as many clues as you can. Then enter each answer in the grid, beginning in the square corresponding to the clue number and proceeding in any horizontal, vertical, or diagonal direction. (The direction can be determined by logic and by the crossing letters of other answers.) Work back and forth between grid and clues to finish. When you're done, every square in the grid will be filled.

Answer, page 186

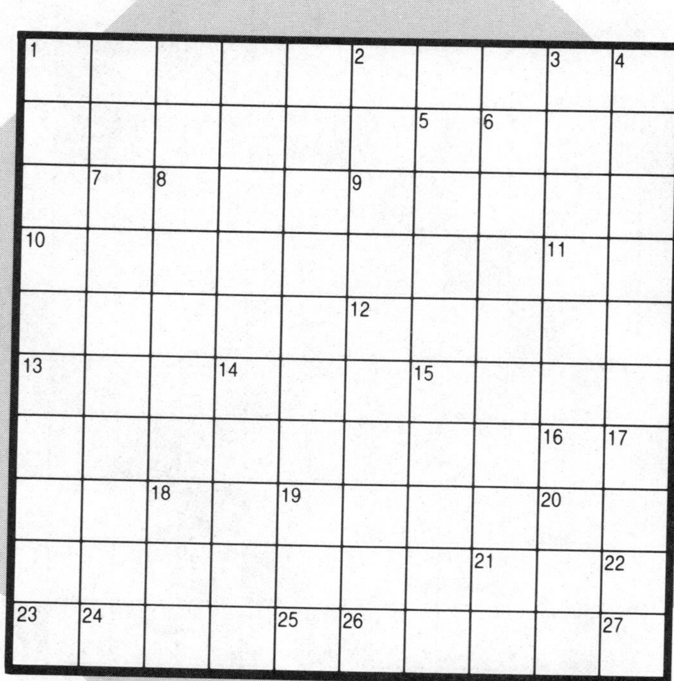

CLUES

1 BROADEN RASPED
2 ASSUME DIVERTS
3 TURTLES TRANSPIRE
4 COURSE MASTER
5 NEST MAILED
6 COLLAPSE BAKE
7 ANOINT REPUBLIC
8 DIRE MARGINAL
9 ANGLE REAP
10 RELAY PREMATURE
11 POUND SHAM
12 CENTER EARTH
13 SCATTER PRESIDES
14 LOPE SPAR
15 SCANTY SPEARS
16 ATTIRE MINARET
17 SKEPTIC STAKES
18 SIRE ASCEND
19 STATE SAVOR
20 EVENING THING
21 ADMIRES PISTOL
22 CLEAN DELUSION
23 STAR AUTOCRAT
24 LOAFER RILED
25 VISION GENIES
26 ASTUTENESS PRIEST
27 PLUG SWALLOW

Wraparounds★★

by Brian Greer

Each numbered clue leads to a word of four to seven letters. Every answer starts in one of the three hexagons around its number, then circles the number either clockwise or counterclockwise, overlapping itself by one or more letters. Thus, the fourth letter will be the same as the first, the fifth letter (if there is one) the same as the second, and so on. For example, BULB, ESSES, and CHA-CHA are possible answers.

Answers to clues marked "cc" are entered counterclockwise; all other answers are entered clockwise. The starting space and length of each answer are for you to determine.

Answer, page 186

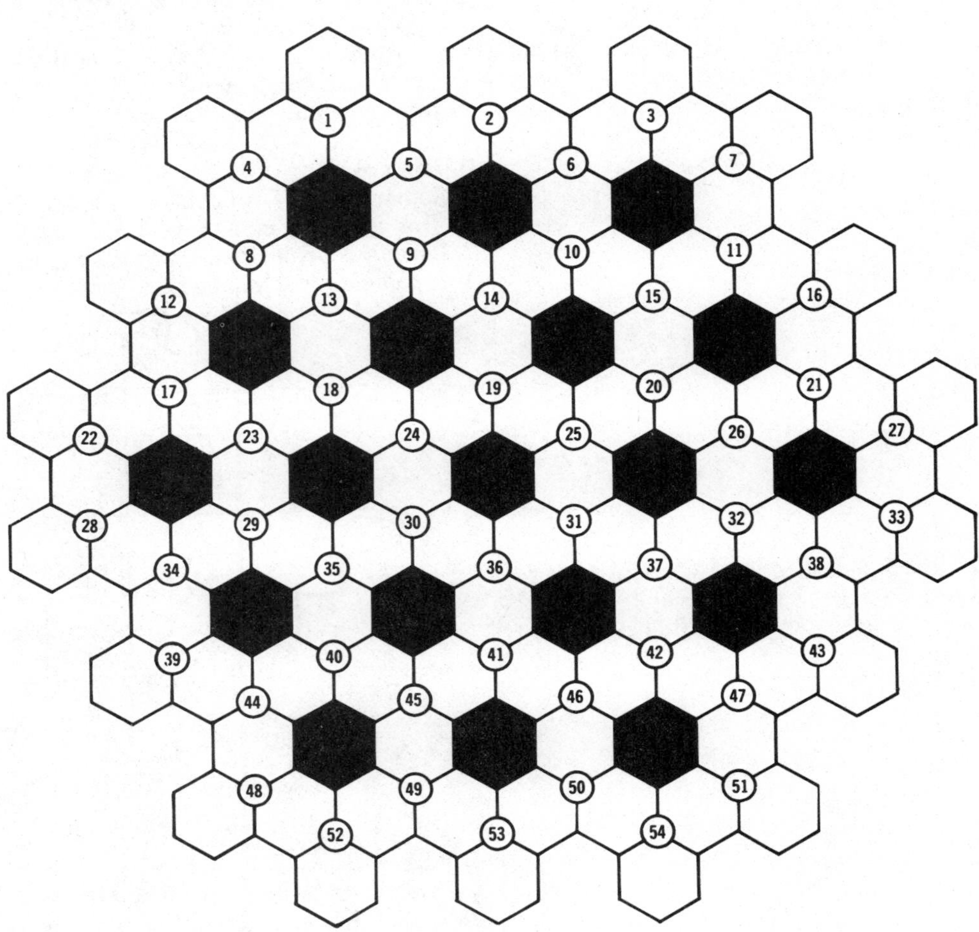

CLUES

1 Vim and vigor
2 Bubbling brook's sound (cc)
3 Lone Ranger's sidekick
4 *Enterprise*'s leader
5 ___ school (private school before college) (cc)
6 American Indian drum
7 Chocolate-covered candy (cc)
8 *Metamorphosis* author (cc)
9 Orange juice thickener
10 Red or Spanish vegetable (cc)
11 Sharp sticker on a wire (cc)
12 Tattle (cc)
13 Kind of sprouts for a salad (cc)
14 What an adjective modifies
15 TV's ___ *Vice*
16 Brisk gait
17 Temporary calm
18 Greasy spoon's specialty
19 Comment from Leo
20 ___ and circumstance (cc)
21 Pinball penalty (cc)
22 Swedish auto (cc)
23 ___ money (a bribe to keep quiet) (cc)
24 Gaelic (cc)
25 Banana-shaped fruit (cc)
26 Dayton's state (cc)
27 Jazzy Latin music
28 Mistake, to a toddler
29 Norway's capital (cc)
30 Alliance between nations (cc)
31 Cuts wood (cc)
32 Like a soprano's C (cc)
33 *M*A*S*H* star Alan
34 Dresden's river (cc)
35 Oriental attention-getter
36 African fly
37 Largest continent (cc)
38 Moved by inches (cc)
39 Otherwise
40 Molten rock in the earth (cc)
41 Accomplishment
42 Hearing, sight, or touch
43 Something to cram for
44 ___ mater
45 Verdi opus (cc)
46 Gas in a glowing sign (cc)
47 Backpacker's shelter (cc)
48 27th president (cc)
49 Buffalo's water source
50 Theatrical failure
51 Moulin Rouge dance
52 ___ sauce (seafood accompaniment) (cc)
53 Toodle-oo
54 1987 movie *La* ___ (cc)

Word Geometry★☆

from the *Games* Library

Before the crossword puzzle was invented in 1913, puzzle solvers worked "forms," geometrical shapes made of interlocking words. The first form published in the English language (in 1859) was a word square, which literally squared the circle as in the example. The same words go across and down, and in the same order.

The word square caught on, and soon puzzlemakers were building forms in other shapes as well: half-squares, diamonds, stars, pentagons, and more. Eventually, with the innovation of the black square to allow more than one word on a line, these elementary forms led to the modern crossword puzzle.

The forms presented here, seven of them culled from old puzzle journals and two of them newly made, are remarkable for being large and yet sticking (mostly) to everyday language.

To solve a form, note that numbers are given only for the across words. The down words are the same as the acrosses, and proceed in the same order, from left to right, as the acrosses go from top to bottom. In the hexagon, the down words proceed diagonally backward; the diagram is shaded to show how they are filled in. *Answers, page 186*

Ex.

C	**I**	**R**	**C**	**L**	**E**
I	**C**	**A**	**R**	**U**	**S**
R	**A**	**R**	**E**	**S**	**T**
C	**R**	**E**	**A**	**T**	**E**
L	**U**	**S**	**T**	**R**	**E**
E	**S**	**T**	**E**	**E**	**M**

1. SQUARE

1. Clear-cut, as a victory 2. Conceitedness 3. Figures out on a MacIntosh 4. Powerless 5. Sweet, white table wine 6. Confined, as during a war 7. Citizens of Austria's capital 8. Town of Erie County, New York, an eponym of a Biblical garden (2 wds.)

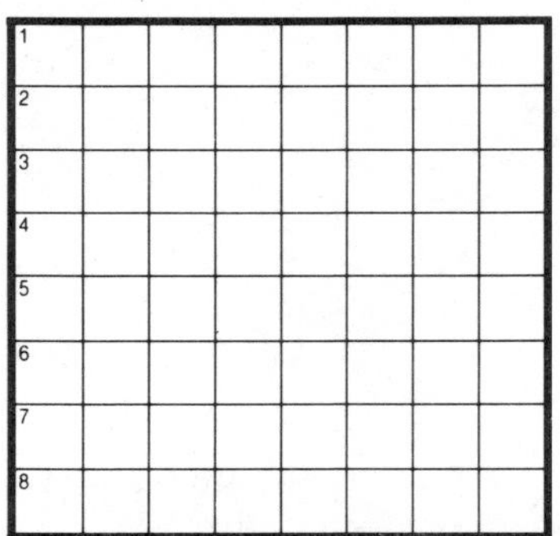

2. HALF-SQUARE

1. Superman's symbol 2. Symbol for iron 3. Long feathered scarf 4. Placid 5. Waits in hiding 6. Musician of ancient Greece 7. Museum's head 8. Between tenor and bass 9. Burl Ives's repertoire (2 wds.) 10. Betsy Ross, for one

3. DIAMOND

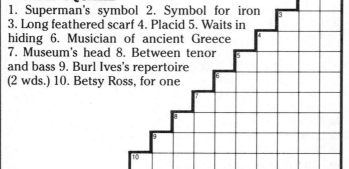

1. Roman five 2. ___-de-lance 3. Flogged 4. Homes for kings 5. Designed, as clothes 6. Fresh air circulating system 7. Readying a rifle again 8. Tooth material 9. River of Paris 10. Spaniel or chihuahua 11. Symbol for nitrogen

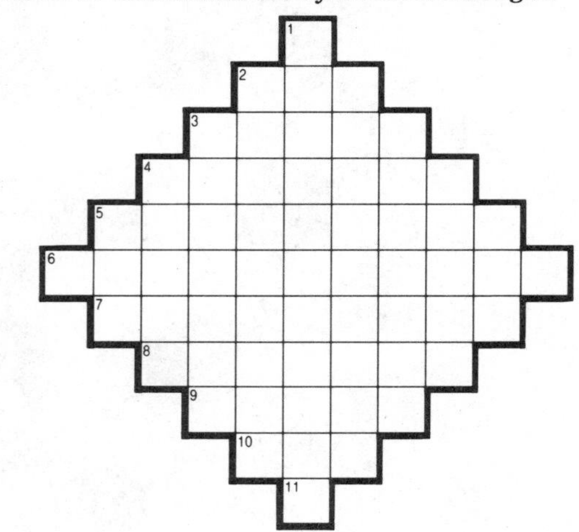

4. HEXAGON

1. Civilian dress 2. Elevated region 3. Exhibitionist, or a traffic light 4. Adorned with dangling ornaments 5. Received as a legacy 6. Fragile 7. Captured again 8. Discover, as Sherlock Holmes 9. Parking lot mishaps

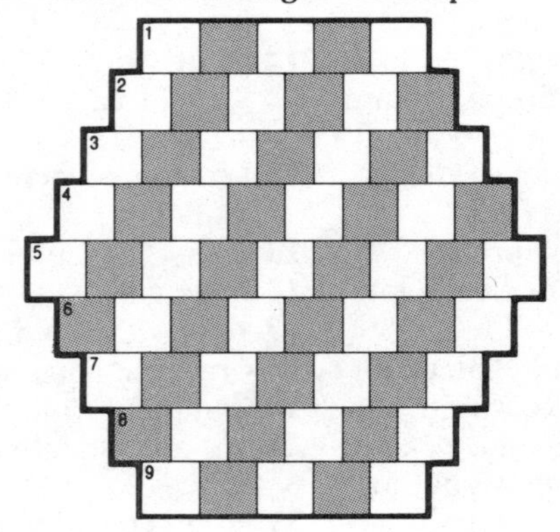

5. DIAMOND

1. 4-___ Club 2. On the ___ (in flight) 3. Challenges 4. Strips the clothing from 5. Underground bombs (2 wds.) 6. In a reckless manner 7. Having curative powers, as cough drops 8. Ernest Hollings or John Glenn, e.g. 9. More parched 10. Make foam 11. James Bond's supervisor

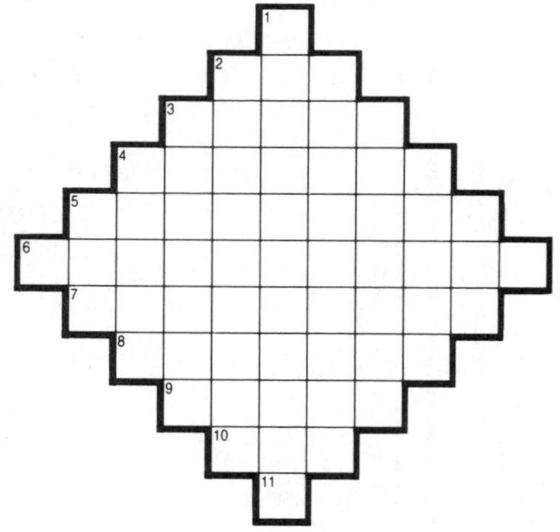

6. HEPTAGON

1. Soft minerals, used to make bath powder 2. Idolized 3. Brought down 4. Fissures 5. Pertaining to a family of caddis-flies *(Sericostomidae)* 6. Things that decay 7. Dangerous outlaw 8. Closet's use 9. Oklahoma Indian 10. Ancient Iranian 11. Spanish gold 12. Exists 13. Grade just above failing

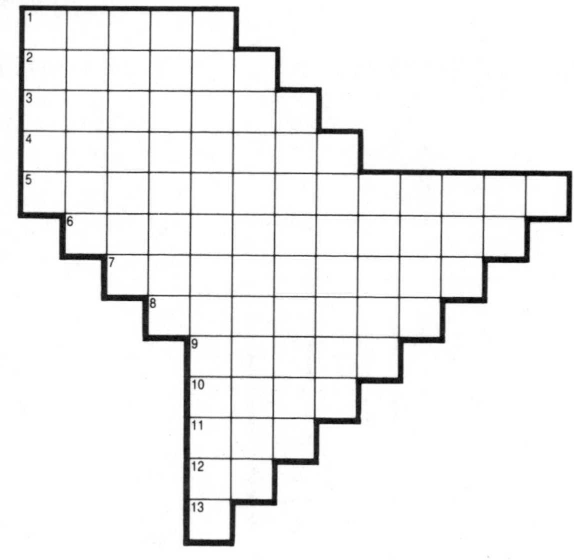

7. SQUARE

1. Stable hands of old 2. Small, parentless child 3. Make a mess, as a tomato falling on the floor 4. Then (2 wds.) 5. Frameworks of crossed slats 6. Those who lure 7. Come into view again 8. Emphasized

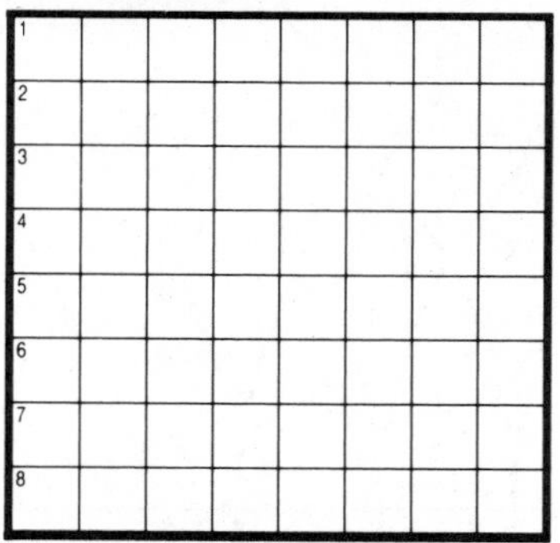

8. HEXDECAGON

1. Cleopatra's suicide weapon 2. Needlefish 3. Prickly bush 4. Jean Harlow and Marilyn Monroe, e.g. 5. Study of grasses, derived from the Greek *agrostis* 6. French island near Madagascar, named for Jesus' mother 7. Most frequent 8. Reaches shore again 9. Small marshland birds 10. Martini ingredient 11. Thus far

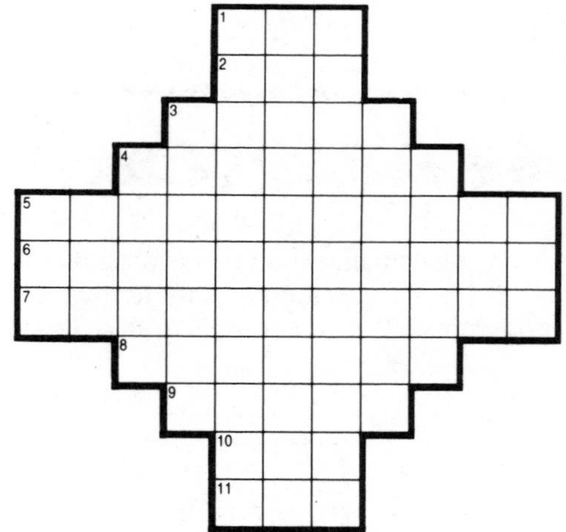

9. OCTAGON

1. The "m" of "$e = mc^2$" 2. Shredded (2 wds.) 3. Stuck bricks together 4. Craftsmanship 5. Marine reptile (2 wds.) 6. Extra charges 7. Made coffee 8. Hair colors

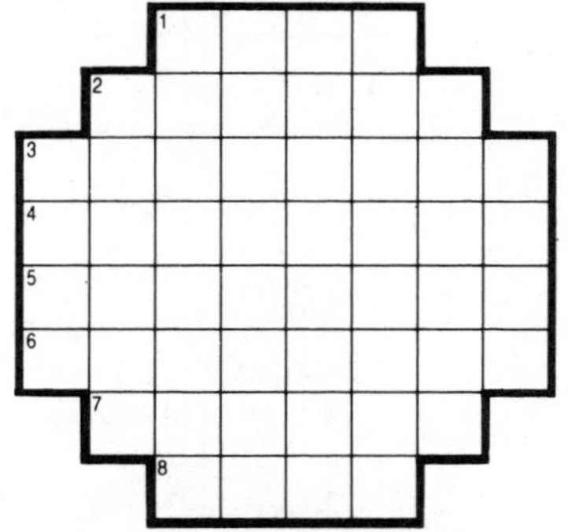

Boomerangs★★

by Penny A. Roman

Fill each six-letter answer in the grid from top to bottom, either clockwise or counterclockwise as indicated. The numbers before each clue indicate the spaces for the answer's first and last letters.

Answer, page 186

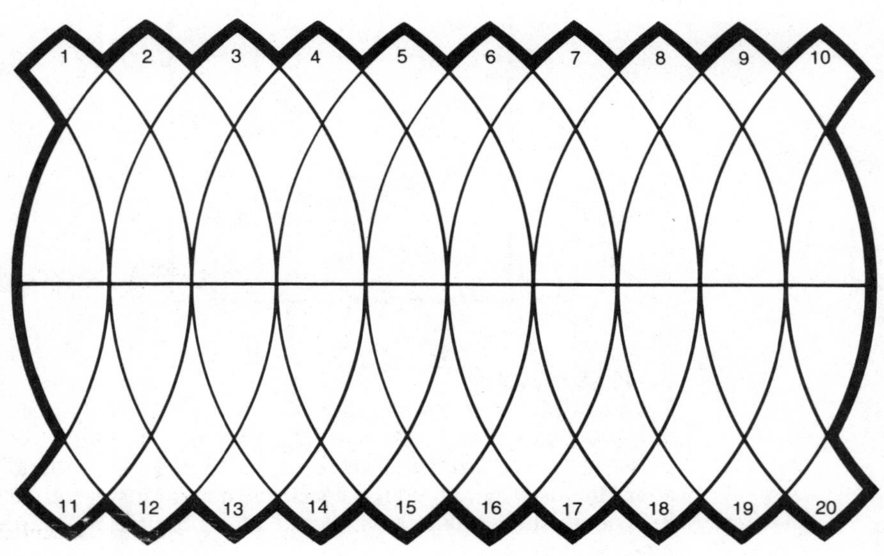

CLOCKWISE
1–11 Middle Eastern capital
2–12 *The Real McCoys* actor Richard
3–13 ___ oneself of (uses)
4–14 Queen of mystery
5–15 Salad, entree, or dessert
6–16 Word with flea or super
7–17 In an early stage of development
8–18 Men of the cloth
9–19 *Brave New World* author

COUNTERCLOCKWISE
2–12 Locust
3–13 Certain Nordics
4–14 In equal portions
5–15 Actress Bloom of *Limelight*
6–16 Bother
7–17 One of an old comedy team
8–18 Hooded jackets
9–19 Invisible rabbit of stage
10–20 Hepburn or Meadows

Cross Anagram★★

by A. Braine

Here's a puzzle for anagram fanciers. With the help of the letters in the grids, answer the clues to discover six pairs of six-letter anagrams. Each answer in grid A has the same letters, rearranged, as the answer on the same line in grid B. (Answers read across only, not down.)

Answers, page 186

A

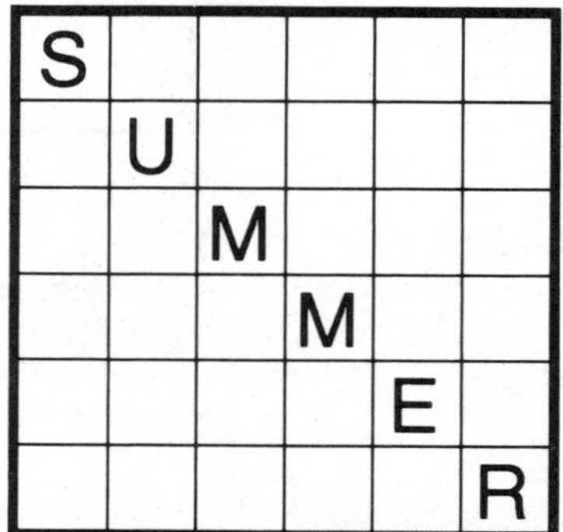

1 2 3 4 5 6

B

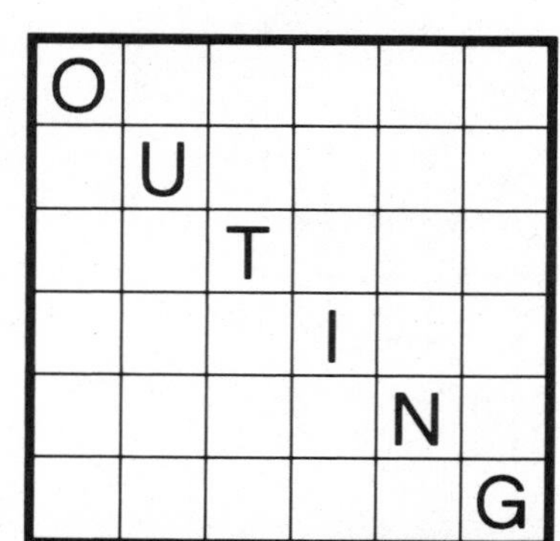

CLUES A
1 South Seas wrap-around
2 From the country
3 Hard-to-get-to
4 Inconceivably vast
5 Bumblebee's relative
6 Film director Bergman

CLUES B
1 Church instruments
2 Actor Tony
3 Shooting star
4 Sunday newspaper section
5 Bathroom "seat"
6 Preparing for war

Missing Links★★

by Gary Disch

The crisscross grid on the right has been left unfinished. Insert the 16 missing letters, listed on the left, into the appropriate squares to complete a pattern of common words reading across and down. You may cross off the missing letters as you solve, because none will be used more than once.

Answer, page 186

MISSING LETTERS

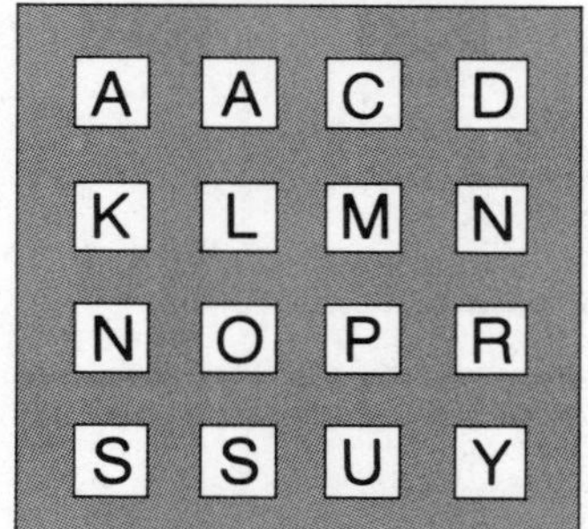

		T	R	I	M			
			U		Y			E
S	T	A	R			C		S
H		M	A			A	R	T
I			L	I	E	S		E
N	I	L			N	E	A	R
E		E			T			
	A	D	D	L	E			
			O		R	E	L	Y

To the Nines★★

by Trip Payne

Answer each clue in this puzzle with a nine-letter word that combines three of the letter triplets at the side of the grid. (The triplets are used as units; you do not need to rearrange letters within them.) Each triplet will be used only once. When you have found all the words, transfer four letters from each into the grid as indicated by the boxes. For example, in number 1, place the third, first, seventh, and fourth letters of the nine-letter word in that order in the top row of boxes. When all the boxes have been filled, a quotation will read down the grid column by column. Two of the 26 triplets at the side will not be used; when put in proper order, they will spell the name of the quotation's author.

Answer, page 187

1. "Dull as ___" ________________

2. Saloon employee ________________

3. Village ________________

4. Turns to mist ________________

5. Stereo component ________________

6. Tucked-in item ________________

7. False front ________________

8. Warm memory ________________

3	1	7	4
5	2	9	8
7	9	5	3
7	3	9	4
9	2	1	3
6	5	8	4
2	4	6	3
4	8	3	9

TRIPLETS

ACE	LOW
AFT	MUN
AIL	NIN
BAR	NTA
BLE	ORI
COM	PHO
DER	RTT
DIS	SHI
ERG	TEN
ESS	TER
HOR	TUR
HWA	VAP
ITY	ZES

Cross Comics★★

The grid below is made up of four different comic strips, two reading across and two reading down. All but two of the panels, however, have been removed from the grid and scattered randomly around these two pages.

1

5

9

10

11

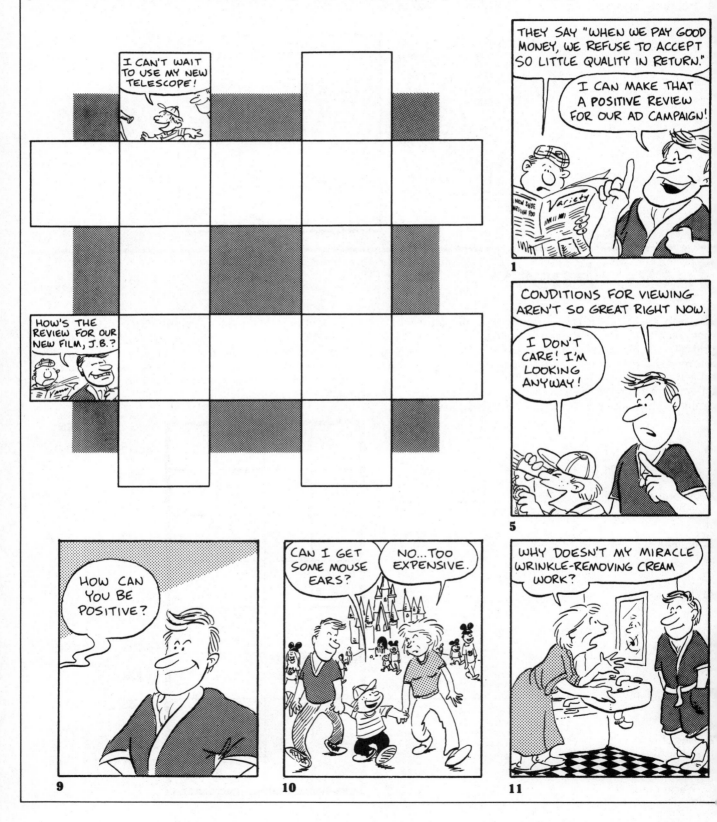

by Robert Leighton

Using logic and your funny bone, can you correctly place each panel in the grid? Note that four of the panels must make sense in two different directions.
Answer, page 187

2

3

4

6

7

8

12

13

14

Left and Right★★

by Will Shortz

There are only two directions to this puzzle—left and right. Each answer is a six-letter word, which is to be entered in the grid one letter per square according to the numbers. Half the answers will read from left to right, as in the example, SUMMIT (1–2). Half will read from right to left, as in the answer to 2–3, which begins TIM-. Work in both directions to complete the puzzle.

Answer, page 187

1 S	U	M			
			M	I	T 2
3					
					4
5					
					6
7					
					8
9					
					10
11					
					12
13					
					14
15					
					16
17					
					18
19					
					20
21					
					22
23					
					24
25					
					26
27					
					28
29					
					30
31					
					32
33					
					34
35					
					36
37					
					38

CLUES

1–2 Meeting of leaders
2–3 Lumberjack's cry
3–4 Provides evidence against
4–5 House of King James I
5–6 Emotional shock
6–7 Charm
7–8 Bank employee
8–9 Put down again, as tiles
9–10 Crown
10–11 "Greatest hits" pastiche
11–12 Cried out, as a dog
12–13 Expel from the country
13–14 Fighting forces
14–15 To the victor go these
15–16 Splinter
16–17 Book or movie critique
17–18 German "republic"
18–19 Put through without discussion
19–20 Attic window
20–21 Stay
21–22 Vitamin B_3
22–23 French woman's name
23–24 Leaves via ladder?
24–25 Kind of tank
25–26 Lemon's relative
26–27 Europe's northernmost NATO member
27–28 Expressed boredom
28–29 Pertaining to canines?
29–30 The second of two
30–31 Part of the eye
31–32 "20 Questions" category
32–33 Gave birth, as a sheep
33–34 Trash
34–35 Brightest star
35–36 Courting man
36–37 Spoiled
37–38 Below

Split Ends★★

by Will Shortz

Each clue in this crossword has been cut into two parts, and the parts have been given numbers from 1 to 78. To solve the puzzle, find and rejoin each matching pair of clue parts to produce the original clue. Enter the answer to each clue at the grid space indicated by the sum of the numbers of the clue's two parts. For example, #70 and #29 below combine to form the clue "Popular television/canine." The answer, LASSIE, is filled in at #99 (70 + 29). Either part of the clue may appear first in the numbered list. Every part will be used exactly once in the completed puzzle.

Answer, page 187

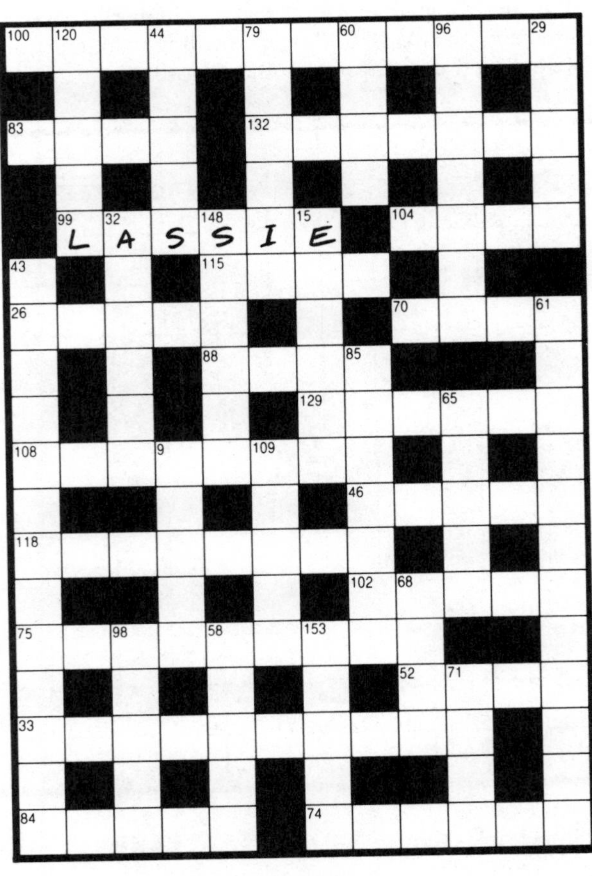

CLUES

1 Ocean
2 People who have no
3 Swings on
4 B&O Railroad
5 Drink popular
6 What a door
7 Prohibition's
8 Two
9 Opposite of
10 Around Christmas
11 Dirty dishes
12 Money
13 Miss
14 "Filthy"
15 Basketball team
16 Person of
17 Injury
18 Speed or fire
19 Tennis star
20 Boys
21 Club
22 Any whole
23 Person who reads
24 Or seawater
25 Not
26 Amendment
27 For breeding
28 Noted Harlem
29 Canine
30 Low IQ
31 Northernmost
32 Red ink
33 From Stockholm
34 According to
35 Invention
36 Item shown in
37 Turkey is eaten
38 Bumps on the head
39 Golf
40 Alexander Graham Bell
41 The Soviet government
42 Clothes on
43 Under, in
44 Center of
45 Hearst
46 Census
47 Amount of
48 Of perfection
49 Quite
50 William
51 Overnight
52 Word after
53 Stock ___
54 Standard
55 New York
56 Stallion kept
57 What follows
58 Data
59 Bird that has
60 Like pretzels
61 Or Bryan, e.g.
62 Ankle or wrist
63 Holiday on which
64 Law
65 Playwright
66 Poetry
67 The "O" in
68 Clay
69 Place to stay
70 Popular television
71 Precipitation
72 Nap
73 A comb
74 Number
75 Performance
76 A Mexican
77 Place for
78 Met

Marching Bands★★

by Mike Shenk

The words in this puzzle march around the grid in two ways. In one formation ("Rows"), words march across—two words for each numbered line, reading consecutively from left to right. The dividing point between these answers is for you to determine, except in row 7, where the words are separated by a black square. In the second formation ("Bands"), words march around each of the six shaded and unshaded bands, starting at the lettered squares (A, B, C, D, E, and F) and proceeding in a clockwise direction, one word after another. For example, Band "A," when filled, will contain seven consecutive words (a through g) starting in square "A" and reading around the perimeter of the grid. Band "B" will contain a series of six words (a through f) starting in square "B." Again, the dividing point between these answers is for you to determine. All clues are given in order. When the puzzle is completed, each square in the grid will have been used once in a Row word and once in a Band word. *Answer, page 187*

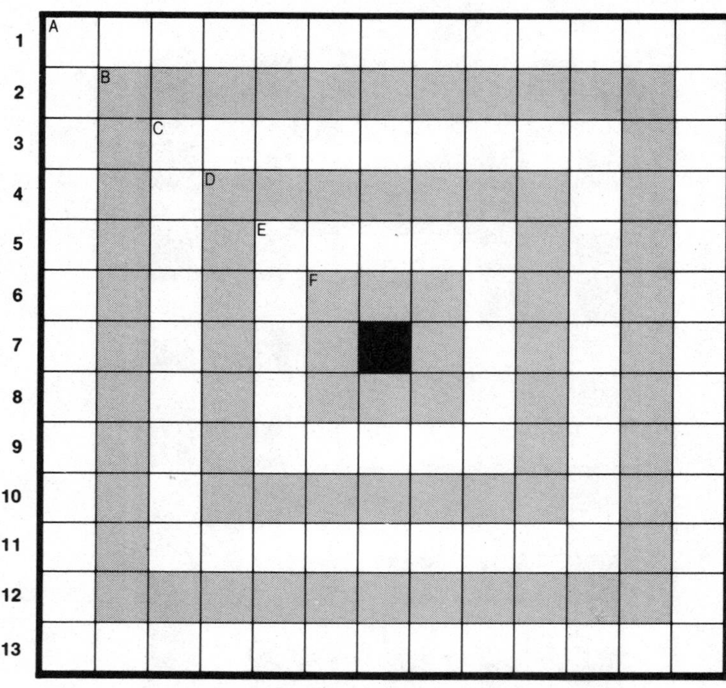

ROWS

1 a Obscured by fog
b Pompously intellectual

2 a Like better
b Rosy

3 a Interoffice note
b Don Pardo or Johnny Olsen

4 a Agency of the United Nations
b Tidal wave

5 a Convene again
b Angelic babes

6 a Fantasy world creatures
b Moderate orange color

7 a Storybook sailor
b Overrun

8 a ___ Van Gleason III (Jackie Gleason role)
b Caravan stopover

9 a Like some typing paper
b B. B. King's music

10 a January birthstones
b Black Sea port

11 a Pends
b Boisterous merrymaking

12 a Famed lexicographer
b Personal strong points

13 a Peculiarity
b Car from Japan, e.g.

BANDS

A a Struck the wrong key
b Evil personified
c Written theme
d Razor-sharpening aid
e Botch the telegraph message
f Wealthy widows
g High card

B a Alluded (to)
b Divests of real existence
c Slowing-down rocket
d Worries
e Warning word
f "Goodnight" girl

C a Make wailing sounds
b Person, place, or thing
c Soviet region
d Voting booth items
e Pageant crown
f Another fantasy world creature

D a Highlanders
b Peerless
c Open to view

E a Engraver
b Dynamite inventor
c Hackneyed

F a Flavorful
b Lass's sibling

Pathfinder★★

by Scott Marley

You'll need some straight thinking to work your way through this twisty crossword. Every answer makes one or more right-angle turns through the grid, beginning at the appropriately numbered square and proceeding in a path for you to determine. The letter after the clue number indicates the answer's starting direction—north, south, east, or west. The number in parentheses after the clue indicates the length of the answer. It will help you to know that each letter in the completed grid will appear in exactly two words—no more, no less. The first answer has been filled in as an example.

Answer, page 187

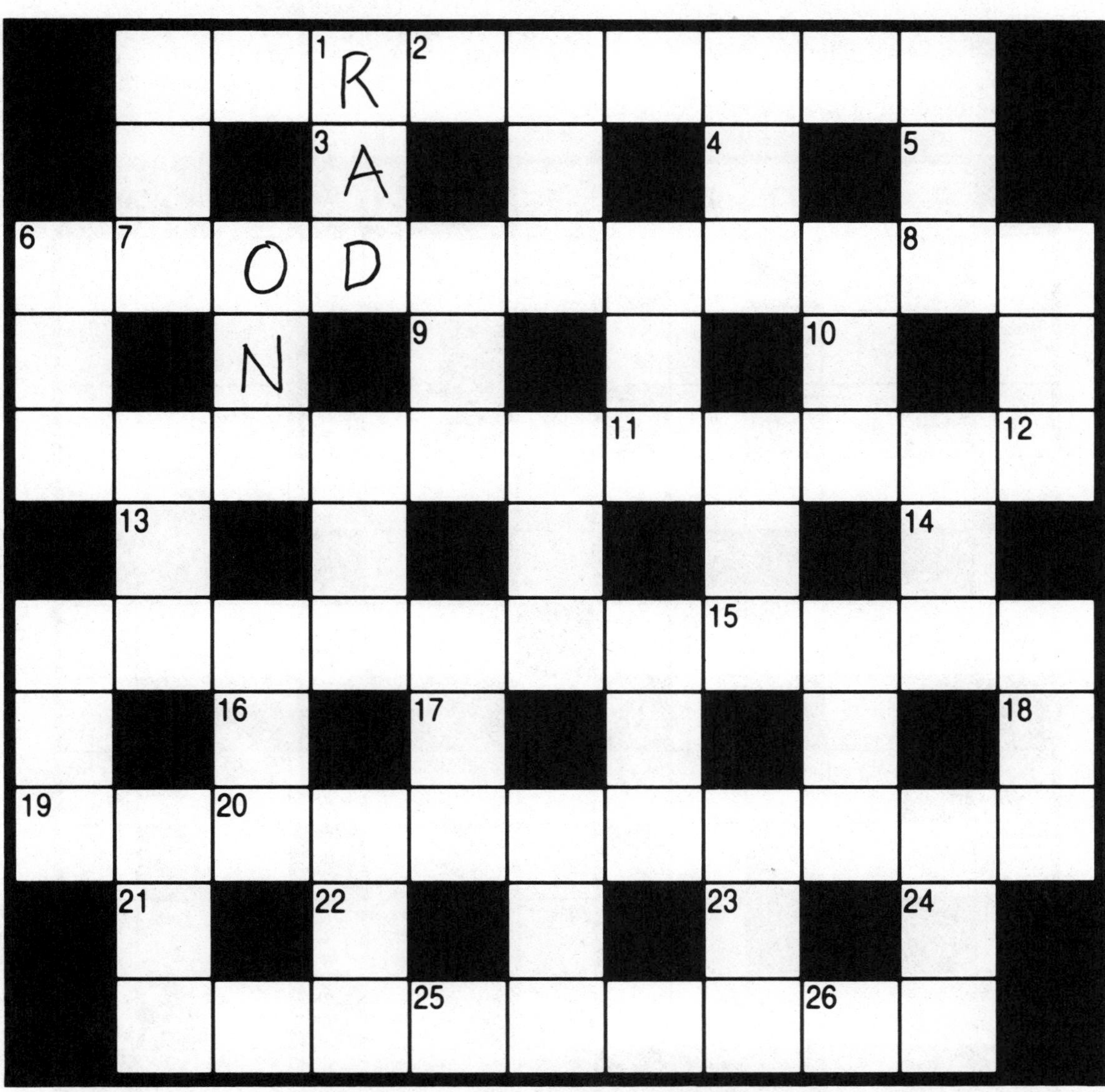

CLUES

1S Inert gas (5)
2W Film star Garbo (5)
2E Festive celebration (4)
3S Highly proficient (5)
4N Blossom part (5)
5N Commencement (5)
6S Leisure suit material (9)
7N Despise (4)
8W *Queen Mary*, for one (4)
9N WW2 attack site (5, 6)
10N Spin like a dervish (5)
10S Have on (4)
11W "Mister" in Munich (4)
12N Individuals (7)
13N Instrument played with hammers (9)
14N Gallup's rival (5)
15W Easter hats (7)
16N Pueblo plaster (5)
17N President John Quincy . . . (5)
18N . . . and his predecessor (6)
19E Exotic citrus fruit (7)
20N Sir's counterpart (5)
21N Coin-operated phonograph (7)
21S City once called Zion (9)
22N Military flight formation (8)
22S Certain (4)
23N Musician's timekeeper (9)
24S Carouse (5)
25E Evil incarnate (5)
26E Limerick or sonnet (5)

A to Z★★

by Will Shortz

This crossword contains 26 clues, each of which begins with a different letter of the alphabet. These initial letters have been removed and replaced by blanks. First fill in as many of these initial letters as you can be sure of. Then enter these letters in the correspondingly numbered squares in the grid.

Next, answer as many of the completed clues as you can. Each of the 26 answer words *also* begins with a different letter of the alphabet—always different from the initial letter of its clue.

Answers cannot be entered at the corresponding numbers in the grid, because their first letters will not match the initial letters you've already filled in. Instead, they should be filled in at the correct initial letters, wherever these may be. For example, clue #1 has been completed as "Furrowed," and the letter F filled in at square 1 in the grid. Clue #19 has also been completed as "Viking harbors." Viking harbors are FJORDS. So FJORDS gets filled in starting at the F. Also, the letter V from clue #19 is entered in square 19. Now look for a clue whose answer starts with V. Work back and forth between grid and clues to complete the puzzle.

Answers, page 187

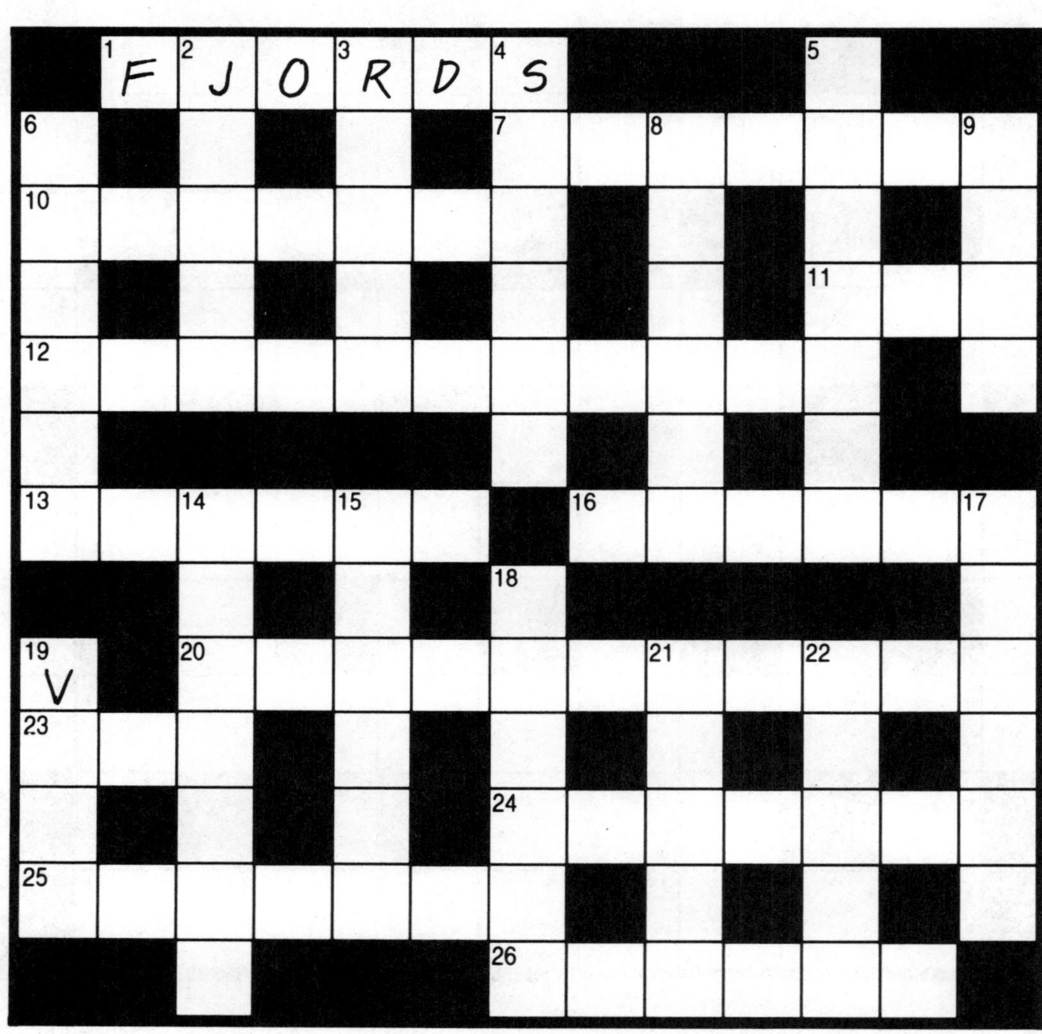

CLUES

1 F urrowed
2 ___unk paper receptacle
3 ___ailroad worker
4 ___ister
5 ___uite
6 ___art of a belt
7 ___ind of jump or theory
8 ___urger order, maybe
9 ___aire, for example
10 ___ift
11 ___ine of these make a game, usually
12 ___ith good fortune
13 ___aft
14 ___yclist's headgear
15 ___ate for a goose
16 ___eavy gas
17 ___ake off, as soldiers
18 ___frican fly
19 V iking harbors
20 ___nit of weight
21 ___mas present for a child, maybe
22 ___'Hare employee
23 ___quipping with weapons
24 ___sraeli collective
25 ___ears and years
26 ___ive too little light to, as film

WARNING: TOP SOLVERS ONLY

Magic Rings★★★

by Cal Q. Leytor

Can you place the numbers from 1 to 14 into the small circles at right so that the six numbers in each of the four large rings total 50? Each of the numbers should be used only once. Five numbers have been filled in to give you a head start. *Answer, page 188*

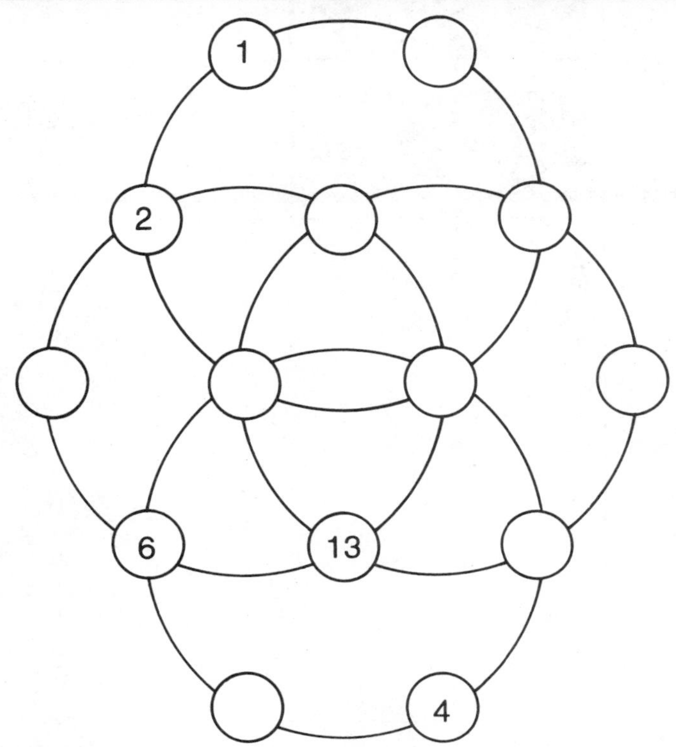

Card Addition★★★

by Marek Penszko

The aces, kings, queens, and jacks (four of each) from a deck of cards have been arranged to form a correct addition. Each digit is replaced by a card, and equal digits are replaced by cards of equal rank. (Thus, all aces stand for the same digit, and so on.) Aces stand for a higher digit than kings do; similarly, kings are higher than queens, and queens are higher than jacks.

Some of the cards in the addition have been turned face down, and one face-down card is left over. What is the rank of the extra card?

Answer, page 188

Figure Eights★★★

by Will Shortz

Each answer in this puzzle is an eight-letter word that is to be entered in the grid in the shape of a figure eight, crossing itself at the appropriately numbered box. All answers proceed in the same direction (see diagram), but the starting point is up to you to determine. The first answer, INTERNAL, has been filled in as an example; it starts at the I, proceeds diagonally downward to the T, and then curls back and up to the L. Note the letter N is used twice, and that its two appearances are separated by exactly three other letters. Each of the other 31 words will have a similarly repeated letter, which will go in the shaded box (although this letter will not always appear in the second and sixth positions of the answer word). Be sure you have your balance before beginning . . . and happy skating! *Answer, page 188*

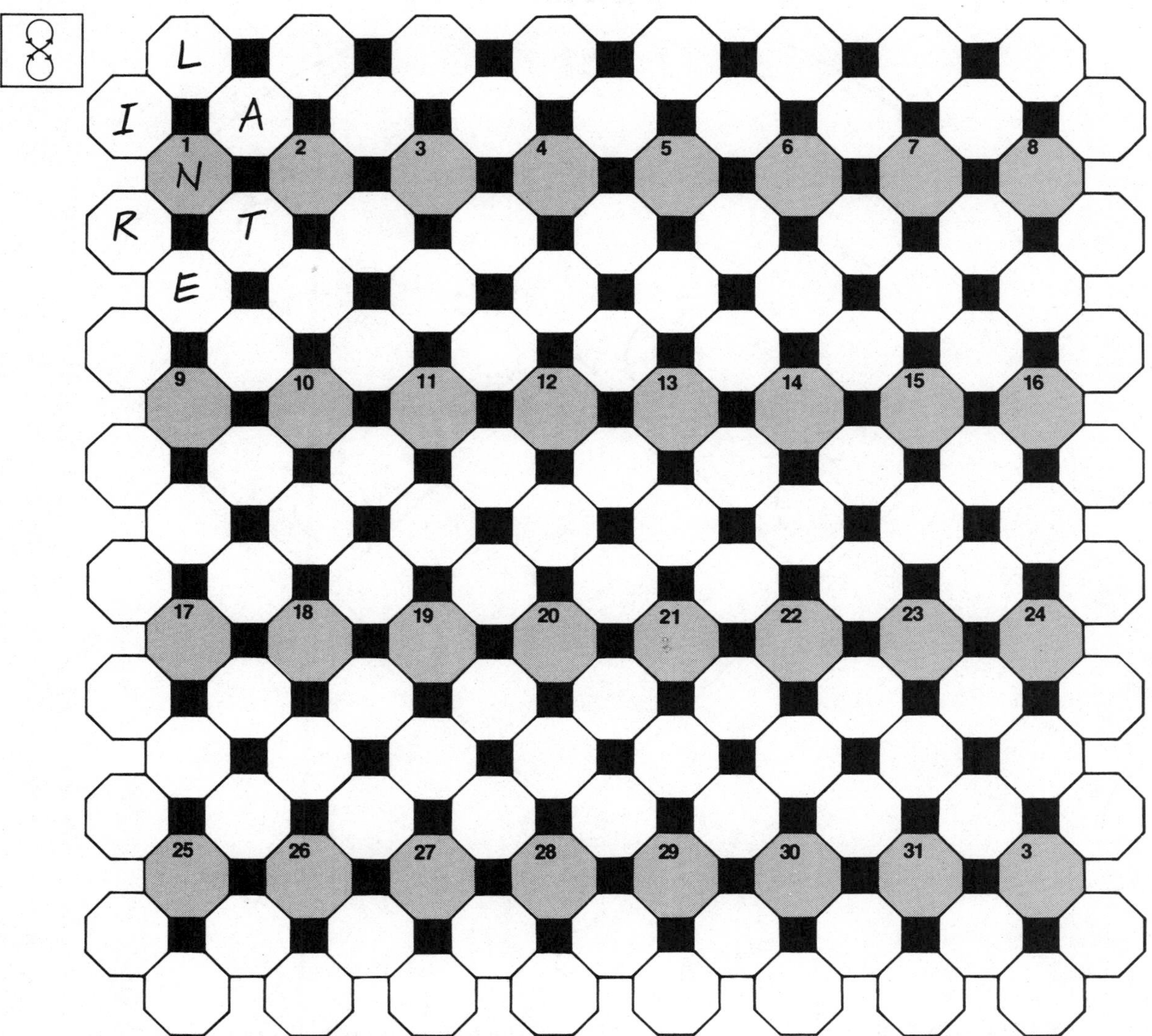

CLUES

1 The "I" of IRS
2 Adherent to the old regime
3 Wallet
4 Coin in a Spanish treasure chest
5 Befuddle
6 Diabolical
7 Sweat
8 More idiosyncratic
9 Loony bin
10 Covers, as a sword
11 Worthless bum
12 Hiawatha's father, or a sign of a storm? (2 wds.)
13 Circumnavigators
14 Natural tendency
15 Trespass (upon)
16 Shaking, as a pillow
17 Somewhat pale
18 Airplane's body
19 Playing "Turkey in the Straw," for example
20 Female devil
21 Sends by special post (hyph.)
22 Bowling game
23 Daydreams
24 Reduce as much as possible
25 Cuspid
26 Personal guidance and instruction
27 Sensation of excitement
28 Monotonously rhythmic, as a voice
29 Makes rough
30 Witty reply
31 Principal division of a symphony
32 Where touchdowns are scored (2 wds.)

Baseball Lineup★★★

by Emily Cox and Henry Rathvon

Manager Grubb watched from the dugout as his baseball team took the field. It was the ninth inning and his boys, the Dustville Crickets, were locked in a 9-9 tie with the Louisville Slugs. Grubb studied the nine players he had positioned on the field: Simmons, Roe, Blow, Schmoe, Schmidt, Whitt, Kitt, Kent, and Kowalski. His attention soon became absorbed by the curious fact that his nine players wore on their uniforms the numerals 1, 2, 3, 4, 5, 6, 7, 8, and 9. The more he looked at his players and their numbers, the more he noticed. Grubb's observations are given below as clues, from which you should be able to deduce who played which position, wearing which number. *Answer, page 188*

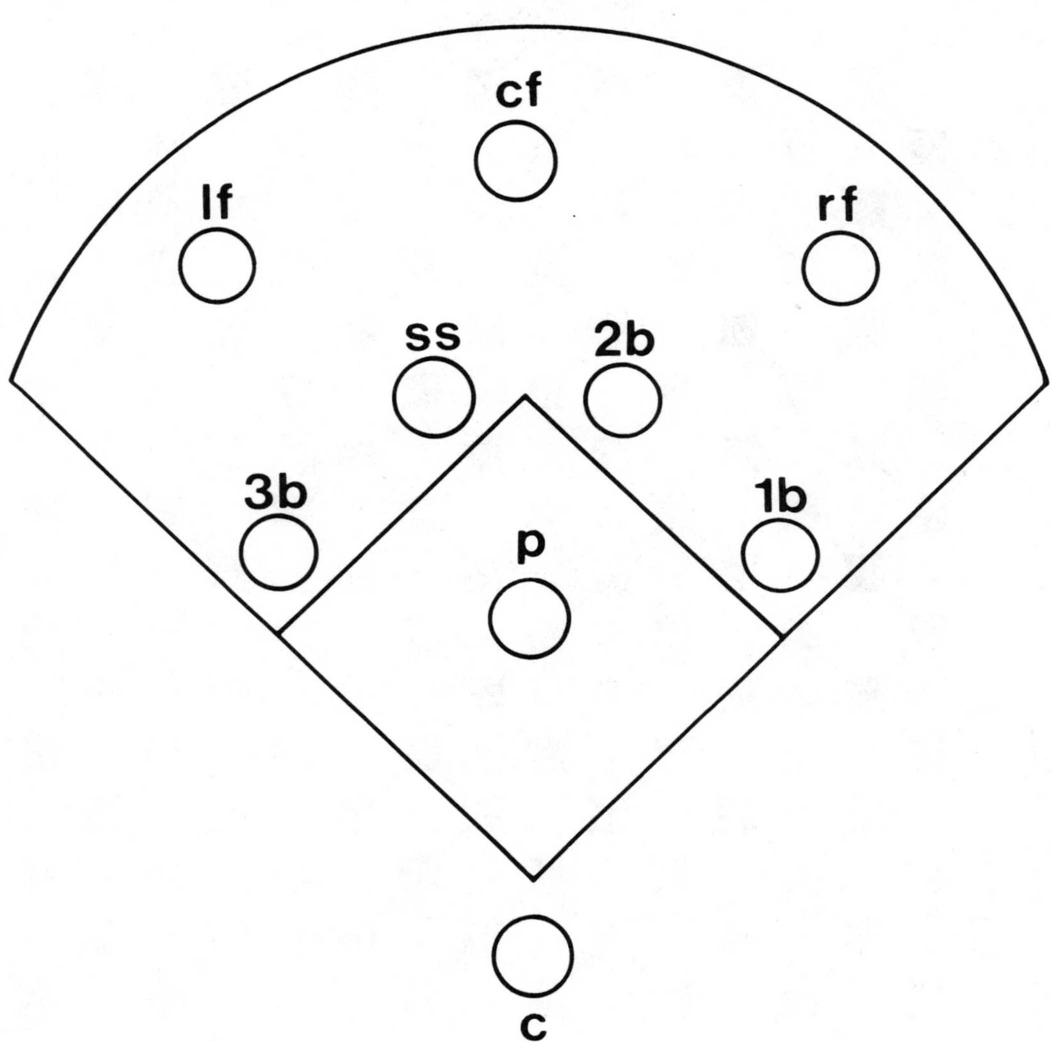

CLUES

1. The outfielders' names rhymed.

2. The outfielders' numbers, from left field around to right, increased and were consecutive.

3. The names of the catcher, third baseman, and left fielder all began with the same letter.

4. The numbers of the catcher, first baseman, and right fielder had no curves in them.

5. The man with the longest name had the highest number.

6. The sum of the outfielders' numbers equaled the sum of the infielders' numbers (pitcher and catcher not being considered infielders).

7. The number of letters in the pitcher's and catcher's names, added together, was equal to the sum of their uniform numbers.

8. The four infielders, reading from first base around to third, were positioned alphabetically.

9. The second baseman's number was half the number of letters in the center fielder's name.

Mystery Theme★★★

by Stephanie Spadaccini

The nine unclued answers in this puzzle (indicated by shaded squares in the diagram) all have something in common. What is it? When you're done, can you name any other items that fit the same theme? *Answer, page 188*

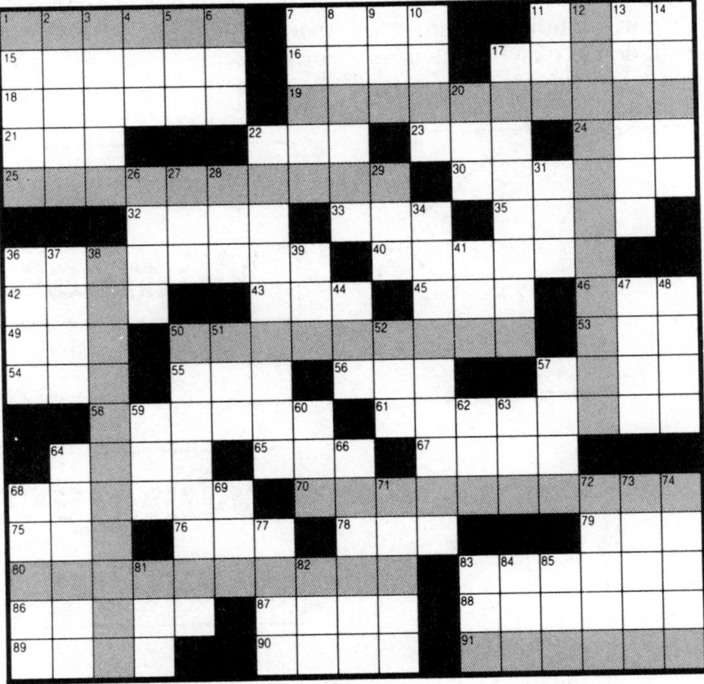

ACROSS

1 SEE INSTRUCTIONS
7 "Blue Velvet" or "Blue Bayou," e.g.
11 Fight souvenir
15 Looooong winter
16 "Alas" from a lass?
17 Slalom skier Phil
18 1986 Best Actor
19 SEE INSTRUCTIONS
21 Adaptable truck
22 Manila's Cardinal ___
23 Newman/Neal film of 1963
24 Didn't do a thing
25 SEE INSTRUCTIONS
30 Actresses Blair and Drake
32 Dorothy's companion
33 "... what I ___, and that's all..."
35 Some dental work
36 Features of some receptions
40 Relative of the frug
42 Literally, "high wood"
43 More than an era
45 "Krazy" one of comics
46 Furniture wood
49 Word with room or hall
50 SEE INSTRUCTIONS
53 Bill's partner
54 And that's not all
55 Make a mistaek
56 It's a wrap
57 Erté's art
58 Consumes
61 Does court work
64 Her, to Herr?
65 Final figure
67 "___ Heartache" (Bonnie Tyler hit)
68 *Fantasy Island* structure
70 SEE INSTRUCTIONS
75 Cipher grp.
76 Polit. label
78 Root word?
79 Screwball
80 SEE INSTRUCTIONS
83 Get, in a way
86 Twiddles one's thumbs
87 Tons
88 Most unfriendly
89 Spiritedness
90 Wacko
91 SEE INSTRUCTIONS

DOWN

1 Betty Grable, notably
2 Prefix with soluble or morphine
3 Kind of post
4 New Cornelia Tailings, e.g.
5 A Khan
6 Not a Rep.
7 *Kiss of the Spider Woman*'s Braga
8 *The Four Million* author
9 Radar dir.
10 "Gee whiz!"
11 Maple staple
12 SEE INSTRUCTIONS
13 Matrices
14 Takes ten
17 Trimmed back
20 "Cheers," e.g.
22 Come home?
26 ___ *Jury*
27 60-Down's mate
28 Aitch's ancestor
29 "Too many cooks...," for one
31 Prof's aides
34 Birthday party request
36 Civil rights org.
37 Be an accessory to
38 SEE INSTRUCTIONS
39 Junior, to senior
41 Longest river in Scotland
44 Cribbage card
47 Mathematical points
48 Kind of shine or stone
50 Pink blooms
51 Organization that takes many forms
52 Lays out
57 Grayish
59 They deal with lemons
60 27-Down's mate
62 Lithper's trouble thpot
63 Simile center
64 Guise
66 Source of excitement
68 Spanish seaport
69 Small colonist
71 Yecchy
72 Printshop employee
73 City on the Arkansas
74 Leaves alone, editorially
77 Mexican president Porfirio
81 Was the welcome wagon for
82 Just like
83 Rice, to René
84 Hotshot
85 Scratchy point

How Far to Zequop? ★★★

by Scott Marley

The seven towns of Tidville, Ubania, Vogton, Wimpster, Xendic, Yunjar, and Zequop are indicated on the map below by the letters A to G, not necessarily in order. The roads connecting the towns run strictly north-south and east-west, and the distance between adjacent dots is exactly one mile. Thus, the town labeled C is five miles (by road) from the town labeled E. Each town contains a sign that gives the length of the shortest route to two other towns. These seven signs, one from each town, are shown below. The last sign, though, has been left incomplete. Can you discover which town is where, put each sign in its correct town, and give the correct distance to Zequop? *Answer, page 188*

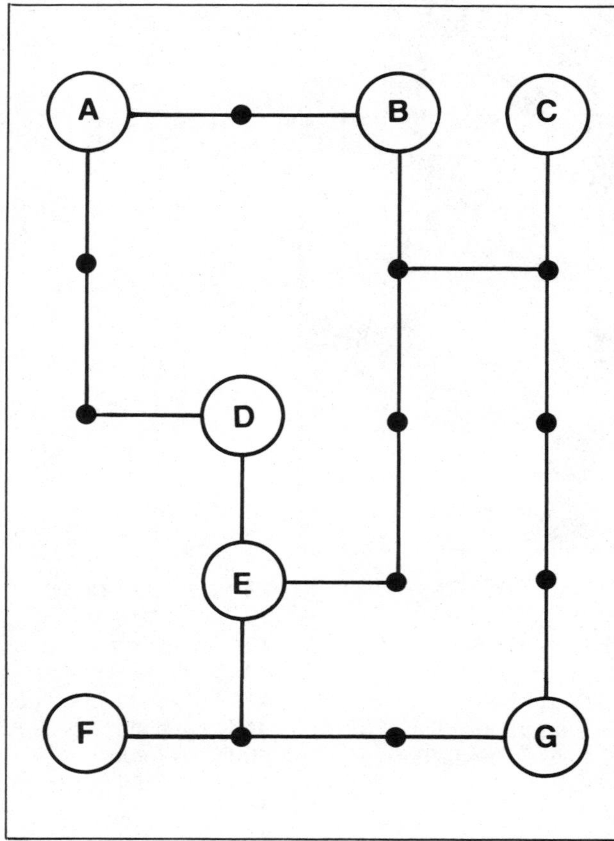

1
Tidville 3
Ubania 4

2
Ubania 7
Vogton 3

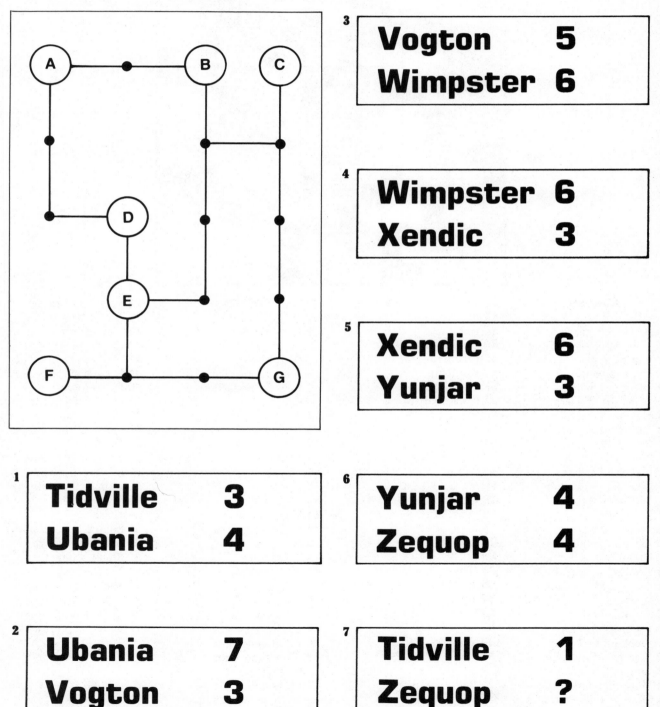

3
Vogton 5
Wimpster 6

4
Wimpster 6
Xendic 3

5
Xendic 6
Yunjar 3

6
Yunjar 4
Zequop 4

7
Tidville 1
Zequop ?

Spoonerisms★★★

by Emily Cox & Henry Rathvon

In a spoonerism, two consonant sounds in a word or phrase are transposed, creating new words. For instance, CLOCKWORK would "spoonerize" to WOK CLERK, NEW DELHI would become DO NELLIE, and BIRD IN THE HAND would turn into HEARD IN THE BAND. Note that spelling changes appropriately in the newly formed words. In this puzzle one third of the clues (12) must have their *answers* spoonerized before entry in the diagram; another third of the clues are written with spoonerisms occurring in the *definitions* of the answers; the remaining third are normal cryptic clues.

Answers, page 188

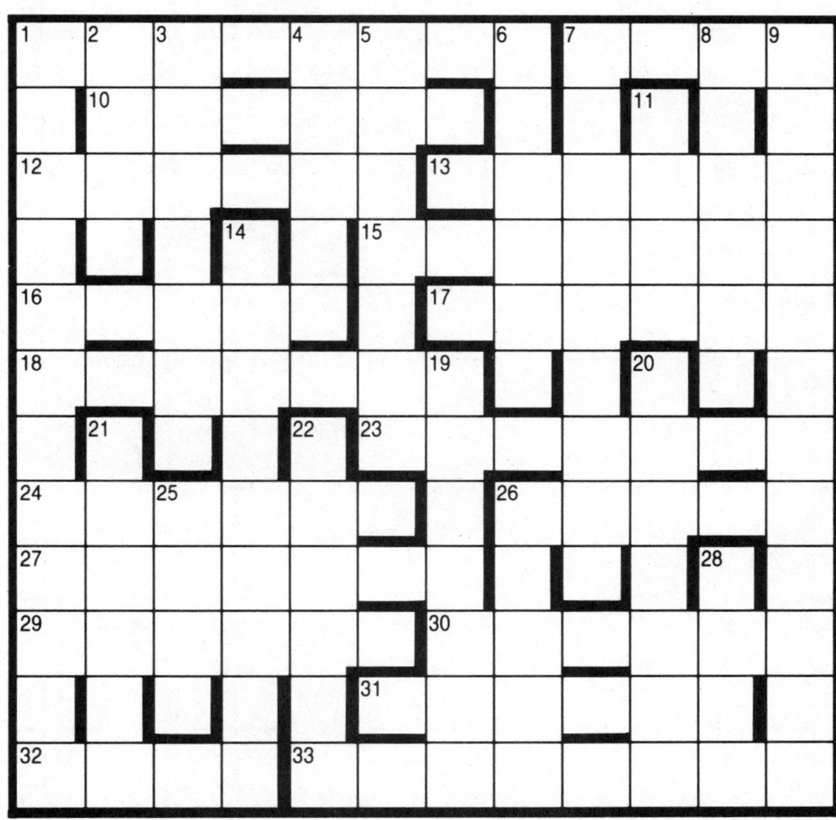

ACROSS

1 Cryptic grid's new birds (8)
7 Reconstruct Hal's kind with boards (4)
10 Court to study tilt of beak, perhaps (6)
12 Superlative about English dog (5)
13 Went ahead around nuts I've collected (6)
15 ID for guard sent back (7)
16 Sets gear for buggy rides (5)
17 Roue has me back in form again (6)
18 Consents to chop kernels, we hear (7)
23 Turning, see fossil fuel in the ground (7)
24 Deity vocalized first note backwards (3,3)
26 Diver's need in southern Caribbean site (5)
27 Raise key—a hip transposal (3,4)
29 Artist finally peruses Saturns on a pole (6)
30 With tide out, some hesitation in storing bait (6)
31 One hundred wild dingoes made marks together (2-6)
32 Burns Tad in heartless Haley opus (4)
33 Dreiser's novel is better suited? (8)

DOWN

1 Wandering herds wait for liquid (9)
2 Hear of evergreen's shady leap (4)
3 Refusal to sleep with diamonds (2,4)
4 Date in March maintaining one's views (5)
5 Lee's TNT wrecked plants (7)
6 Appeared to look Democrat up (6)
7 Pairing in a scoreless tennis contest? (4,5)
8 At song's beginning, Kate's flubbed B-tones (6)
9 Merl's game—he'd fabricated a whopper? (12)
11 Ship nickel and sodium (4)
14 Fluid, say, spewed in racetracks (9)
19 Matador's foe packs small trunk (5)
20 Stupidly, I hound one tragic mix master (7)
21 Queen upset at our sage pies (6)
22 Ailing dove I'd wiped out (6)
25 Nymphet extremely negative to Soviets (4)
26 Guys to train snakes eating a mouse! (5)
28 In Parisian street, 500 having mad banners (4)

Word Quest★★★

by D. A. Nafis

Before you can be crowned King of Greater Thesauria, you must prove your royal worthiness by passing through the maze pictured below. The rules of this arcane rite appear at the bottom of the page. Keep a careful eye on your purse—your goal is to earn enough money to escape through the bottom right door. *Answer, page 189*

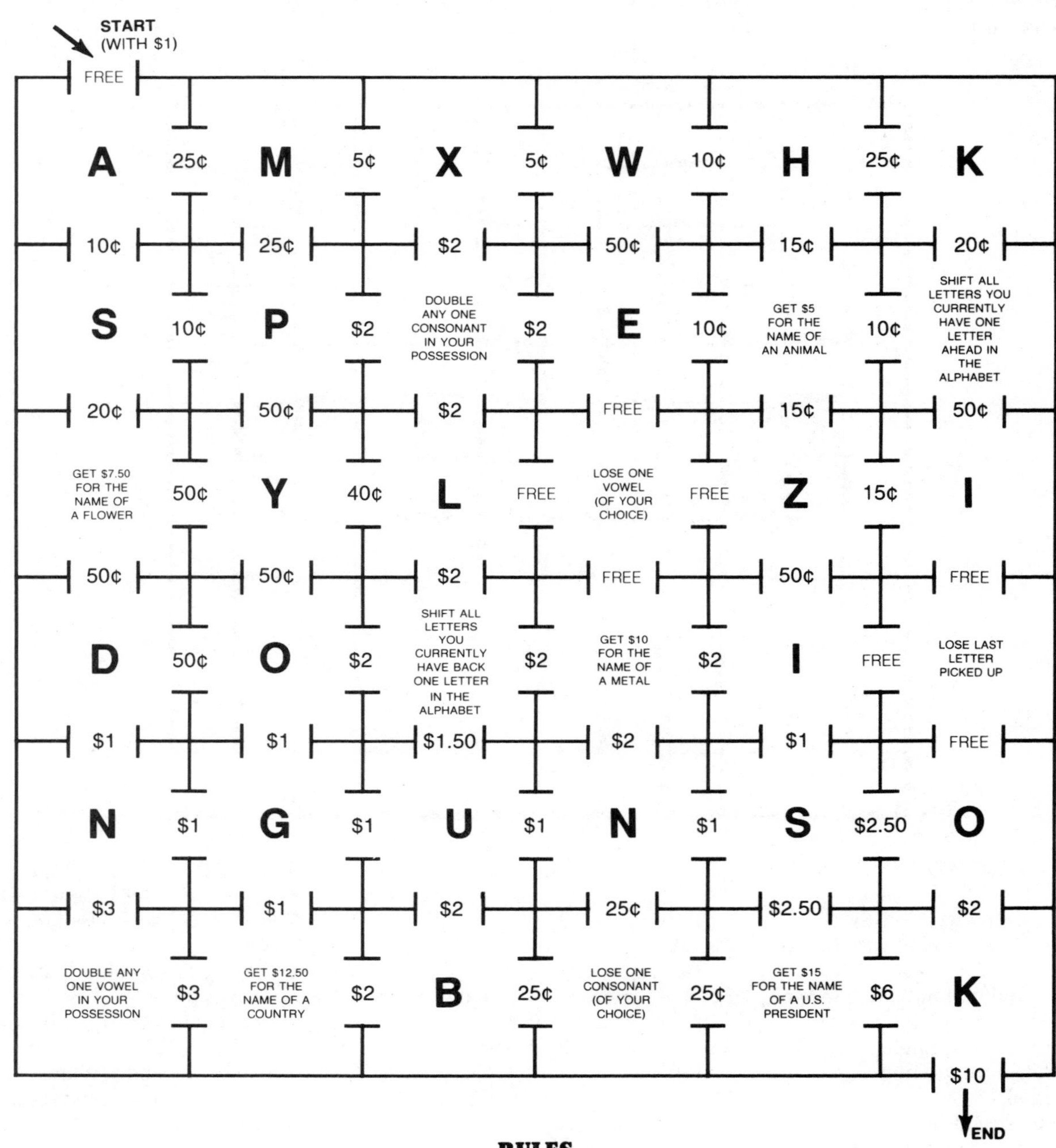

RULES

You have $1.00 to start with as you enter the door in the upper left corner. Every time you go through a door you must pay the toll shown. If you don't have enough money left, you can't use that door.

You may enter any of the rooms as many times as you wish. Some rooms contain a letter, which you may take if you like. A letter can be picked up only once; if you decide not to take it, you can still pick it up on a later visit.

In some rooms you can earn money by using some or all of your letters to form a word that fits the given category. Once you have sold a word, those letters are gone and cannot be used again. You don't have to sell a word if you don't want or if you don't have the right letters.

Other rooms contain instructions that must be followed, if possible. (If you are told, say, to lose a vowel, and you have no vowels, you don't lose anything.)

Full House★★★

by Norton Rhoades

This diagramless crossword puzzle is 18 squares wide by 17 squares deep and has an asymmetrical design. The location of the starting square and other solving tips appear at the bottom of the page.

Answer, page 189

ACROSS

1 Fusses
5 Hockey player Leach
8 Old soft shoe
9 Galena, for one
10 There was an ___ . . .
12 Yalie
13 Lavish party
14 Something to put forward
16 Who lived in ___ . . .
17 In reserve
21 She had so many ___ . . .
24 Chemists get a charge out of it
25 One with sea legs
26 She didn't know what ___ . . .
28 Lack
30 Long, long time
32 She gave them some ___ . . .
35 Sympathy's companion
37 Some dorm dwellers
40 Learn by heart
45 Footpaths
48 ___ *pro nobis*
49 Without any ___ . . .
51 Analogous
54 Foot or hand, e.g.
56 CPA's jottings
58 Aesopian ending
60 Fork feature
61 She whipped them all ___ . . .
62 Mental picture
63 Order to Fido
64 Mel Brooks movies, e.g.
65 And put them ___

DOWN

1 Microscopic "blob"
2 Where D.C.'s DC's land
3 A bit past one's prime
4 Put in stitches
5 Subject of "Wherefore art thou?"
6 Sonneteer's Muse
7 *The Maids* playwright
11 Rankles
15 Awl, e.g.
18 Afghanistan neighbor
19 Media star
20 Computer key
21 Footnote
22 Cager's target
23 Prefix with Chinese or European
27 Twice tetra-
29 Johnny's bandleader
31 Basil, for one
33 Little tyke
34 That very woman
36 Buenos ___
38 Abner's and Donald Duck's girlfriends
39 Actor Alastair
40 Foot-and-___ disease
41 Bert's *Sesame Street* sidekick
42 Where the Penobscot flows
43 Philosophers of Citium, Elea, and Sidon
44 Consume
46 55, usually
47 Sportscast feature, for short
50 SPECTRE villain
52 Beautiful horse
53 Fad
55 ___ Aviv
57 Last single words
59 Directed

TIPS FOR NEW SOLVERS

A diagramless puzzle is a combination of crossword and logic problem. The object is not just to answer the clues, but to discover—by logic and the crossing of words—where the answers go in the grid. It's not as hard as it sounds. Remember:

• Each answer word is at least three letters long, and each letter is part of two answers, one reading across and one down.

• When solving, put a number in each square that starts a word, either Across or Down.

• Put a black square before and after each word (except, of course, where the word is bounded by the edge of the grid).

• To start, note that the length of 1-Across must be one letter less than the number of the second word across. Thus, in the puzzle above, 1-Across is four letters long (and *hint*: it begins in the first square of the top row).

• As in all the diagramless puzzles published in GAMES, the shape of the completed grid is appropriate to the theme of the puzzle.

Locker Room Mystery★★★

by Marek Penszko

The men down at the 13th precinct suspected an inside job when a prankster stole all the handles from their locker doors. Worse yet, no one could remember which lockers opened on the left and which on the right. One officer did recall that each horizontal row contained a different number of right-handled lockers, and the custodian remembered that each vertical column had a different number of left-handled lockers. The officers have managed to pry open two of the lockers, as shown. They've also found an old overhead view of the lockers that shows nine of the doors open. By comparing the two views, and using some logical reasoning, can you figure out where each handle goes?

Answer, page 189

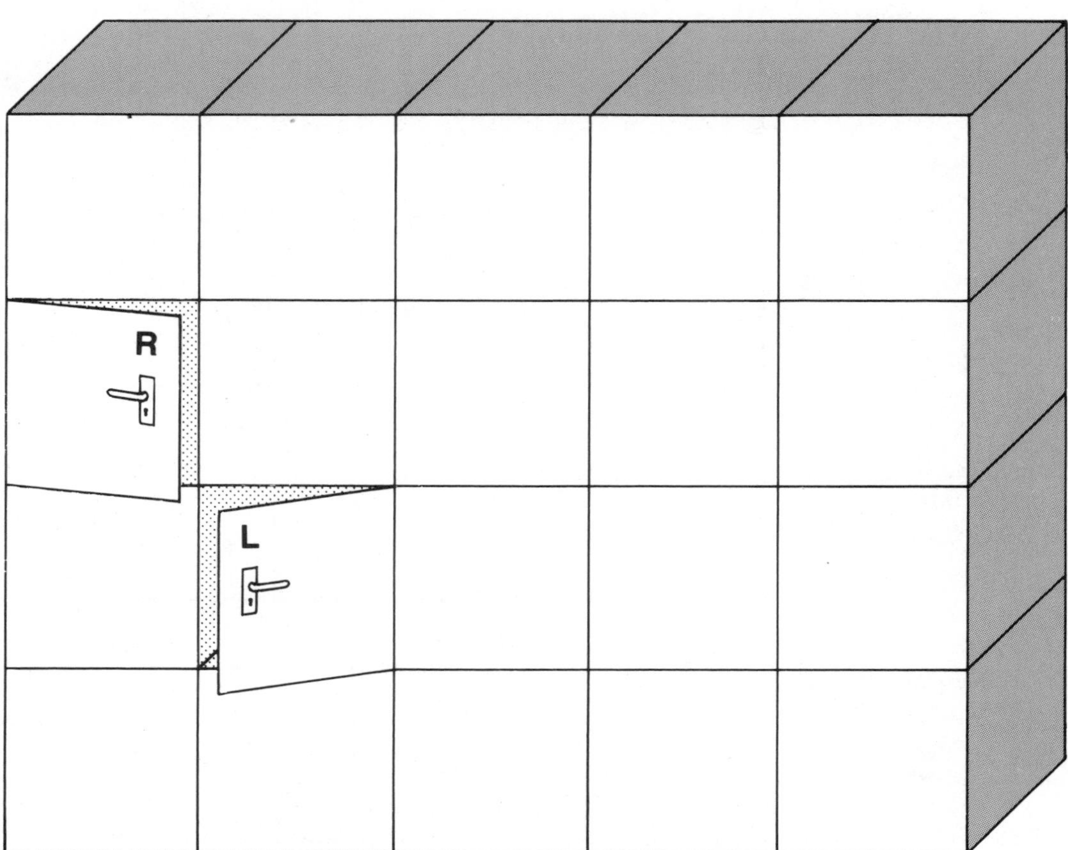

OVERHEAD VIEW

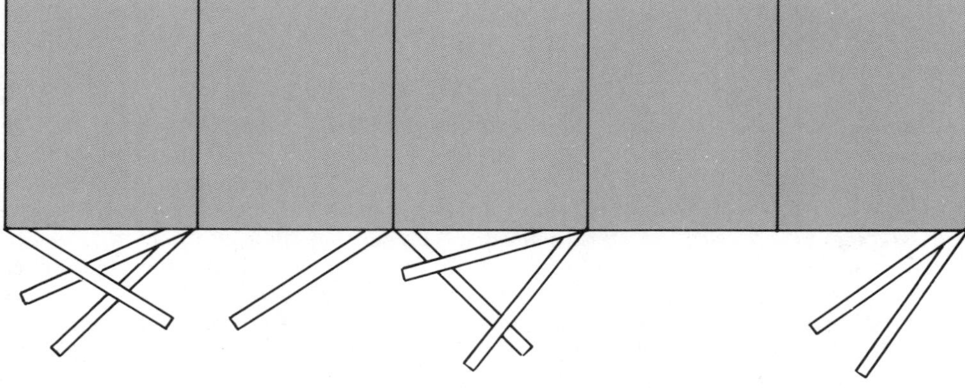

Pentathlon★★★

by Roger Hufford

Five young athletes named Jay, Ken, Lee, Mike, and Nick took part in a contest of five events: the high jump, the shot put, the mile run, the hurdles, and the 100-meter dash. It was agreed that a first-place finish would receive 1 point, a second-place finish 2 points, and so on; and that the competitor with the lowest point total would be declared the overall pentathlon winner. As it turned out, there were no ties in any single event, and no ties for overall points in the pentathlon. When the meet was over, the five athletes made a number of statements, which are recorded below. These statements, all true, will enable a dedicated logician to determine the placement of all the athletes in each event and in the final standings.

Answer, page 188

STATEMENTS

JAY: 1. Mike beat me in the high jump, but lost to Lee in the shot put.
2. Ken finished with 14 points in the pentathlon.

KEN: 3. Mike was first in two events, but he did not win the pentathlon.
4. Jay did not finish last in the mile or the shot put, but Nick was last in the hurdles.

LEE: 5. Nick beat me in the shot put and in just one other event, and he beat Jay in the high jump; but Nick did not place first in either the shot put or high jump.
6. Jay finished one place ahead of me in the hurdles, but lost to me in the shot put.

MIKE: 7. Ken beat Nick in the mile, but lost to him in the 100-meter dash; neither man placed first in either event.
8. I did not win the mile, and Jay did not finish second in the 100-meter dash.

NICK: 9. Jay finished in a different position in each event.
10. Without winning either event, Lee beat Mike in the high jump, and beat Ken in the mile.

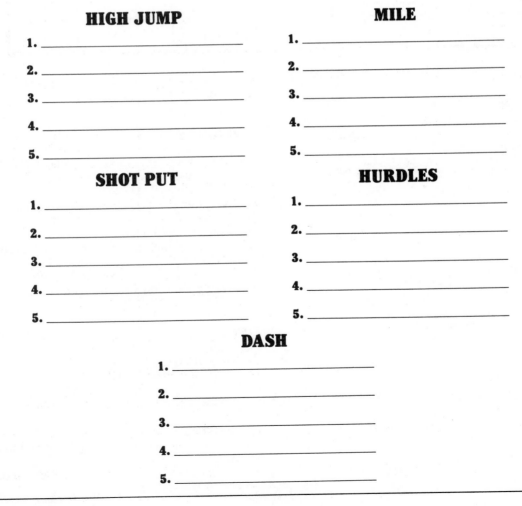

HIGH JUMP

1. __________
2. __________
3. __________
4. __________
5. __________

MILE

1. __________
2. __________
3. __________
4. __________
5. __________

SHOT PUT

1. __________
2. __________
3. __________
4. __________
5. __________

HURDLES

1. __________
2. __________
3. __________
4. __________
5. __________

DASH

1. __________
2. __________
3. __________
4. __________
5. __________

Word Games ★★★

by Scott Marley

This puzzle is really five games in one. The clues are presented in five sections, each posing a different challenge. We've given an example in each category below to get you started. First answer as many of the clues as you can. Then enter the letters in the diagram, as indicated by the letter/number pairs. (Thus, A1 represents the upper left corner square, R8 the lower right corner square, etc.) Many squares are used in more than one answer, so every clue you solve will provide some help toward others. When the puzzle has been completed, you will find a bit of original light verse reading across the diagram, line by line, beginning in square A1. *Answer, page 189*

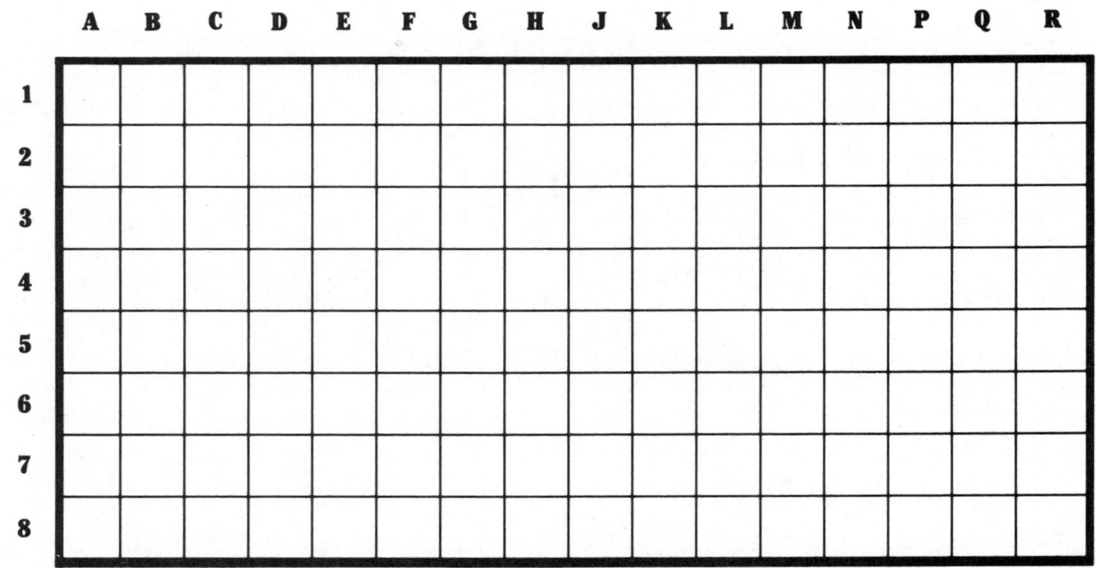

MISSING LINKS

Ex. tennis ______ grease: ELBOW
1. better ______ pint: F7 H5 F3 Q5
2. other ______ wise: K6 M2 K8 K3 D4 Q1 E3
3. chain ______ plank: R2 B4 C5 E7
4. legal ______ hearted: D8 J3 B2 A5 C6 Q6
5. Chinese ______ food: M4 L5 M3 J4
6. rock ______ dollar: L8 Q3 G7 D5 G1 D2

OPPOSITES

Ex. white: BLACK
1. out: H5 L8 Q1 C2 B6 N3
2. short: H3 L4 F8 H6 N4 J2 A4
3. his: E7 L3 M2 F2 K5 M6 R4 B1
4. fine: K8 L4 H7 G4 A8 F2
5. rough: H1 J7 G3 D6 Q7 B4 J5
6. blank: R5 P7 M6 R3 J8 A5

RATIOS

Ex. rooster : hen : : ram : EWE
1. cup : pint : : bit : P8 K1 J7 H4 M5 F5 J2
2. lain : rowed : : paws : Q7 L1 B5 F6 R6 D8
3. egad : gained : : fits : L2 D7 N1 P5 G4 B7 H6 B8 (2 wds.)
4. diagnose : San Diego : : insertable : D3 D1 E4 G7 K5 R1 N8 K3 E6 P2 (2 wds.)
5. devil : existed : : desserts : J3 G2 Q4 N5 A3 B1 D7 B6 C8 Q2
6. Romeo : Juliet : : H8 B5 H2 K6 M8 M5 E5 F8 : L7 G3 N1 B2 A7 G6 D1 K4 A3

COMMON FACTORS

Ex. pipe; flower; wristwatch; wineglass: STEM
1. sleeper pajamas; yardstick; poetry; crows: N6 D3 P5 D5
2. toast; freeway; jazz combo; radio signal: M4 L6 D2
3. coatrack; fishing line; boxer; golf stroke: H8 R7 P6 K2
4. tennis; baseball; contract bridge; movie stunts: Q2 A2 N2 G5 B3 R8 E4
5. sea; beer; shaving cream; seat cushion: H1 A2 J6 R3
6. supermarket; cloakrooms; game chest; Nixon: N7 E8 A7 P1 J4 E2 R5 P3

LISTS

Ex. two; four; six; EIGHT
1. nine; ten; eleven; C4 G1 A6 M3
2. forty; thirty; fifteen; B3 P6 E1 M1
3. Albany; Annapolis; Atlanta; Augusta; A1 Q8 P3 F4 E6 C4
4. bed; grange; mellow; preen; F6 F3 M7 F1
5. scratches the surface; dirt; de Milo; J1 N4 G3 N7 K2 K7 D7 C3 E1 F5 N8
6. cappella; movie; note; day; Q4 C1 K1 Q6 B5 C7 N2 B8 Q8 G8 M7 P4 (2 wds.)

Crytpic Crosswodr ★★★

by Henry Hook

The clues in this cryptic crossword follow the usual rules, but the answers don't. To solve, you must switch two consecutive letters in each answer before entering it in the diagram. Thus, the word PRINCE might be entered as RPINCE, or as PIRNCE, PRNICE, PRICNE, or PRINEC. Deciding which is right is part of the puzzle. *Answers, page 189*

ACROSS

1 Pair is atop jail (6)
6 Pacino and Winnie return in commotion (6)
11 Wrongly puts together opening of Monet with wild Matisse (8)
12 Runny oriental sauce holds up (5)
13 Moves slowly in unending board game (6)
14 Ship's gone sailing, circumnavigating everything (7)
15 Italian island is cold before All Fools' Day (5)
16 Portion of wealth I eventually steal (6)
18 Smash hit—*Lear* act for the stage (10)
20 Crazy Ava loiters in washrooms (10)
25 Er... shortstop's last to anger referee (6)
27 Sound of German car: nothing (5)
28 After Monday, looked wealthy (7)
29 Accepting no money, keeps part of sundial (6)
30 Bit of cork in champagne makes you cringe (5)
31 Time to break ship's doors with axes (8)
32 Woman at "K" train gives Israeli coin (6)
33 Less meaningful in an emergency room (6)

DOWN

1 Regarding mail distributed to pals (6)
2 High-fiber food for witch in red (8)
3 Ruined post office covered by sediment (6)
4 Limp elbows yielding to force (5)
5 Something new in tavern: *Cheers* (10)
7 Ball game's slugger, you say? (6)
8 Bad review hurt style (7)
9 The filling or else (5)
10 Attack donkey and get sick (6)
13 Trust in men playing piano, for instance (10)
17 Perseverance for mixing nice paté (8)
19 Bad actor simulated a place to sleep (7)
20 Lug has nutty Snickers (6)
21 Alternatively I cheer bird (6)
22 Middle Eastern yarn is unraveled (6)
23 Book was a guide to Germany (6)
24 Poet has appointment about noon (5)
26 Write Capone concerning punishment (5)

Puzzle Decathlon

This puzzle is really 10 brain-twisters in one: 10 individual puzzle "events," forming a "Decathlon." The puzzles have been designed to test the widest possible range of solving skills.

Each event (numbered 1 through 10) consists of a puzzle to be solved. For each, the final answer is a single word, number, or string of letters.

Answers, page 190

1. TEN TAKEAWAY

This "10" sculpture is made of nine blocks. Imagine that you and one other person are playing a game in which the two of you take turns choosing one of the blocks. The block a player chooses is immediately removed from the sculpture, *along with any block(s) wholly or partially above it.* The object is to be the player who removes the last block.

For example, if you choose block number 4 (a bad choice), blocks 1, 2, and 3, as well as 4, will be removed; your opponent can then win by choosing block 9, which causes all the rest of the blocks to be removed.

If you play first, one of the blocks (1–9) can be chosen to guarantee you a win, no matter how your opponent plays. Which block should you choose?

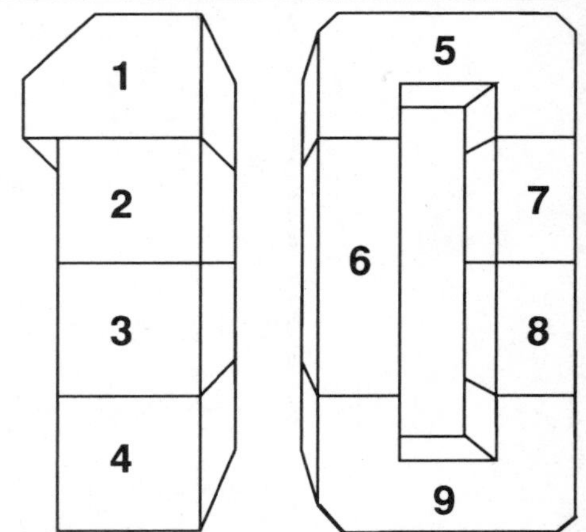

2. CRISSCROSS

Fill in the words below so they interlock in crossword fashion in the grid. The middle (shaded) word, not given in the list, is to be determined from the crossing words. What is this word?

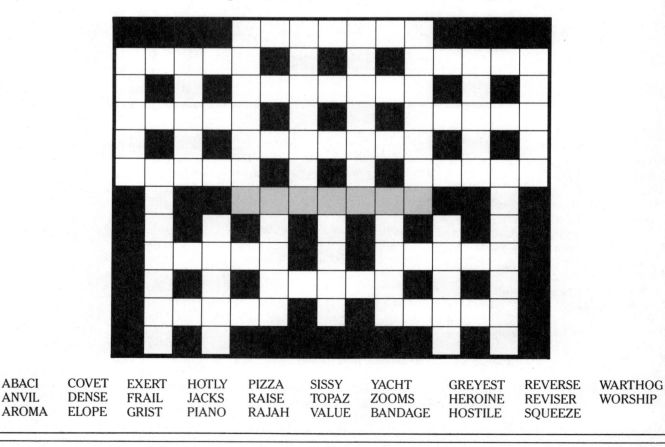

ABACI	COVET	EXERT	HOTLY	PIZZA	SISSY	YACHT	GREYEST	REVERSE	WARTHOG
ANVIL	DENSE	FRAIL	JACKS	RAISE	TOPAZ	ZOOMS	HEROINE	REVISER	WORSHIP
AROMA	ELOPE	GRIST	PIANO	RAJAH	VALUE	BANDAGE	HOSTILE	SQUEEZE	

3. DOUBLE-CROSTIC

Answer the clues for words to be entered on the numbered dashes. Then transfer the letters on the dashes to the correspondingly numbered squares in the puzzle grid to spell a quotation reading from left to right. Note that spaces between words in the grid are not indicated. The message in the completed grid will reveal further instructions. Follow them to determine the final answer.

1	2	3	4	5	6	7	8	9	10	11
12	13	14	15	16	17	18	19	20	21	22
23	24	25	26	27	28	29	30	31	32	33
34	35	36	37	38	39	40	41	42	43	44
45	46	47	48	49	50	51	52	53	54	55
56	57	58	59	60	61	62	63	64	65	66
67	68	69	70	71	72	73	74	75	76	77
78	79	80	81	82	83	84	85	86	87	88

A. Minos's subjects — 33 15 50 7 86 42 69

B. Extemporaneously (3 wds.) — 78 54 70 84 75 63 49 34 88 3

C. Magazine founded in 1933 — 65 53 59 12 77 32 9 22

D. "___ Dreams" (#1 song by Heart) — 35 52 45 83 68

E. Appraise — 27 37 10 56 18 41 1 21

F. Nautical spar — 31 47 79 60 74

G. Mischievous dwarf — 26 44 72 39 57

H. "Why should ___, because 'tis light?" (Donne) (2 wds.) — 23 38 71 67 19 76

I. Pressed — 4 24 29 61 14 85

J. Atlantic tern — 30 58 80 43 16

K. One who stays up late (2 wds.) — 5 36 62 8 65 17 13 81

L. Adam Smith, e.g. — 20 28 55 11 2 73 25 46 51

M. Mideastern capital — 66 82 40 48 6 87

4. COMPLETE THIS SEQUENCE

The four numbered items (1–4) below form the beginning of an unusual sequence. How should the four lettered items (A–D) be arranged to best continue the sequence?

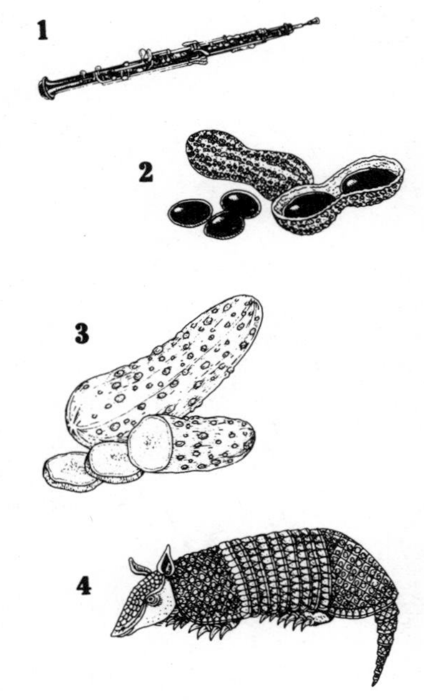

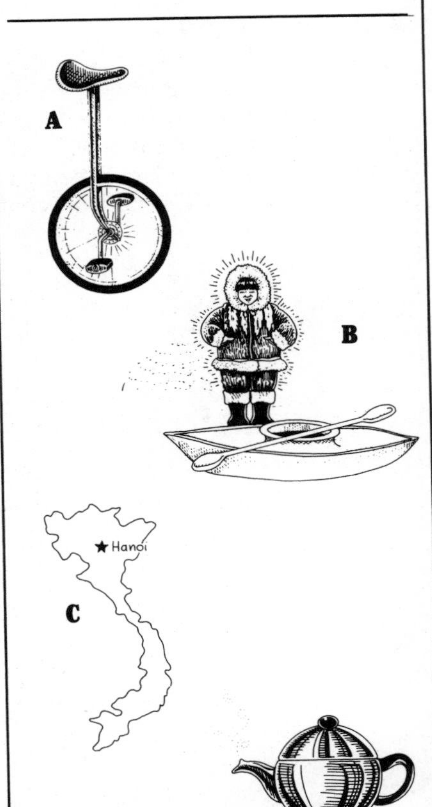

5. COUNT THE TRIANGLES

How many triangles of all sizes are in this figure? Triangles count even if they contain one or more other triangles or shaded diamonds.

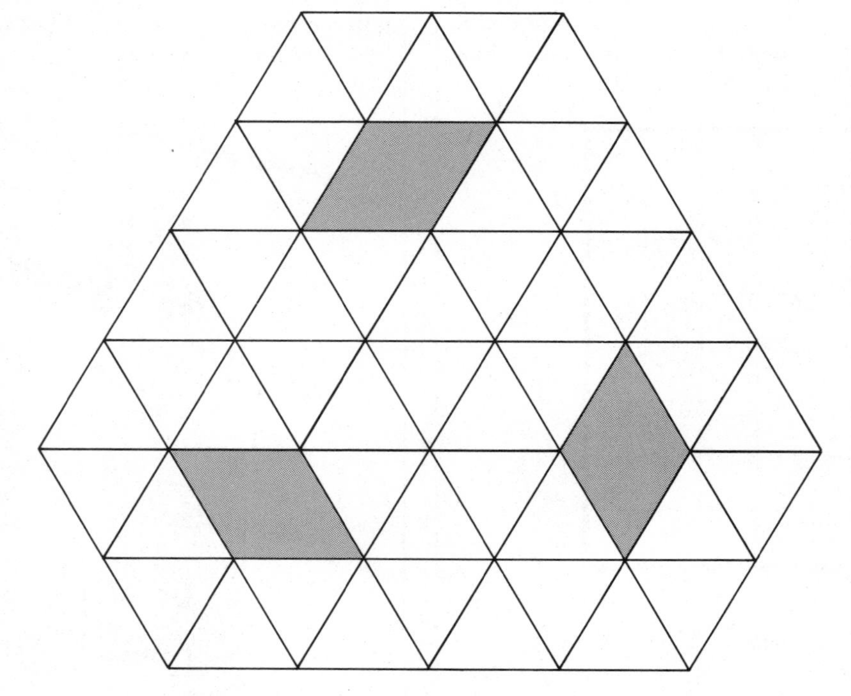

6. WORD SEARCH

The names of a number of world capitals (that is, capital cities of independent countries) are hidden in this grid. Each reads in a straight line horizontally, vertically, or diagonally. Find and circle them all. When the puzzle is done correctly, the leftover letters can be rearranged to spell the name of another country whose capital is not included here. What is it?

```
H S O E D I V E T N O M
A D S Y A J O R I A C A
S I A L K T A C S U M C
U R E Y E O O K S U A C
N D I P I S T R A L V R
C A N N I R S U C R E A
I M M A N A G U A K T W
O S L O M O T I R A N A
N S I N U T B R A B A T
R U T D A M A S C U S T
E H E L S I N K I L A O
B T S E P A D U B L I N
```

7. DIGITITIS

We've removed most of the digits from the mathematically correct long division below, and replaced them with dashes. The missing digits can be determined by using logic and simple arithmetic. (No number starts with zero.) Find the five-digit quotient (the number on the top line) of the completed problem.

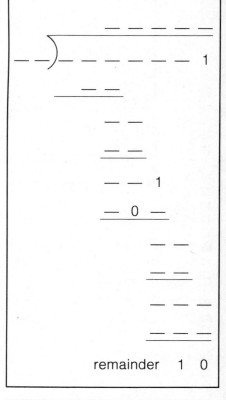

```
              _ _ _ _ _
       ____________________
_ _ ) _ _ _ _ _ _ _ 1
      _ _
      ---
        _ _
        _ _
        ---
        _ _ 1
        _ 0 _
        -----
            _ _
            _ _
            ---
            _ _ _
            _ _ _
            -----
remainder   1 0
```

8. CRYPTOGRAM

Solve this puzzle by breaking the alphabet code. Letter substitutions remain constant throughout the message. The resulting message asks a question. What is its answer?

JDEH JMAS
BNEICIZ "GNEXD"
XMITCTHT MY E
TLIMILB YMA
"GAMESXETH"
EAMPIS "XNAHECI
DECATHLON?"

9. CROSSWORD

If this crossword puzzle is solved correctly, the letters in the six shaded squares can be rearranged to spell a familiar word. What is it?

1	2	3	■	4	5	6	7	■	8	9	10	11
12			■	13				■	14			
15			16					■	17			
18					■	19		20			■	■
■	■	■	21		22	■	■	23			24	25
26	27	28		■	29	30	31		■	32		
33				■	34			■	35			
36			■	37				■	38			
39			40		■	■	41	42		■	■	■
■	■	43			44	45	■	46		47	48	49
50	51			■	52		53					
54				■	55				■	56		
57				■	58				■	59		

ACROSS

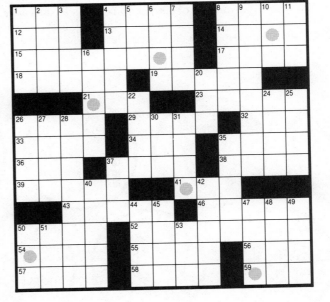

1 *Studio One* setting
4 Buoyant buggies
8 Hissen Habré's home
12 Gone shopping, perhaps
13 Check
14 Leonato's daughter
15 "The most gratuitous form of error": Eliot
17 Company VIP
18 Queening, e.g.
19 Crowd scene constituent
21 Zeus's babysitter
23 Fleming's figure
26 Cancer time
29 Film technique
32 School of the future
33 Charge
34 Mum, e.g.
35 Bear of story
36 Tanning need
37 Hamburger's better half
38 Dubai bigwig
39 Kennedy or Clark
41 Lafitte milieu
43 Key character
46 Cause
50 Slips separator
52 Literally, "roast sunshine"
54 *Douleur* : bread : : *unbehaart* : ____
55 See 54-Across
56 Covet, e.g.
57 Lincoln's and Gray's
58 Like omega
59 This, in a way

DOWN

1 Lola's workplace
2 Result of a pat on the back
3 Bottom-of-page SAT instruction
4 Had smarts?
5 *Finnegans Wake* finish
6 Miami doings
7 Mother of Zeal
8 Abelard, to Héloïse
9 Magen David
10 119.6 square yards
11 Roy Atwell supplied his voice
16 Exercises
20 Starting point, for some
22 Remote African language
24 Huruingwuhti worshiper
25 Toot
26 Danny's lift man
27 One's one
28 Light meal
30 Like
31 God, to Gregory
35 British Arctic explorer-turned-admiral
37 It's felt overhead
40 Pulls down
42 Eleanor Southworth's married name
44 With colleagues, perhaps
45 Comic Jay
47 Inch, perhaps
48 Homologous
49 Strain
50 Yaw angle, in aeronautics
51 Ammonium, e.g.
53 *Cuba libre* ingredient

10. PINBALL MAZE

First, complete the Pinball Maze by placing one of the arithmetic symbols below into each of the 10 "bumpers" (the circles), in front of the number 10. Each bumper must have a symbol, and all 10 symbols must be used.

Next, travel from START to FINISH, hitting each of the 10 bumpers at least once. Travel along the paths, changing direction, if you wish, at any bumper. You may not use any path more than once, but you may cross earlier parts of your route at bumpers.

When you leave START, your score is zero. Each time you hit a bumper, adjust your score by performing the arithmetic indicated there. (For example, when you hit a "+10" bumper, add 10 to your running score.) What is the highest score with which you can reach the FINISH?

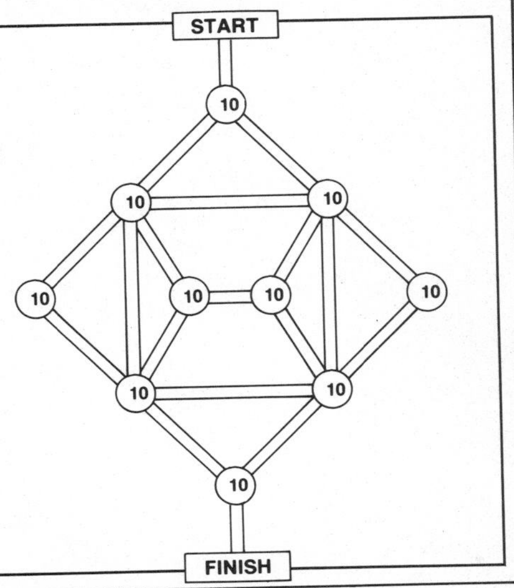

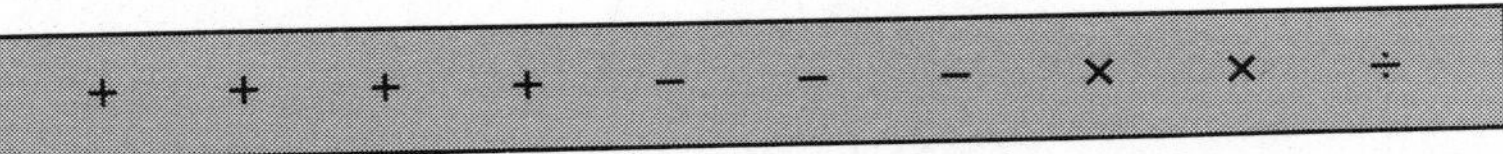

The Last Roundup★★

by Karen Anderson

This last puzzle will test how well you were paying attention as you worked through the games in this volume. The seventeen circles below contain pieces of illustration and type reproduced from the preceding pages, with no change in size or orientation. Find the page on which each illustration appears, and assign the first letter of the title of that puzzle to the number beside the circle. Then, substitute that letter every time the corresponding number appears under a blank below. When entered correctly, the letters will form a quote by James Thurber. *Answer, page 190*

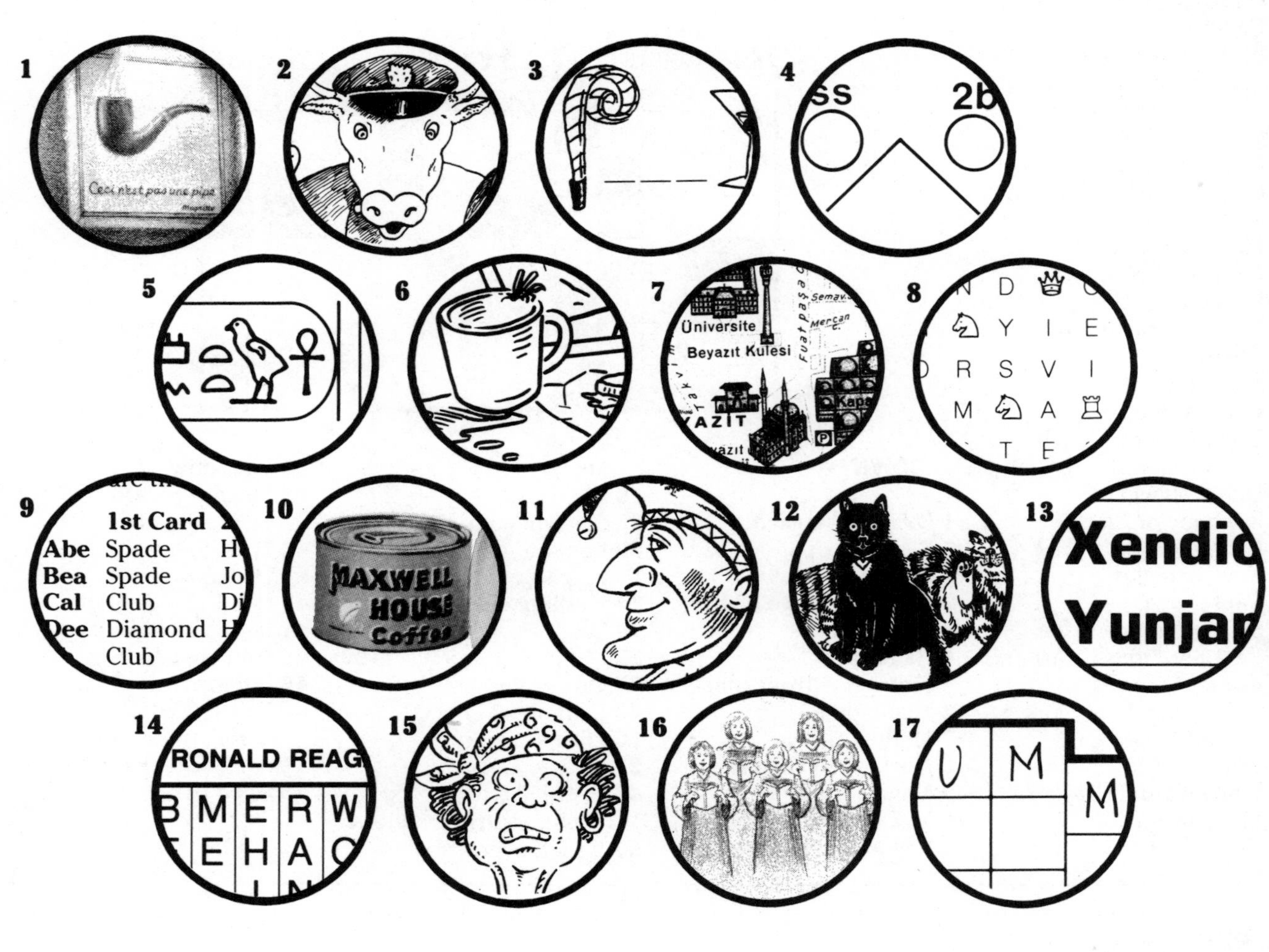

1 2 3   4 5 2 2 5 6   2 7

8 9 7 10   3 7 11 5   7 12

2 13 5   14 15 5 3 2 1 7 9 3

2 13 16 9   16 17 17   7 12

2 13 5   16 9 3 10 5 6 3.

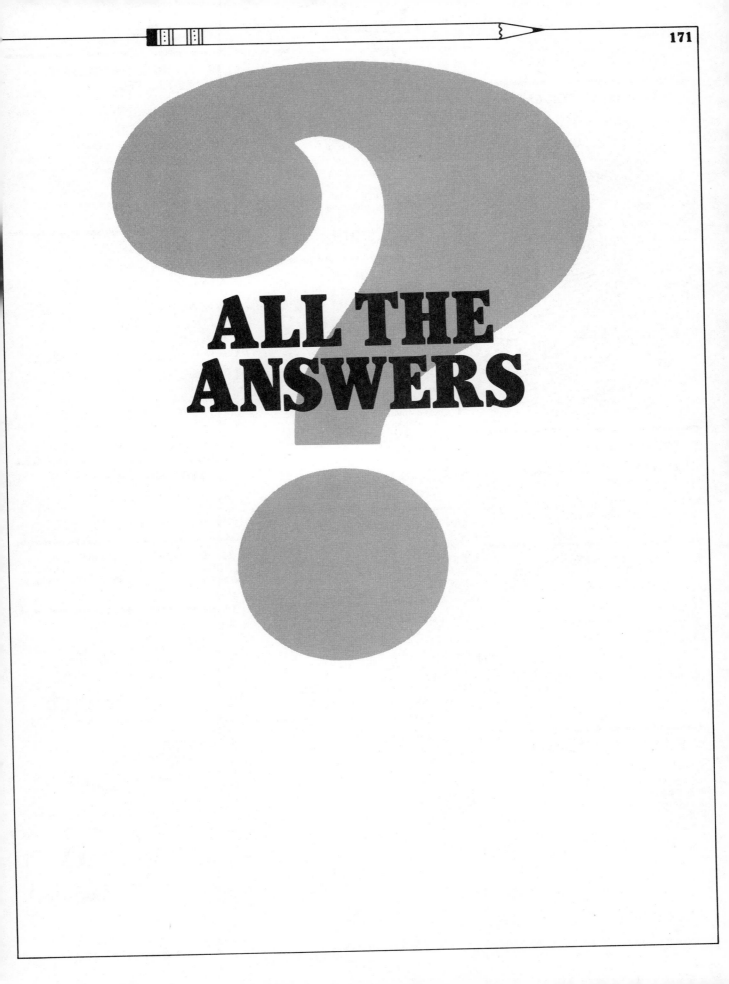

ALL THE ANSWERS

1

7 WHERE IN THE WHORL?

8 QUOTE BOXES

1. "On the whole, human beings want to be good, but not too good and not quite all the time."
2. "I have left orders to be awakened at any time in case of national emergency, even if I'm in a cabinet meeting."

8 COMPOUND INTEREST

1. Armstrong (arm strong)
2. Callas (call as)
3. Campbell (camp bell)
4. Chamberlain (chamber lain)
5. Rockwell (rock well)
6. Redgrave (red grave)
7. Mansfield (man's field)
8. Chopin (chop in)
9. Springsteen (springs teen)
10. Unitas (unit as)
11. Lamour (lam our)
12. Carpenter (carp enter)

9 DIRECTORY ASSISTANCE

1. Bridal shops
2. Chiropractors
3. Towing services
4. Plumbers
5. Beauty salons
6. Funeral directors
7. Employment agencies
8. Burglar alarms
9. Veterinarians

10 INITIAL REACTIONS

1. Vulture Cutting Rope
2. Napoleon Frying Lobster
3. Uncle Sam Selling Radio
4. Pirate Tossing Anchor
5. Bald Yankee Oiling Bat
6. Ballerina Milking Old Cow
7. Fat Dinosaur Icing Cake
8. Arnold Schwarzenegger Playing Chess Alone
9. Tarzan Giving Indian Fish
10. Neil Armstrong Addressing Christmas Present
11. Pilgrim Dunking Queen
12. Magician Balancing Apples

12 STRIP TEASE

1. Telephone directory
2. *TV Guide*
3. Crossword magazine
4. Superman comic book
5. Chinese restaurant menu
6. Bible
7. Cereal box
8. Traffic ticket
9. Theater playbill
10. *Guinness Book of World Records*
11. Chess manual
12. "Ripley's Believe It Or Not" book
13. Thesaurus
14. Credit card application
15. Seed catalog
16. Atlas index
17. Mother Goose book
18. Bank statement

14 CHARACTER STUDY

1. (f)	5. (g)	9. (a)
2. (b)	6. (e)	10. (h)
3. (d)	7. (i)	11. (k)
4. (l)	8. (j)	12. (c)

15 FAMILY PICTURES

The five families are:
Baseball Terms: bat, pitcher, plate.
Broadway Musicals: *Cats, Hair, Oklahoma!*
Card Suits: club, heart, spade.
Things with Tails: comet, formal jacket, kite.
Words Ending "-key": jockey, monkey, turkey.

16 CARTOONERISMS

1. Weeping lizard/leaping wizard
2. Bunny phone/funny bone
3. Churning bear/burning chair
4. Head dog/dead hog
5. Quart shaker/short Quaker
6. Duck store/stuck door
7. Polar bear/bowler pair
8. Reading spider/speeding rider

18 ADDRESS CORRECTION REQUESTED

1. Mary Richards *(The Mary Tyler Moore Show)*
2. Mindy McConnell *(Mork and Mindy)*
3. Herman Munster *(The Munsters)*
4. Andy Taylor *(The Andy Griffith Show)*
5. J. R. Ewing *(Dallas)*
6. Lucy Ricardo *(I Love Lucy)*
7. Fred Flintstone *(The Flintstones)*
8. Jed Clampett *(The Beverly Hillbillies)*
9. Rob Petrie *(The Dick Van Dyke Show)*
10. Archie Bunker *(All in the Family)*

19 SKETCHWORDS

1. Television
2. Melody
3. Yield
4. Skiing
5. Carpenter or Carpentry
6. Wizard
7. Hawaii
8. Rodeo
9. Moses
10. Justice
11. Touchdown
12. Party
13. Sherlock
14. Pacman
15. Santa
16. Toothpaste

20 SCRAMBLED COMICS

Blow-Up—C, G, A, E, B, F, D
About a Bout—D, G, E, B, A, F, C
Buy Lines—B, D, G, A, E, C, F

22 PICTURE DOMINOES

The chain proceeds as follows: A–C, C–F, F–H, H–B, B–G, G–D, D–E, E–A.

24 BON APPETIT!

1. Campbell's Homestyle Vegetable Soup
2. Peter Pan Creamy Peanut Butter
3. Reddi Whip instant whipped cream
4. Ragu Spaghetti Sauce
5. Seven Seas Viva Italian! salad dressing
6. Sun-Maid Raisin Bread Cinnamon Swirl
7. Beech Nut Yellow Cling Peaches baby food
8. Fig Newtons
9. V8 vegetable juice
10. Kellogg's Rice Krispies
11. Alpo dog food
12. A.1. Steak Sauce
13. Hellmann's Real Mayonnaise
14. Calvin Cooler Passion wine cooler
15. Dannon Original Strawberry Lowfat Yogurt
16. Stouffer's Chili Con Carne
17. Celeste Cheese Pizza

23 SIGNS OF TROUBLE

The signs are positioned as shown below.

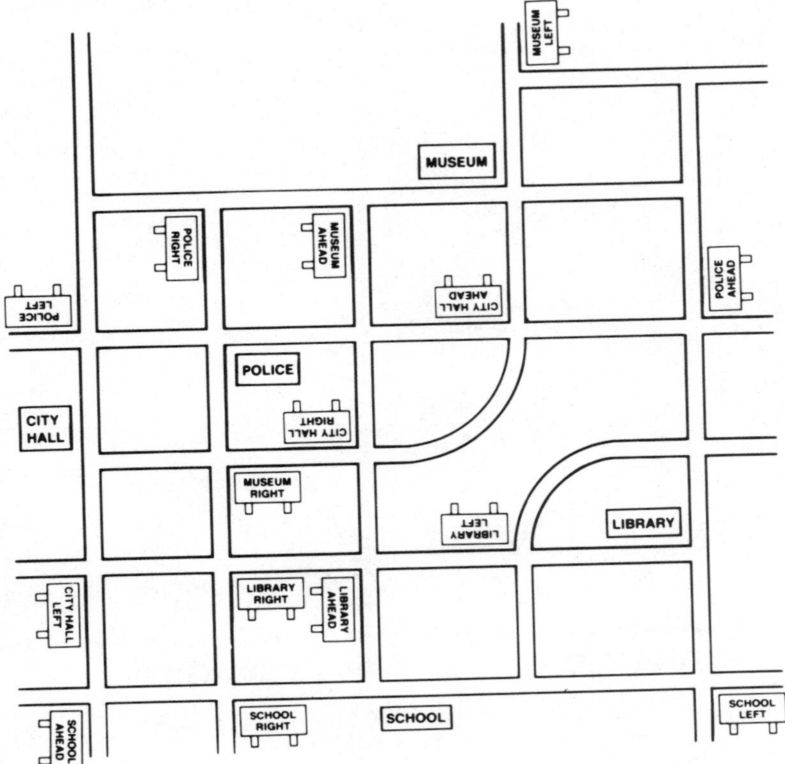

26 WHAT'S SO FUNNY?

1. G
2. E
3. K
4. A
5. I
6. C
7. L
8. F
9. B
10. J
11. D
12. H

28 THE BEADLESS ABACUS

1. To give a total of the operations in any three cells in a row, perform the operation in the next cell beyond the row of three, at either end of it, and subtract the result from 34.
2. A row of four is even easier: Its total will *always* be 34.
3. All you need to do is glance at the operation in the central cell of the cluster, perform it, and subtract that answer from 68. The result will be the sum of the operations in all seven cells.

29 TERROR INCOGNITUS

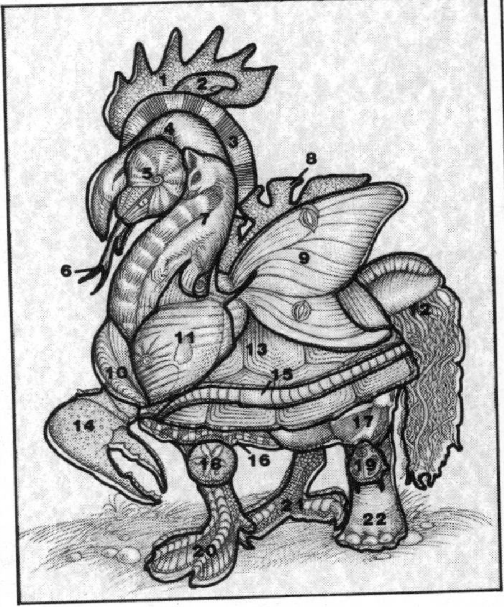

1. White leghorn rooster (comb)
2. Paramecium
3. Zebra (mane)
4. Flamingo
5. Nautilus
6. Snake (tongue)
7. Ring-tailed lemur
8. Elkhorn coral
9. Luna moth
10. Mussel
11. Queen triggerfish
12. Portuguese man-of-war
13. Galapagos tortoise
14. Fiddler crab
15. Earthworm
16. Tiger salamander
17. Skunk
18. Sand dollar
19. Ladybug beetle
20. Grebe
21. Eagle
22. Elephant

2

30 EYE EXAM

1. b
2.

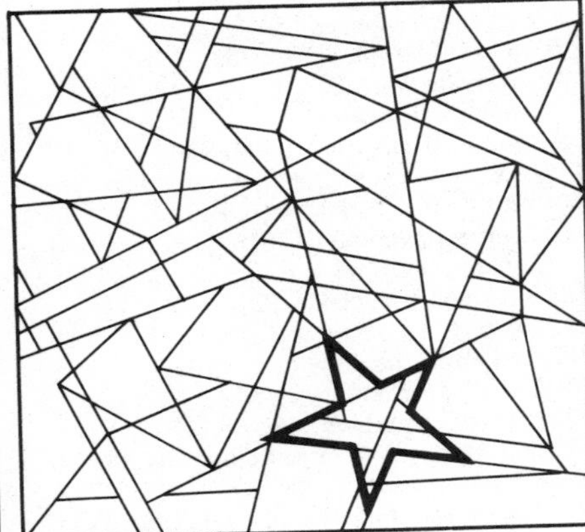

3. K
4. a) dime—4
b) penny—5
c) quarter—9
5. b
6. c
7. 16

32 MATCH PLAY

Sketch #3 is perfect. The areas with mistakes in the other sketches are circled below.

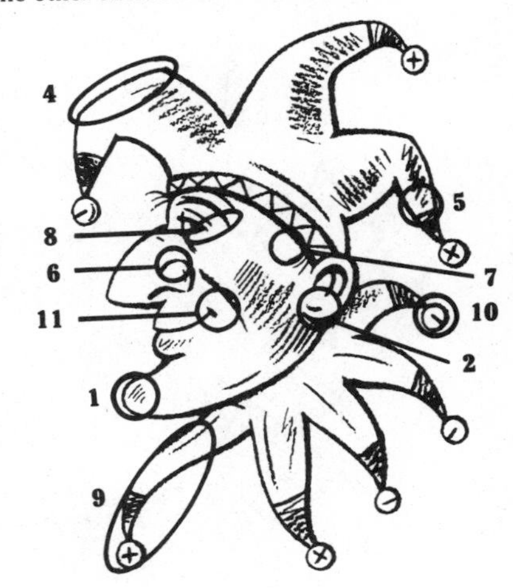

33 OUT OF THIS WORLD

1. Antarctica
2. Hiroshima (Japan)
3. Saudi Arabia
4. Spokane (Washington)
5. Fiji (the island of Viti Levu)
6. Istanbul (Turkey)
7. Delaware
8. Mars
9. New Jersey (Sandy Hook)

36 THE BUCK STARTS HERE

FRONT

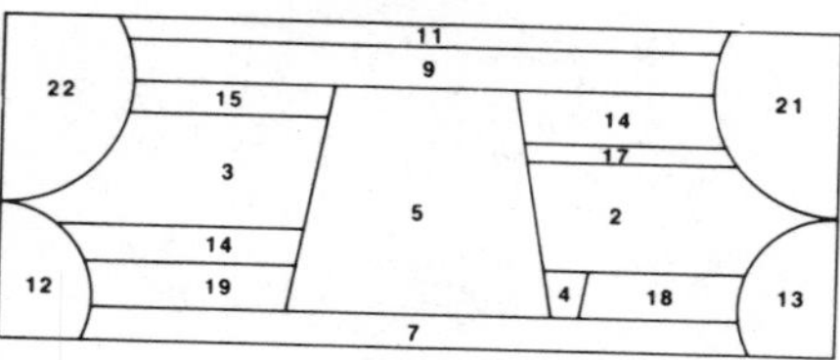

BACK

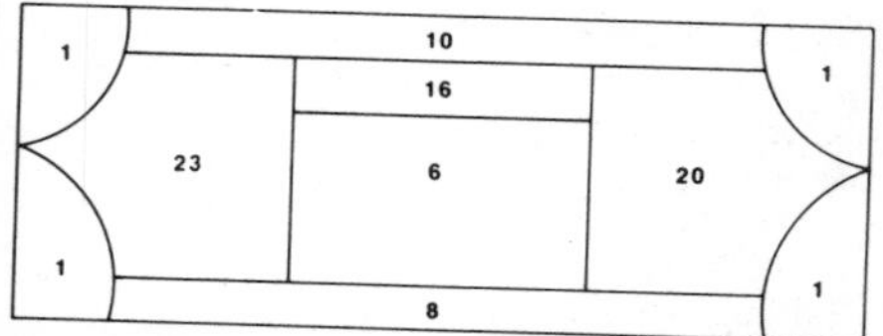

41 SIGNS OF LIFE

A 2 (cat)
B 11 (spider)
C 9 (owl)
D 12 (turtle)
E 5 (elephant)
F 10 (snake)
G 6 (giraffe)
H 8 (monkey)
I 3 (deer)
J 7 (kangaroo)
K 4 (duck)
L 1 (butterfly)

Based on *The Perigee Visual Dictionary of Signing* by Rod Butterworth.

42 MUMMY DEAREST

The correct sequence is G, D, J, A, K, B, E, L, I, H, C, F. The pyramid schematic gives a three-dimensional view of the path.

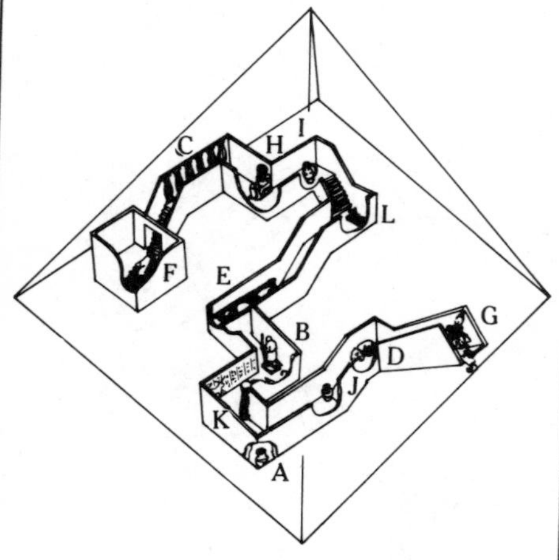

34 A BETTER MOUSETRAP

It's really quite simple:
Mouse (1) pulls cheese (7), turning switch "on" (3). Fan (8), starting up, blows ship with pin (2) forward to pop balloon (4), bringing weight down and feather up. Feather tickles bird (10), who squawks and lets go of rope, upsetting milk bottle (15). Milk pours down funnel into beaker (6), upsetting seesaw and pulling rope attached to stack of blocks (5). Stack collapses, dropping pole (12) through hole in shelf, and magnet on end of pole (19) falls to shelf-level. Magnet on cart pulls candle under rope (12), burning the rope and freeing it (19) to let mallet (20) land on bell-board (21). Rope on board's end pulls stopper from bird-feeder (18), letting pellets drop into cart (14). Cart teeters off when full, pulling wedge out from under bowling ball (11). Bowling ball falls, letting crowbar trip mousetrap (22), pulling cork out of water jug (17). Water spills into bucket (16) till its weight pulls pole (9) out from under sack (23). Sack drops, pulling knife (24) across frayed rope, dropping trap (13) onto completely unsuspecting mouse (1).

37 A SWITCH IN TIME

We identified 22 anachronisms:

1. *American Gothic* painting (painted by Grant Wood in 1930)
2. President Washington poster (Washington took office in 1789)
3. Flag with 15 stars (adopted in 1795, after the admission of Vermont and Kentucky to the Union)
4. Light bulb (invented around 1878)
5. Clock with a second hand (introduced in the 19th century)
6. Bananas (first shipped to the United States in 1804)
7. Zipper (invented in 1893)
8. Bic pen (introduced in 1958)
9. Ice cream cone (introduced in 1904 at the St. Louis World's Fair)
10. *Alice in Wonderland* (published in 1865)
11. Loose-leaf, hole-punched notebook paper (invented in the 20th century)
12. Tin can (invented in 1810; popularized during the Civil War)
13. Tophat (introduced in 1797)
14. Cigarette (invented in 1797)
15. Friction match (invented in 1826)
16. Bow tie (first popularized in the 1920s)
17. *New York Times* (founded in 1851)
18. Doberman pinscher (developed as a breed in the 20th century)
19. Postage stamp (first sold in the United States in 1847)
20. Chicago (founded in 1804 as Ft. Dearborn)
21. ZIP code (adopted in 1964)
22. Sneakers (introduced in 1917)

In case you wondered, the following were *not* anachronisms: *Robinson Crusoe* (published in 1719); *Gulliver's Travels* (published in 1726); the rifle (a model known as the "Brown Bess," popular during the 18th century); eyeglasses (which date back to 13th-century Italy); and the wristwatch (popularized in the 17th century).

40 RADIO ACTIVITY

The following call letters are suggested by the picture:
WALL
WAND (on the poster)
WARP (on the record)
WASH (the wet socks)
WASP
WAVE (on the Beach Boys album)
WEEK (circled on the calendar)
WELL (pencil holder)
WEST (on the weather vane)
WHIP
WICK (on the candle)
WINE (bottle)
WING
WINK
WIRE
WOLF
WOOD (the chair)
WOOL
WORM
WREN

In addition, you may have found WAKE (behind the surfer) and WORD.

44 MAKING TRACKS

The circus passed through the cement in this order:

1. Mouse
2. Elephant (large round prints)
3. Clown (big shoe prints)
4. Bear
5. Acrobat (person walking on his hands)
6. Ostrich (three-toed bird tracks)
7. Kangaroo (larger three-toed tracks with tail prints)
8. Stilt walker (rectangular tracks)
9. Pony (hoofprints)
10. Unicyclist (single wavy line)

38 EVERYBODY'S A CRITIC

47 TWELVE BRATS OF CHRISTMAS

The name of each gift rhymes with something worn by the child receiving it:
Roz (glasses)—passes (5)
Beth (mittens)—kittens (10)
Morton (hat)—bat (8)
Shelby (tie)—pie (3)
Louise (robe)—globe (1)
Lance (collar)—dollar (11)
Dave (sandals)—candles (6)
Wallace (zippers)—flippers (7)
Sue (pocket)—locket (4)
Nancy (sling)—ring (9)
Buddy (jacket)—racket (2)
Harold (sneakers)—speakers (12)

48 INFERIOR DECORATOR

Foreground, left to right:
The Grand Canyon pillow should say "Arizona."
"Dictionary" is misspelled "Dictionary."
The flower stems disappear in the glass bowl.
The rear leg on the round table is in front of the crossbar.
The tiger's stripes disappear between two legs of the table.
Chess pieces have replaced the salt and pepper shakers on the plate.
The digital clock on the robot has no room to show the hours 10 or 12.
The sun is too low in the sky for the correct time to be 2:13, A.M. or P.M.
One of the robot's antennae extends behind a pillow on the couch.
Salt and pepper shakers have replaced chess pieces on the chessboard.
The telephone should have 12 buttons, not nine.
The plant on the right is behind, not in, the planter.

Left wall:
Smoke is coming from the Magritte painting.
The skyscraper in the glass orb is upside down.
The television in the fireplace is on fire.
One andiron is resting on the book in the foreground.
A six-pack is in the log holder.

The Greek bust is wearing a necktie.
The pedestal holding the bust changes from circular marble to a block of wood.
The bust is reflected in the mirror on the same wall.

Rear wall:
The painting on the left is a continuation of the scene outside the window.
Part of the road passes in front of the windowpane.
The still-life painting on the right includes a real bowl of fruit resting on the lampshade.
The light over the still-life painting is shining upward.

Right wall:
The stairway leads up while the bannister is going down.
The globe shows a mirror image of the Western hemisphere.
The "octopus" on the vase has only seven legs.

Center of the room:
The rug is resting on the tabletop in the foreground.
The lamp on the end-table has no harp, or shade support.
The end-table is missing a rear leg.

46 METERS & GAUGES

1. Battery tester
2. Cooking thermometer
3. Parking meter
4. Thermostat
5. Medical thermometer
6. Barometer
7. Exercise bike
8. Blood pressure gauge
9. Electric meter

50 CLASS REUNION

Back row: 3) Phil Harmonick, 6) Clara Nette, 4) Moe Hawk, 1) Matt Adohr
Middle row: 10) Claire Voyent, Ex.) Nick O'Teen, 8) Dick Tator
Front row: 9) Sue Veneer, 5) Jim Nast, 2) Otto Graff, 7) Meg O'Fone

51 STORIES FROM THE SAFARI

The hunter made 11 identifiable errors in his story:

1. "Wrestling with a tiger" (it was a leopard)
2. "Armed with only a knife" (the hunter had a pistol)
3. "The attack occurred around noon" (the sun was low in the sky)
4. "Two miles from ... Bukwimba" (it was two kilometers)
5. "I was all alone" (the hunter had an aide)
6. "I left my canteen back at camp" (the hunter had it with him)
7. "A pride of lions could be seen" (no lions were nearby)
8. "The gun wasn't loaded" (the shot could be seen)
9. "Wrestled the tiger to the pavement" (the road was unpaved)
10. "You can still see the scar where he gashed me" (the hunter already had the scar at the time of the attack)
11. "His head mounted on the wall behind me" (the head is not of the animal that attacked)

3

53 ALTERNATING CURRENCY

The 17-pengo coin is a turquoise square; the 36-pengo coin is a maroon circle; the 55-pengo coin is an olive green triangle.

54 UNTRUE CONFESSIONS

The true confession was made by Leopold Looney. Each of the other "confessions" was flawed as follows:
Bonkers—The telephone was cordless.
McNutt—The glass of brandy was undisturbed on the table.
Noodleton—cobwebs across the window were intact.
Cracklin—The fireplace was fake.
Mayhem—The door to the room opened outward.
Fogpate—Dr. Shrynker wore slippers with no laces.
Bananaman—With a sound effects record playing, Shrynker would not have been alarmed by a creaking floorboard.

56 CAN YOU THINK UNDER PRESSURE?

1. The capital H should be underlined in the first sentence.
2. 1, 2, 3, 4, 5.
3. The words "strike," "out," "baseball," and "bat" should be crossed out.
4. "Africa" should be circled (it's a continent; the others are countries).
5. The four center matches should be crossed out, leaving a single square.
6. The next space should be empty.
7. A wavy line should appear under "8/18."
8. Four of the following states should appear in the blanks: Alaska, Washington, Idaho, Montana, North Dakota, Minnesota, Michigan, New York, Vermont, New Hampshire, Maine.
9. A circle should be drawn in the square.
10. 11.
11. "Forehand" should be circled.
12. 8.
13. The two jacks and two eights should be crossed out.
14. The next space should contain the word ACE.
15. The queen of clubs should be circled.
16. MISSPELL should be spelled correctly in the space (or spelled incorrectly somewhere other than in the space).
17. 16.
18. 6.
19. 6.
20. Italy, Turkey, Hungary, Paraguay. (Other answers are also possible.)
21. The next space should be empty.
22. CORE WRECKED should be written in the right margin.

Scoring Count 1 point for each correct answer. Maximum score: 22.

Ratings
22 points—Whiz. You stay cool and think logically under stress. Your co-workers probably hate you.
19–21 points—Excellent. You are well-suited for, say, directing rush hour traffic in Hong Kong.
16–18 points—Very good. Assembling a bicycle on Christmas Eve is a snap for you.
13–15 points—Good. You can usually complete your jigsaw puzzles.
10–12 points—Fair. When the going gets tough, you go home.
Under 10 points—You consistently make wrong decisions in tense situations. A successful career in government awaits you.

57 POLISH YOUR WITS

1. Number Ring

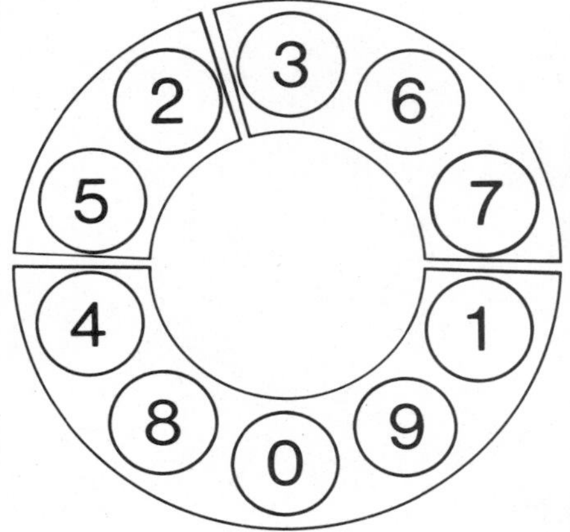

2. Cornering the King

	Queen	King
1.	a2	c1
2.	b3	d2
3.	b1	c3
4.	a2	d3

3. Loop the Loop

52 × 367 = 19,084

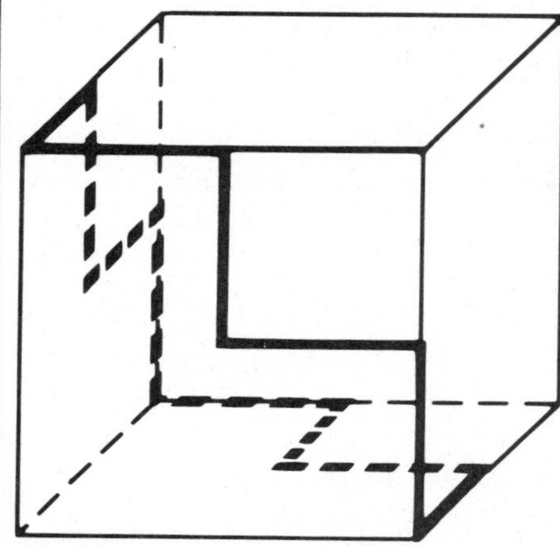

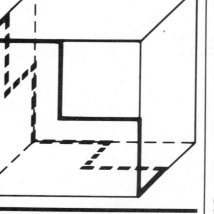

58 WORD DIVISION

	0	1	2	3	4	5	6	7	8	9
1.	P	A	L	I	N	D	R	O	M	E
2.	S	U	B	Z	E	R	O	D	A	Y
3.	T	E	N	O	F	C	L	U	B	S

60 TRAINING EXERCISE

By taking the following trains, Sally will make it to Hope Springs and back by 11:50:
7:20 from Alphaville, eastbound, to Discovery;
8:00 from Discovery, westbound, to Clarksville;
8:20 from Clarksville, eastbound, to Hope Springs;
9:20 from Hope Springs, westbound, to Ephemeral;
10:00 from Ephemeral, eastbound, to Fortuna;
10:40 from Fortuna, westbound, to Alphaville.

58 CUTTING A RUG

The rug can be cut and resewn as shown:

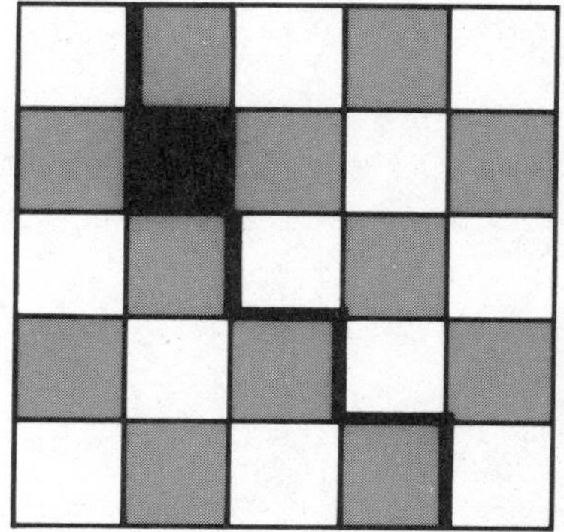

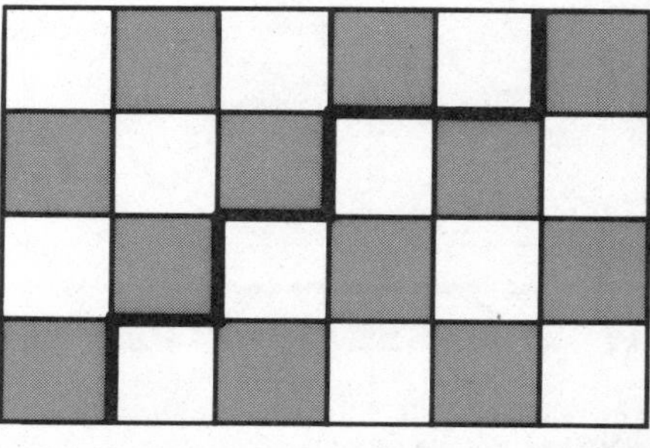

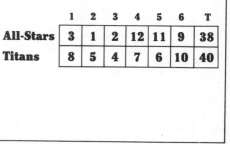

59 SLUGFEST ON PROTEUS

The All-Stars scored twice as many runs in their fourth inning as in their first three combined. Their first three innings must contain at least six (1 + 2 + 3) runs, so their fourth inning must be 12 runs. Their first three innings are therefore 1, 2, and 3 in some order.

Since there are two innings after the fourth, but only one number after TWELVE alphabetically (namely, TWO), it must be the Titans, not the All-Stars, who scored their numbers of runs in alphabetical order.

The two teams were only a run apart after five innings. The most the All-Stars could have after the fifth inning is 29 runs (1 + 2 + 3 + 11 + 12). The fewest the Titans could have is 30 runs (4 + 5 + 6 + 7 + 8). So those must have been the scores. Of the remaining two numbers, NINE and TEN, only TEN comes alphabetically after all of the Titans' other scores. So the Titans' scores, in order, were: 8, 5, 4, 7, 6, and 10. The All-Stars' scores were: (1, 2, 3 in some order), 12, 11, and 9. Since the Titans won 40–38, they are the home team.

The All-Stars, who are the visiting team, scored at least three runs in the first inning and two in the third, so their first three innings scored 3, 1, and 2 runs.

The final scoreboard read:

	1	2	3	4	5	6	T
All-Stars	3	1	2	12	11	9	38
Titans	8	5	4	7	6	10	40

61 LETTER LOGIC

Our answers appear below. Yours may differ.

1

I	M	A	G	E
M	O	R	A	L
G	R	O	S	S
L	I	N	E	N

2

R	O	U	N	D
A	B	U	S	E
R	A	B	I	D
N	O	I	S	E

3

H	O	T	E	L
S	H	O	R	T
R	A	N	G	E
S	L	A	N	G

4

T	O	W	E	R
O	C	C	U	R
A	W	A	I	T
I	S	S	U	E

61 CROSS MATH

1

3	+	1	+	2	=6
x		+		x	
5	+	7	÷	6	=2
–		–		÷	
9	+	8	–	4	=13
=6		=0		=3	

2

3	x	6	÷	9	=2
+		–		–	
2	–	1	+	7	=8
÷		+		x	
5	x	8	÷	4	=10
=1		=13		=8	

62 COIN-OP PUZZLERS

1. Either solution (or its reflection) is correct:

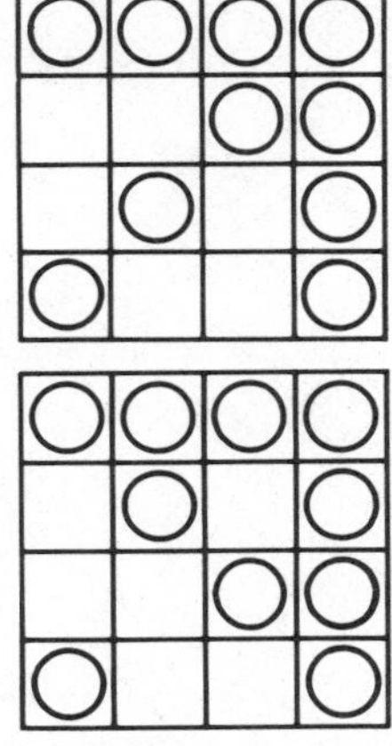

2. Remove four pennies as shown. Except for rotations, the solution is unique.

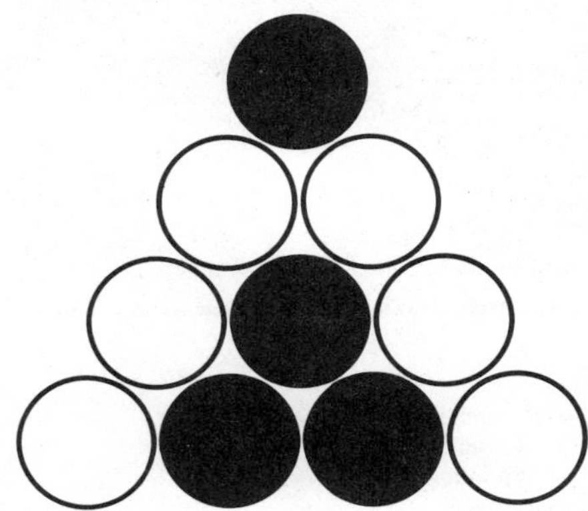

3. Dudeney's solution, in 18 moves, was as follows: 2-3, 9-4, 10-7, 3-8, 4-2, 7-5, 8-6, 5-10, 6-9, 2-5, 1-6, 6-4, 5-3, 10-8, 4-7, 3-2, 8-1, 7-10.

4. If the coins are numbered in order from 1 to 10, they may be jumped as follows: 6-9, 4-1, 8-3, 2-5, 7-10. Other solutions are also possible.

5. Number the top penny 1, the next row of pennies 2 and 3, and the bottom row 4, 5, and 6. The following is one of many solutions in four moves: Slide penny 3 to abut pennies 4 and 5. Slide 6 to abut 3 and 5. Slide 5 to abut 1 and 2 (on the right). Slide 1 to abut 5 and 6.

6. Divide the grid as shown. Each half totals 81¢.

(Game #6 is by Scott Marley.)

64 NINE PSYCHIC GUESSES

First Psychic Guess The cards, in order, are Heart, Diamond, Club.
Second Club, Spade, Heart
Third Heart, Diamond, Spade, Club
Fourth Club, Heart, Diamond, Spade
Fifth Spade, Joker, Club, Heart, Diamond
Sixth Club, Joker, Heart, Diamond, Spade
Seventh Club, Heart, Diamond, Spade, Joker
Eighth Heart, Spade, Diamond, Club
Ninth Club, Heart, Diamond, Joker, Spade

These puzzles are from Roger Hufford's book *Challenging Puzzles in Logic* (Dover Books).

4

65 RIDDLE MAZE

The riddle reads: What common thing is seen every day, but rarely alone, can be found on a tree, travels extensively, may squeak, is associated with horns and horses, may have a prominent tongue, moves often but never changes jobs, and is known to pinch people? The answer: *A shoe.*

66 MAKING CONNECTIONS

In addition to the beaver and man-made dams, we found the following parallel functions:
Hawk's wings; hang glider
Cacti; water tank
Elephant's trunk; garden hose
Shark fin; airplane's tail fin
Kangaroo pouch; baby carrier
Rose thorns; barbed wire
Horse's tail; fly swatter
Deer's coloration; camouflaged tent (or tank)
Maple-seed wings; helicopter
Bee's nest; house
Woodpecker's beak; jackhammer
Armadillo; tank
Squirrel's cheeks; lunch box
Dog's paws; steam shovel
Mole's tunnel; subway tunnel

Puzzle idea: Mark Mazut

68 BUTTERFLIES

The orange Monarch butterflies are identical. Of the other pairs, the butterflies shown uppermost in the illustration are correct: The lower green Malachite is missing a green section from its upper left wing; parts of the wings of the lower yellow Eastern Tiger Swallowtail are straight instead of scalloped; and the lower Bluewing has white spots on its body. (In nature, no two butterflies are ever exactly alike.)

69 BRINGING UP BABY

The photos of Alison were shot in the following chronological order: 9, 10, 4, 2, 8, 12, 7, 1, 3, 6, 11, 5.

70 THE EGG HUNT

The two identical eggs are outlined in white.

72 MURDER FOR BREAKFAST

Kojumbo arrests Peppard. Peppard lied in his captions to photos #2 and #3; the positions of the shadows prove that the pictures had been taken many hours, not just a few minutes, apart. Another clue was provided by the victim, who lived long enough to grab the pepper shaker from his tray in an attempt to name his killer (see photo #6; note he is not holding the salt shaker, which appears in photo #5). Less direct evidence was the typed note that seemed to implicate one of the deceased's partners: A killer with time to ransack the bookshelves would have had time to read the note and remove it if it implicated him. So Kojumbo suspected it was a plant. Vera Dayton, meanwhile, seemed to have no motive, but if she had, surely she would have removed her photo from Lawless's desk.

Peppard was trying to implicate Schirmer in the murder, and he finally admitted he had taken photo #3 not on Sunday morning but on Friday afternoon, when Schirmer came to visit Lawless. Peppard took care to give Kojumbo a picture in which Schirmer, though visible, was not clearly recognizable, just in case Schirmer had an alibi as to his Sunday morning whereabouts. Peppard also stole the jade ring from Lawless's finger and typed the note found in his typewriter, all in an attempt to steer suspicion away from himself.

In fact, it was Peppard who had engineered the jade robbery three months earlier. Lawless had guessed the truth, and—not content with the insurance money the company would receive—had demanded that Peppard give him half the jade in return for his silence. The payoff was to have been made that Sunday morning; but Peppard, not a generous sort, decided to eliminate Lawless instead. After killing him, Peppard typed the note and ransacked the room a bit to suggest robbery might have been the motive, then exited through the window. He threw his weapon in a garbage can, planning to retrieve it later, then raced around the block to get into his car. But when he saw Miss Dayton on the steps, and it seemed that she had noticed him, he boldly stepped forward and introduced himself, carrying out the plan he had prepared for just such an eventuality. He had even jammed the phone at the corner so that his story about being unable to call the police would check out. But despite all his planning, he had fallen far short of committing the perfect crime.

74 GOOD HEAVENS!

Left third, roughly left to right and top to bottom

Star Trek (Captain Kirk and Mr. Spock)
Milky Way candy bar
Mercury (in thermometer)
Willie Stargell
Venus flytrap
Star Wars (C-3PO)
Pluto
Sunny-side-up egg
Bronze star
Moon Unit Zappa
Cosmos (flower)
Sunset Boulevard (Gloria Swanson)
Starkist Tuna
Star of David
Five-star general (Dwight D. Eisenhower)
Sunmaid raisins
Mars bar (in Moon Unit's pocket)
Ringo Starr (on pink purse)

Center

Moonraker (Roger Moore)
Texaco star
Star 80 (Mariel Hemingway)
Sunfish
Moon Mullins
Chicken and Stars soup
Bill Haley and the Comets (album cover)
Sunbather
Suntan lotion
A Star Is Born (newspaper headline)
Venus de Milo
Nova (green car)
The Moonglows
The Sunshine state (Florida)
Sunflower
Bart Starr
The Lone Star State (Texas flag)
Mercury (winged FTD messenger)
Van Gogh's *Starry Night*
Ziggy Stardust (David Bowie)
Sunglasses
Sundae

Right

Sunkist orange
The Stars and Stripes
The Sundance Kid (Robert Redford)
Comet cleanser
Starfish
Telstar
Sundial
Starling
Vega (red car)
Carl Sagan's *Cosmos*
The Powers of Matthew Starr
Brenda Starr
Hollywood stars
The Honeymooners
The Star newspaper
Reverend Sun-Myung Moon

Based on an idea suggested by the 1984 "Stars" exhibit at The National Air and Space Museum, Washington, DC.

76 SCENIC ROUTE

The joke was on the driver: His passenger turned out to be president of the taxi company. The route is shown below, leading from the train station to the house she was visiting (indicated by the X). The sights she saw are outlined in black, and the dots mark the points from which she saw them. The driver was fired and now makes deliveries for the doughnut shop. On a bike.

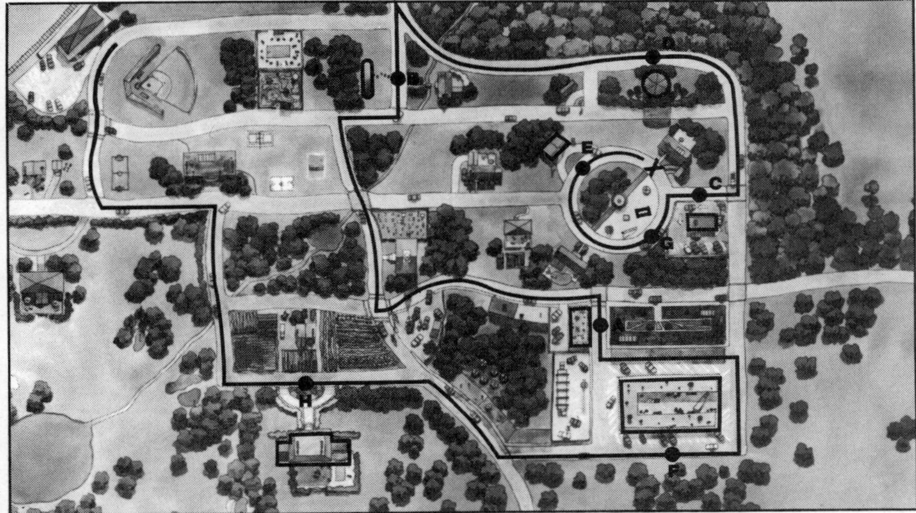

78 FINAL CURTAIN

Eleanor is the murderer. Jealous of Forrest's backstage visits with Arlene, she replaced the blanks with bullets.

Stella Brandt caught on quickly. Looking in Delia's dressing room mirror during their interview, she noticed Forrest heading up the hall toward Arlene's office, and later, on stage, she spotted boa feathers from Arlene's wrap on his clothing.

When Eleanor first left her dressing room to change the blanks, she was startled to see Chris's door open. Clearly she didn't want to be seen heading toward the stage, so she camouflaged her intent by asking Chris for matches that she didn't need. Chris gave her a blue matchbook, but later Stella noticed she had a nearly full red matchbook in her dressing room.

Returning to her dressing room, Eleanor tapped on the connecting door to Forrest's room (marked on the Fire Exit floorplan and similar to the door between Chris and Delia's rooms). When she got no reply, she went through his dressing room to the hall and from there to the stage (this exit was not in the line of vision of Chris's dressing room). In doing so, she left Forrest's door slightly ajar. Quickly replacing the blanks, she hurried back into Forrest's room, shutting the door behind her, while Stella was consulting with Basil. By the time Stella knocked on her dressing room door, Eleanor was back, out of breath from her endeavors, a state she attributed to "aerobics." In her haste to get back from the stage, she closed the connecting door on her jacket sleeve.

Thanks to Stella's keen observations, the police got the murderer, Eleanor got 20 years, Chris and Delia got the lead roles, Arlene and Basil got a divorce, and Stella? She got the biggest story of her career.

81 WUMBLE'S CANDY

Divide the bar as shown.

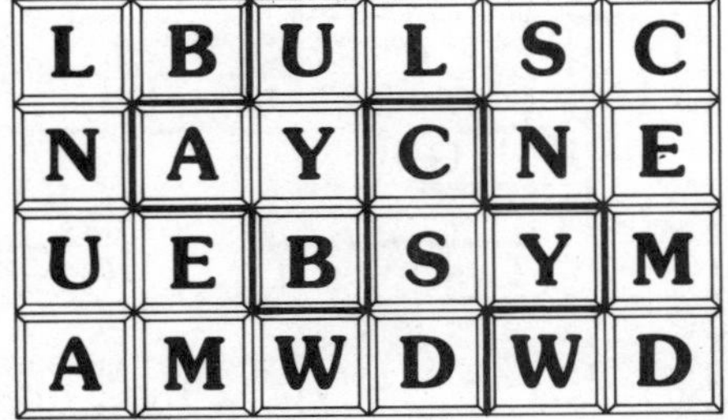

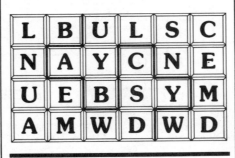

82 WIT TWISTERS

1. Items, mites, smite, times, emits
2. Bleary, barely, barley
3. Señor, Norse, snore
4. Huts, shut, tush, thus
5. Limes, miles, slime, smile
6. Safer, fears, fares
7. Paired, diaper, repaid
8. Mothers, thermos, smother

82 ALPHASWITCH

The winning words, for a score of 52, are:

1. CRYSTAL (7)
2. SUBPOENA (8)
3. BANKRUPTCY (10)
4. UPHOLSTERY (10)
5. SCHMALTZY (9)
6. PTOMAINE (8)

83 CAVEAT EMPTOR

THE BIG BANG! A matchbook
ART LOVERS, REJOICE! A paper clip
THE WONDERS OF ENGRAVING! Four coins (penny, nickel, dime and quarter)
MOVIE SETTING SOUVENIRS! A vial of sand
YEARS OF BACKYARD FUN! An acorn
DEFY GRAVITY! A straw
RANDOM DIGIT GENERATOR! A die
CRYSTALS! CRYSTALS! CRYSTALS! A sugar packet

84 KNIGHT MOVES

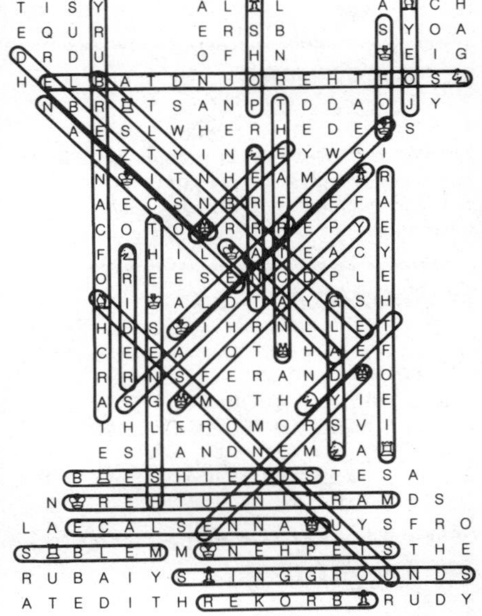

85 REBUSINESS

The seven names are:

1. Ringo Starr (ring-ghost-R)
2. Flip Wilson (flip-will-sun)
3. Captain Hook (cap-ten-hook)
4. Frankenstein (frank-N-stein)
5. June Lockhart (June-lock-heart)
6. Pat Sajak (pats-A-jack)
7. Chico Marx (cheek-O-marks)

86 PRO TEST

1. Proceeding (seeding)
2. Proclaiming
3. Profound
4. Proposing
5. Profiling
6. Propounding
7. Propane (pain)
8. Provision *or* protest
9. Proportion
10. Protractor
11. Promoter (motor)

90 EVOLUTION

Our answers are, in alphabetical order:

APE (ace)
BADGER (badges)
BEAR (pear)
BEAVER (beaker)
CAMEL (cameo)
CAT (cap)
COW (bow)
FOX (box)
GIBBON (ribbon)
GOAT (coat)
HORSE (house)
LEOPARD (leotard)
MINK (milk)
MOUSE (house)
PUMA (pump)
SABLE (table)
SHEEP (sheet)
SHREW (screw)
SLOTH (cloth)
TIGER (timer)
YAK (oak)

92 LIMBERICKS

1. Quite, flight, burned, learned, Wright
2. Relic, angelic, extremes, dreams, Selleck
3. Gavotte, yacht, drowned, ground, plot
4. Gofer, chauffeur, brood, shrewd, loafer
5. Gourmet, disobey, cheese, please, weigh

94 WORD LADDERS

Our answers (other steps may be possible):

1. FOOT, BOOT, BOLT, BOLL, BALL
2. FALL, FAIL, FOIL, COIL, COAL, COAT
3. RAKE, LAKE, LANE, LAND, LEND, LEAD, LEAF
4. COLD, TOLD, TOAD, ROAD, ROAR, SOAR, SOAP, SNAP

94 TWO BY TWO

1. Mishap
2. Napkin
3. Deejay
4. Boxcar
5. Morgue
6. Stodgy
7. Dynamo
8. Enzyme
9. Velvet
10. Dimwit
11. Nebula
12. Unique
13. Outfox

88 HALF AND HALF

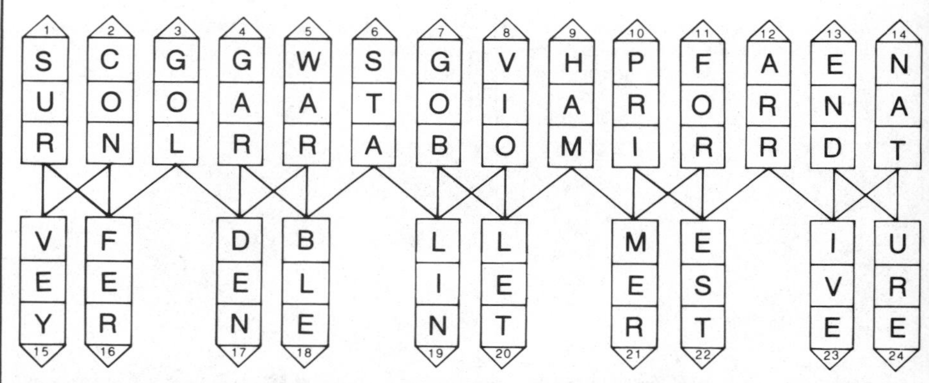

89 OPPOSITES ATTRACT

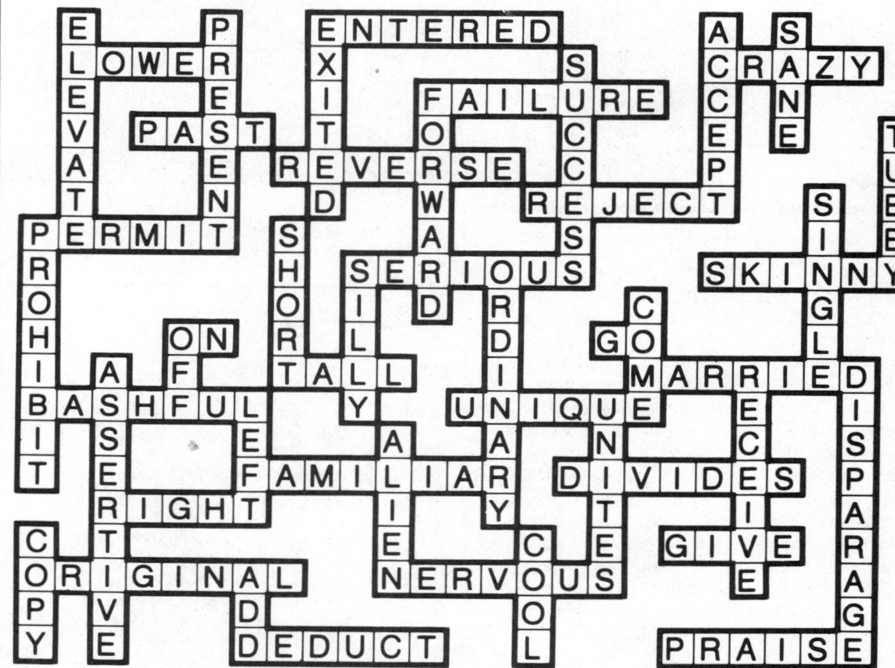

95 ALPHABET SOUP

1. Cherry (CHAIR + E)
2. Pecan (P + CAN)
3. Seesaw (C + SAW)
4. Acorn (A + CORN)
5. Belief (B + LEAF)
6. Treaty (TREE + T)
7. Entire (N + TIRE)
8. Pansy (PAN + Z)
9. Elfin (L + FIN)
10. Extent (X + TENT)
11. Organdy (ORGAN + D)
12. Croquet (CROW + K)
13. Esquire (S + CHOIR)
14. Unite (U + KNIGHT)
15. Piccolo (PICKLE + O)

96 LITERARY CONNECTIONS

The answers, reading from left to right and top to bottom, are: *Tom Jones, Dracula, Lord Jim, Candide, Beowulf, Oliver Twist, Of Mice and Men, The Jungle Book, Vanity Fair, Animal Farm, Jane Eyre,* and *King Lear.*

97 SOLITAIRE HANGMAN

I. MOONBEAM
II. FRICTION
III. WHOEVER
IV. SPORADIC
V. YACHTING
VI. EMBEZZLE
VII. TENACITY
VIII. SYCAMORE
IX. WRECKAGE
X. BABYISH

93 WACKY WORDIES

Contributors' names appear in parentheses following their answers. When the same puzzle was submitted by more than one person, one name was chosen at random.

1a Buckle up (Elizabeth Swain, Vincennes, IN)
1b In between jobs (Ryan Spain, Seattle, WA)
1c "Three Little Pigs" (Linda Duncan, Hartsdale, NY)
1d Division of labor (Betsy Sirk, Silver Spring, MD)
1e Bathtub ring (Keith Moyer, Big Piney, WY)
2a "Smoke Gets in Your Eyes" (Ed Gardner, Winter Park, FL)
2b Growing older (Bub Bufford, Tempe, AZ)
2c Baseball double-header (Noble Reasoner, Bloomington, IN)
2d Postscript (Jerry N. Carolson, Old Bethpage, NY)
2e My cup runneth over (Ken H. MacLeish, Manheim, PA)
3a Coffee break (Betsy Sirk, Silver Spring, MD)
3b Mixed company (Noble Reasoner, Bloomington, IN)
3c A fistful of dollars (Tim Cooper, Tuscaloosa, AL)
3d Microwave ovens (Brian Misialek, Chicago, IL)
3e "Accentuate the Positive" (Barbara Nestingen, Milwaukee, WI)
4a Come out with your hands up! (Ryan Spain, Seattle, WA)
4b Freudian slip (Evanne Kofman, Phoenix, AZ)
4c *The Good, the Bad, and the Ugly* (Jerry N. Carolson, Old Bethpage, NY)
4d By and large (Monica Tenniel, Cudbury, CT)
4e High five (John McCann, Chicago, IL)
5a Sidestepping the issue (Evanne Kofman, Phoenix, AZ)
5b Flat broke (Barbara Nestingen, Milwaukee, WI)
5c Balance of power (Donna Roberts, North Miami Beach, FL)
5d Good up to a point (Edward Ridler, Depew, NY)
5e Three strikes, you're out! (Betsy Sirk, Silver Spring, MD)
6a Close shave (Barbara Nestingen, Milwaukee, WI)
6b Five o'clock shadow (Caroline Ellis, Arlington Heights, IL)
6c *Last of the Red Hot Lovers* (Jerry N. Carolson, Old Bethpage, NY)
6d Vegetable shortening (Humphrey Dudley, Denver, CO)
6e Repeating decimal (Alex Knight, Los Angeles, CA)
7a Outer limits (Betsy Sirk, Silver Spring, MD)
7b Upward mobility (Jerry N. Carolson, Old Bethpage, NY)
7c Second cousin once removed (Norma Holzhauer, Gillett, AR)
7d In a holding pattern (Ken H. MacLeish, Manheim, PA)
7e Tax on capital gains (Noble Reasoner, Bloomington, IN)

98 WORD GOLF

Our pro's answers are below; yours, of course, may be different.

Words	Strokes
1. Tunes, daily	2
2. Coin, detainers	2
3. Chores, rat, into	3
4. Moans, bum, clean	3
5. Fun, tour, neatly	3
6. Maids, antipasto	2
7. Pennate, mutilate	2
8. Misperceived (adding M), since	4
9. Friends, machines, net	3
Total	24

Ratings
Over 40: Duffer
36–40: Weekend player
32–35: Talented amateur
25–31: Pro material
Under 25: Masters winner

99 ANALOGRAMS

1. SCHOOL is to FISH
2. EYE is to HURRICANE
3. INCH is to FOOT
4. DOES is to FAWNS
5. WATCH is to HAND
6. INVENTOR is to PATENT
7. FAN is to BREEZE
8. DAGGER is to SWORD
9. ISLAND is to OCEAN
10. HEAD is to BEER
11. NOTE is to SCALE
12. ENGLISH is to SHINGLE (anagrams)
13. SAW is to TOOTH
14. MOUTH is to ROOF
15. RAMPART is to HORN (charades)
16. ICE is to CAKE
17. SKATE is to BLADE
18. BEE is to SEE (homophones of successive letters of the alphabet)
19. FIN is to SAWBUCK
20. DISK is to DRIVE

100 MOONLIGHTING

The night jobs (with their daytime counterparts in parentheses) are:

1. REPORTER (REWRITER)
2. BEAUTICIAN (MORTICIAN)
3. CARPENTER (CARETAKER)
4. BUTCHER (BUTLER)
5. GUNSMITH (TINSMITH)
6. DOGCATCHER (DISPATCHER)
7. TRANSLATOR (LEGISLATOR)
8. PHYSICIST (PHYSICIAN)
9. FERRYMAN (DAIRYMAN)
10. CARTOONIST (BASSOONIST)
11. BOOKKEEPER (BOOKBINDER)
12. DRESSMAKER (GLASSMAKER)
13. ARCHITECT (ARCHIVIST)
14. WEATHERMAN (FISHERMAN)
15. ENGRAVER (ENGINEER)
16. ACTRESS (ACTUARY)
17. BRICKLAYER (BALLPLAYER)
18. BLACKSMITH (LOCKSMITH)

101 DSZQTIONARY

TUTOR. 1. Teacher employed to give private lessons. 2. Trumpet player not quite up to symphony level.
PRO AND CON. 1. Opposite sides of an argument. 2. Description of ball player jailed for narcotics possession.
DOWN-IN-THE-MOUTH. 1. Feeling of gloom or depression. 2. Problem encountered while eating raw duck.
FLY-BY-NIGHT. 1. Shady, irresponsible, and risky. 2. One way that travelers can save on airfare.
PALISADE. 1. Barricade of pointed stakes used for defense. 2. Low-interest loan for repairing king's residence.
FOUNTAIN OF YOUTH. 1. Mythical source of eternal life. 2. Favorite drugstore hangout during high school days.
LISTLESS. 1. Sluggish or weak from exhaustion. 2. How absent-minded shopper arrives at supermarket.
WITHDRAWALS. 1. Removals of funds from bank accounts. 2. How Southerners speak to each other.

102 ADDED ATTRACTIONS

The paired words are:
HAIR + C = CHAIR
CANE + O = CANOE
CROW + N = CROWN
BRIDE + G = BRIDGE
TOWEL + R = TROWEL
ROD + A = ROAD
WINE + T = TWINE
HOSE + U = HOUSE
BOW + L = BOWL
CORN + A = ACORN
PLANE + T = PLANET
PANTS + I = PAINTS
CAT + O = COAT
SAIL + N = SNAIL
NET + S = NEST
The 15 added letters, when put in proper order, spell CONGRATULATIONS.

103 BLANKETY-BLANK

Quote: "Words are the physicians of a mind diseased."

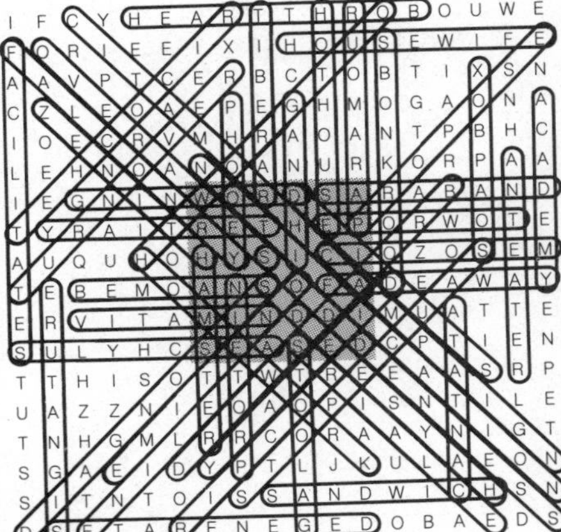

104 EGYPTOGRAMS

Traveler
1. E
2. F
3. B
4. C
5. A
6. D

Visitor
1. D
2. E
3. A
4. B
5. F
6. C

Native
1. D
2. C
3. F
4. A
5. E
6. B

Expert
1. **2.**
3. **4.**
5. **6.**
7. **8.**

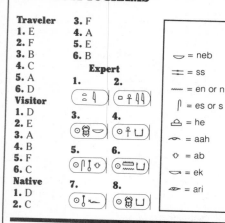

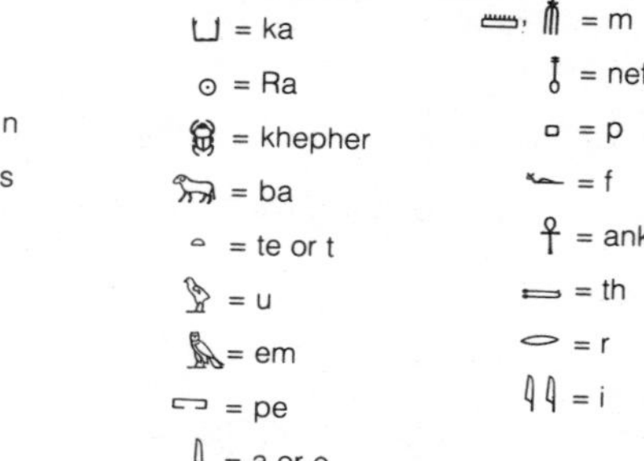

106 RHYME AND REASON

1. Swept (pest + W)
2. Baker (bark + E)
3. Plaids (sapid + L)
4. Cater (race + T)
5. Rhine (hire + N)
6. Stitch (chits + T)
7. Shriek (hiker + S)
8. Guessed (segued + S)
9. Shaking (asking + H)
10. Whitest (theist + W)
11. Smash (hams + S)
12. Fleas (safe + L)
13. Sleighs (gishes + L)
14. Wicket (twice + K)
15. Tepee (pete + E)
16. Groan (rang + O)
17. Anchor (ranch + O)
18. Pastor (ports + A)
19. Preach (parch + E)
20. Third (dirt + H)
21. Dancer (cadre + N)
22. Flavor (flora + V)
23. Prime (ripe + M)
24. Boast (stab + O)
25. Royalty (taylor + Y)
26. Score (rocs + E)
27. Wrinkle (rewink + L)
28. Sleuth (lutes + H)

The quotation by Oscar Wilde: "Only the shallow know themselves."

107 TOM SWIFTIES

1. presently
2. hotly
3. rashly
4. sternly
5. exactly
6. flippantly
7. impatiently
8. dolefully
9. mechanically
10. gracefully
11. cryptically
12. crestfallenly

108 THE LAST WORD

1. c. EGGSHELL (words with two pairs of doubled letters)
2. a. YOU (homophones of letters)
3. c. TABLET (words that begin and end with the same letter)
4. b. WEEVIL (words beginning with a pronoun)
5. b. INTERMITTENT (words with one letter appearing four times)
6. c. STINK (words that can be reversed to form other words)
7. a. TRACING (words that become new words when the first letter is removed)
8. a. MIMIC (words consisting of letters that are Roman numerals)
9. b. NUDISM (words whose last letters immediately precede their first letters in the alphabet)
10. b. COLLECTION (synonyms of "set")
11. c. OUGHT (words that become new words when the last letter is shifted to the front)
12. a. ALMOST (words whose letters are in alphabetical order)

6

109 HAIRDOS AND HAIRDON'TS

1. Richard Nixon (with hair from #8)
2. Cher (#9)
3. Phil Donahue (#4)
4. Tiny Tim (#7)
5. Woody Allen (#2)
6. Whoopi Goldberg (#3)
7. George Washington (#1)
8. Shirley Temple (#5)
9. Indira Gandhi (#6)

110 TWISTED TELEVISION

1. Cheeks *(Cheers)*
2. Moonsighting *(Moonlighting)*
3. The Frying Nun *(The Flying Nun)*
4. Slipper *(Flipper)*
5. The Old Couple *(The Odd Couple)*
6. Father Knots Best *(Father Knows Best)*
7. Growing Pawns *(Growing Pains)*
8. Beat the Flock *(Beat the Clock)*
9. Kodak *(Kojak)*
10. The A-Tram *(The A-Team)*
11. Perky Mason or Merry Mason *(Perry Mason)*
12. The Moo Squad *(The Mod Squad)*

112 PICTURE QUIZ

1. The harmonica
2. Alaska
3. January 24, 1935—in Richmond, Virginia
4. Continental
5. Andrews (and give yourself a bonus point if you remembered "Sugar, Sugar")
6. a) Queen Anne's Revenge
7. Franklin Pierce, who was arrested and charged with running over an elderly lady with his horse (the charges were eventually dropped)
8. True—in 1979, for example, 973 patients had been bitten by fellow human beings, whereas only 233 were hospitalized because of rodent bites
9. Green
10. Diego Rivera (the work shown is *Agrarian Leader Zapata*)
11. d) 40,177, to be exact
12. Atlanta

118 COMIC RELIEF

1. "Barney Google and Snuffy Smith"
2. "The Wizard of Id"
3. "Andy Capp"
4. "Hi and Lois"
5. "B.C."
6. "Peanuts"
7. "Pogo"
8. "Doonesbury"
9. "Little Lulu"
10. "Garfield"
11. "Cathy"
12. "Bloom County"
13. "Superman"
14. "Gasoline Alley"
15. "Frank and Ernest"

122 WHAT'S THE DIFFERENCE?

1. Nelson Rockefeller
2. Meryl Streep
3. Joe DiMaggio
4. Rhonda Fleming
5. Golda Meir
6. Julia Child
7. Michael Spinks
8. Lily Tomlin
9. John McEnroe
10. Liza Minnelli
11. Redd Foxx
12. Yoko Ono
13. Calvin Coolidge
14. Buddy Holly
15. Vladimir Nabokov
16. Patrick Swayze
17. Desmond Tutu
18. Rich Little

114 SECOND GUESSING

1. MONTHS
2. CENTURIES
3. MONTHS
4. HOURS
5. WEEKS
6. CENTURIES
7. MINUTES
8. HOURS
9. MONTHS
10. DAYS
11. SECONDS
12. HOURS
13. MONTHS
14. MINUTES
15. SECONDS
16. SECONDS
17. CENTURIES
18. MINUTES
19. CENTURIES
20. CENTURIES

The basis for each answer is given below. We've used estimates where precise figures were not available.

1. $25{,}000 \text{ miles} \times \frac{1 \text{ hour}}{4 \text{ miles}} \times \frac{1 \text{ day}}{24 \text{ hours}} \times \frac{1 \text{ month}}{30 \text{ days}} = 8.7$ MONTHS

2. $\$1{,}000{,}000{,}000 \times \frac{1 \text{ day}}{\$3{,}000} \times \frac{1 \text{ year}}{365 \text{ days}} \times \frac{1 \text{ century}}{100 \text{ years}} = 9.1$ CENTURIES

3. $1{,}000{,}000 \text{ names} \times \frac{1 \text{ minute}}{10 \text{ names}} \times \frac{1 \text{ hour}}{60 \text{ minutes}} \times \frac{1 \text{ day}}{24 \text{ hours}} \times \frac{1 \text{ month}}{30 \text{ days}} = 2.3$ MONTHS

4. $2{,}600 \text{ miles} \times \frac{1 \text{ hour}}{742 \text{ miles}} = 3.5$ HOURS

5. 4 WEEKS

6. $93{,}000{,}000 \text{ miles} \times \frac{1 \text{ hour}}{3 \text{ miles}} \times \frac{1 \text{ day}}{24 \text{ hours}} \times \frac{1 \text{ year}}{365 \text{ days}} \times \frac{1 \text{ century}}{100 \text{ years}} = 35.4$ CENTURIES

7. It took our play-tester 5 MINUTES.

8. $110{,}000 \text{ hairs} \times \frac{1 \text{ second}}{2 \text{ hairs}} \times \frac{1 \text{ minute}}{60 \text{ seconds}} \times \frac{1 \text{ hour}}{60 \text{ minutes}} = 15$ HOURS

9. $3{,}000{,}000 \text{ awards} \times \frac{1 \text{ minute}}{6 \text{ awards}} \times \frac{1 \text{ hour}}{60 \text{ minutes}} \times \frac{1 \text{ day}}{24 \text{ hours}} \times \frac{1 \text{ month}}{30 \text{ days}} = 11.6$ MONTHS

10. $984 \text{ feet} \times \frac{1 \text{ hour}}{16 \text{ feet}} \times \frac{1 \text{ day}}{24 \text{ hours}} = 2.6$ DAYS

11. $238{,}000 \text{ miles} \times \frac{1 \text{ second}}{186{,}000 \text{ miles}} = 1.3$ SECONDS

12. $18 \text{ years} \times \frac{365 \text{ days}}{1 \text{ year}} \times \frac{1 \text{ foot}}{1 \text{ day}} \times \frac{.053 \text{ minute}}{1 \text{ foot}} \times \frac{1 \text{ hour}}{60 \text{ minutes}} = 5.8$ HOURS

13. $5{,}800 \text{ miles} \times \frac{1 \text{ hour}}{3 \text{ miles}} \times \frac{1 \text{ day}}{24 \text{ hours}} \times \frac{1 \text{ month}}{30 \text{ days}} = 2.1$ MONTHS

14. $368{,}000{,}000 \text{ miles} \times \frac{1 \text{ second}}{186{,}00 \text{ miles}} \times \frac{1 \text{ minute}}{60 \text{ seconds}} = 33$ MINUTES

15. $t = \sqrt{2d/g}$, where t = time, d = distance, and g = gravitational acceleration (32 feet/second^2), so:

$$t = \sqrt{\frac{2 \times 29{,}028 \text{ feet}}{32 \text{ feet/second}^2}} = 42.6 \text{ SECONDS}$$

16. 3 SECONDS, according to our play-testing

17. $18{,}000{,}000 \text{ books} \times \frac{250 \text{ pages}}{1 \text{ book}} \times \frac{400 \text{ words}}{1 \text{ page}} \times \frac{1 \text{ minute}}{300 \text{ words}} \times \frac{1 \text{ hour}}{60 \text{ minutes}} \times \frac{1 \text{ day}}{24 \text{ hours}} \times \frac{1 \text{ year}}{365 \text{ days}} \times \frac{1 \text{ century}}{100 \text{ years}} = 114$ CENTURIES

18. Ours burned 11 MINUTES.

19. $1 \text{ square mile} \times \frac{4{,}014{,}489{,}600 \text{ square inches}}{1 \text{ square mile}} \times 0.1 \text{ inches} \times \frac{1 \text{ gallon}}{231 \text{ cubic inches}} \times \frac{1 \text{ day}}{3 \text{ gallons}} \times \frac{1 \text{ year}}{365 \text{ days}} \times \frac{1 \text{ century}}{100 \text{ years}} = 15.9$ CENTURIES

20. $(2^{17} - 1) \text{ days} = 131{,}071 \text{ days} \times \frac{1 \text{ year}}{365 \text{ days}} \times \frac{1 \text{ century}}{100 \text{ years}} = 3.6$ CENTURIES.

116 A HERCULEAN ATLAS QUIZ

Following Directions

1. East **2.** Africa **3.** Yes
4. Darwin, north; Brisbane, east; Melbourne, south; Perth, west

Uphill Climbing

1. Nepal and China (Tibet)
2. Chile and Argentina (all in the Andes mountains). The other peak is in Peru (also in the Andes). The tallest peak is Aconcagua, in Argentina.
3. Mont Blanc; France, Italy, and Switzerland
4. Turkey, the Soviet Union, and Iran
5. The peak is in Turkey

Between the Lines

1. The touching pairs are: Colorado and Nebraska; British Columbia and Montana; Austria and Switzerland; Finland and Norway; Indonesia and Malaysia
2. Colombia, both; El Salvador, Pacific only; Nicaragua, both
3. The order is: Guatemala, Honduras, Nicaragua, Costa Rica, Panama.
4. Antarctica

Going the Distance

1. Ecuador (on the Equator; its name means "Equator"), the Philippines, Australia, Mexico, Tahiti
2. Antarctica, Alaska, the Soviet Union
3. Beijing and Buenos Aires, which are almost exactly at opposite ends of the globe

Tropics Topics

1. The Tropic of Cancer **3.** The Philippines
2. Australia **4.** Pakistan

As Big As All Outdoors

1. California (third), Montana (fourth), New Mexico (fifth)
2. Canada (second); China (third)
3. Lake Superior (second), bordering the United States and Canada; Lake Victoria (third), bordering Kenya, Uganda, and Tanzania

Island-Hopping

1. Indonesia; New Guinea (second) and Borneo (third)
2. Chicago
3. Easter Island, Pacific; Christmas Island, take credit for either Pacific or Indian (two different islands have that name); Seychelles, Indian; Galapagos Islands, Pacific; Canary Islands, Atlantic
4. Greenland; Gothab

120 OFF AND RUNNING

1. b. The 202 votes made Johnson the Democratic primary winner, which in Texas at that time meant certain election to the Senate. The derisive nickname "Landslide Lyndon" came from his opponents.
2. a. Citizens of the District of Columbia couldn't vote for president, having no electoral votes (despite the fact it had a bigger population than several states). This was corrected beginning in 1964.
3. a. In Taylor's day it wasn't unusual to send letters postage due, but the war hero received so many that he left orders that all be sent straight to the dead letter office. A second letter with proper postage was sent later.
4. b. Victoria Woodhull was languishing in cell 11 of New York's Ludlow Street jail on these flimsy charges when she heard that she not only lost the election but didn't get any votes.
5. a. Washington, as was the custom, provided refreshments for the voters. These included 28 gallons of rum punch, 34 gallons of wine, 46 gallons of beer, and two gallons of cider for the 391 voters. He won.
6. d. Before an 1845 law was passed, the date of election day varied widely from state to state.
7. d. Julian Bond withdrew because he knew he was too young.
8. a. Ike was not overly fond of his VP.
9. 1. (e) Gerald Ford made this mistake on national television. **2. (d)** Richard Nixon used his children's dog to emotionally defend on TV what opponents termed his political slush fund. **3. (a)** Roosevelt's "hat in the ring" phrase has become standard political phraseology. **4. (c)** Bryan's "cross of gold" speech and his campaigns based on free silver made him famous. **5. (b).**
10. a. Kefauver had inadvertently crossed the state line as he campaigned from small town to small town.
11. b. "Bloviate" is defined as "to orate verbosely and windily." In Ohio, locals used it to mean goofing off.
12. a. Grant was no speaker, but fortunately for him, a president didn't have to be in his day.
13. b. An assassin's bullet, deflected by a metal eyeglass case and a folded speech, lodged in TR's chest. He insisted on making the speech anyway.
14. b. In the pre-TV era, Buchanan's appearance wasn't much of a drawback. It was Grover Cleveland's admission of fathering an illegitimate child that inspired the insulting ditty in (d).

123 QUIZWORD PUZZLE

The answers to the questions are:
Across
1-d, most are white
9-g, Lewis Carroll
10-a, walk in space
11-b, three days and nights
12-h, a pair of aces and a pair of eights
13-n, Australia, Great Britain, Greece, Switzerland
14-f, Australia
15-c, hearts
Down
2-1, zinc
3-o, a rope ladder
4-i, moons of Jupiter
5-e, Rudolph
6-m, an example of a palindrome (a word, phrase, or sentence that reads the same backward and forward)
7-j, mass
8-k, Al Jolson in *The Jazz Singer*

128 WHEN THE BOOMERS WERE BABIES

The cost of each product in 1950 was:
1. RCA Victor TV, Fairfield model, $299.50
2. Vitalis, 25 cents a bottle
3. Pabst Blue Ribbon beer, 20 cents a bottle
4. Westinghouse electric Rancho stove, $159.95
5. Playtex Living Girdle, $3.50 ($3.95 with garters)
6. Cine-Kodak Reliant movie camera, $79
7. 12-inch long-playing record, $4.85
8. Ethyl gasoline, 26 cents a gallon
9. Mercury Sport Sedan, $2,031
10. Maxwell House coffee, 79 cents a pound
11. Stetson "Stetsonian" man's hat, $12.50
12. Gillette Super Speed Razor, with 10-blade dispenser, $1

132 CAN YOU ANSWER THIS?

1. Each of these words has been proposed as a neutered replacement for the phrase "he or she."
2. Put it on—it's a sweater that buttons like a jacket.
3. Beer.
4. A completed jigsaw puzzle.
5. A violin.
6. Nothing. Adult moths don't eat.
7. A man, by about 5 to 1.
8. The price of gold.
9. Monk.
10. It was quite a success—it was Mark Twain's *Tom Sawyer.*
11. "Happy Birthday to You."
12. Politicians.
13. *"Pardonnez-moi, je vais téléphoner à Hitler."*
14. The echo of the blood pulsing in your ear.
15. Exposure to light may spoil wine.
16. Swallow.
17. All the spectators' clothing. (By the way, the loser was put to death.)
18. What was the name of the first Concorde?
19. False. If you guessed correctly, *gesundheit.*
20. She pursued the "oldest profession."

124 TAKE THE DAY OFF

Holiday In, Holiday Out
2. Groundhog Day was brought to the U.S. by the Pennsylvania Germans. They had long believed that the badger was a good prognosticator of the weather, but finding no badgers here, they adopted the groundhog.

A Claus by Any Other Name
1–d; 2–c; 3–g; 4–a; 5–e; 6–b; 7–f

The Great White North
Memorial Day, which was begun in the South during the U.S. Civil War, is not celebrated in Canada.

A Federal Case
The holidays are: New Year's Day, Washington's Birthday (celebrated on a Monday; it's known as Presidents' Day in some parts of the U.S.), Memorial Day (Monday), Independence Day, Labor Day (Monday), Columbus Day (Monday), Veterans Day (Monday), Thanksgiving Day, and Christmas Day.

Greetings!
According to Hallmark Cards, the holidays, in order, are: Christmas, Valentine's Day, Easter, Mother's Day, Father's Day, Thanksgiving, Halloween, St. Patrick's Day, Jewish New Year, and Hanukkah. (Graduation Day is actually in sixth place on Hallmark's list, but is not a holiday.)

Holiday Handles
1. (b) So says Venerable Bede, the 8th-century English historian. (The holiday itself has been celebrated since the second century, however.)
2. (a) **4. (c)** **6. (c)**
3. (b) **5. (c)**

Practice, Practice, Practice
1. (b) The custom of wearing new clothes and parading in them can be traced to the new white robes worn by the recently baptized in the early Church.
2. (c) Bringing a snowdrop (an early-blooming flower) into the house was considered *bad* luck and would prevent an unmarried woman from finding a husband that year.
3. (a) **5. (d)**
4. (c) **6. (b)**

St. Andrew, by the way, is the patron saint of Scotland and Russia.

126 NUMBER, PLEASE!

The key number is 114.
A. 5 − 3 = 2
B. 101 − 40 = 61
C. 0 + 0 = 0
D. 109 − 88 = 21
E. 15 + 15 = 30
F. 10 + 44 = 54
G. 24 ÷ 2 = 12
H. 15 + 3 = 18
I. 8 × 2 = 16
J. 10 + 4 = 14
K. 10 − 9 = 1
L. 10 − 7 = 3
M. 9 × 4 = 36
N. 13 + 13 = 26
O. 4 × 12 = 48
P. 9 × 3 = 27
Q. 78 ÷ 39 = 2
R. 7 + 24 = 31
S. 144 ÷ 3 = 48
T. 96 − 90 = 6
U. 6 × 5 = 30
V. 12 × 3 = 36
W. 36 − 7 = 29
X. 66 ÷ 22 = 3
Y. 10 + 6 = 16

A	B	C	D	E
2	61	0	21	30
F	**G**	**H**	**I**	**J**
54	12	18	16	14
K	**L**	**M**	**N**	**O**
1	3	36	26	48
P	**Q**	**R**	**S**	**T**
27	2	31	48	6
U	**V**	**W**	**X**	**Y**
30	36	29	3	16

127 FAMOUS FOOTSTEPS

The famous parents are:
1. Robert Alda 2. Patty Duke and John Astin 3. Whitney Blake 4. Ed Begley 5. Harry Belafonte 6. John Carradine 7. Johnny Cash 8. Nat "King" Cole 9. Robert Conrad 10. Bing Crosby 11. Janet Leigh and Tony Curtis 12. James Daly 13. Bruce Dern 14. Kirk Douglas 15. Martin Sheen 16. Debbie Reynolds and Eddie Fisher 17. Henry Fonda 18. Joel Grey 19. Mary Martin 20. Alan Hale 21. Jayne Mansfield 22. John Huston 23. Naomi Judd 24. Barbara Hale 25. Arlene Dahl and Fernando Lamas 26. Jack Lemmon 27. Judy Garland 28. Helen Hayes 29. Dean Martin 30. John Mills 31. Judy Garland 32. Michael Redgrave 33. Carl Reiner 34. Ingrid Bergman and Roberto Rossellini 35. Martin Sheen 36. Frank Sinatra 37. Walter Slezak 38. Danny Thomas 39. Raquel Welch 40. Ed Wynn 41. Frank Zappa

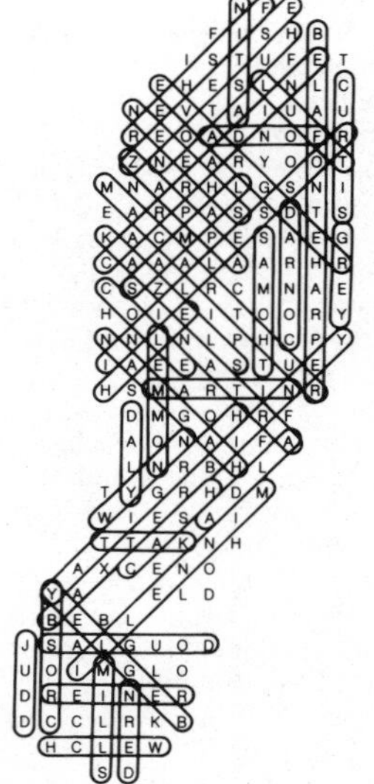

130 THE MELTING POT QUIZ

Howdy, Neighbor! 1-d (Italians, New York City); 2-f (Mexicans, Los Angeles); 3-g (Swedish, Minneapolis); 4-b (Japanese, Honolulu); 5-a (Cubans, Miami); 6-c (Chinese, San Francisco); 7-e (Polish, Chicago)
Fifty Into Three New York, Florida, and California
Foreign Exchange (c) 9 million
Take a Number (b) 270,000. This number, according to the U.S. Department of Immigration and Naturalization Service, actually represents 270,000 household heads, each of whom is also allowed to bring his or her family. The actual number of immigrants is closer to 570,000.
Inside Information Nine; The Bill of Rights; freedom of religion (separation of church and state), freedom of speech, freedom of the press, and the right to petition.
Marquee Benders 1-d (Silverman, Sills); 2-c (Shalhoub, Sharif); 3-a (Andrejewski, Benatar); 4-f (Italiano, Bancroft); 5-g (Konigsberg, Allen); 6-b (Estevez, Sheen); 7-e (Matuschanskayasky, Matthau)
I Just Flew in From... 1-b (Asimov, Russia); 2-a (Borge, Denmark); 3-d (Greco, Italy); 4-e (Houseman, Rumania); 5-h (Humperdinck, India); 6-c (Koppel, England); 7-f (Nichols, Germany); 8-g (Simmons, Israel)
Foreign Flavor 1-c, gnocchi and manicotti (Italian); 2-a, albondigas and tamales (Mexican); 3-b, quenelles and crêpes (French); 4-d, kreplach and blintzes (Jewish); 5-f, won tons and eggrolls (Chinese); 6-e, piroshki and blini (Russian)
Whaddya Say? (c) Spanish; (d) Italian; (e) German; (b) French; (a) Polish; (f) Chinese
O Tannenbaum 1-f (plum pudding, British); 2-d (Christmas trees, German); 3-e (kissing under the mistletoe, Scandinavian); 4-a ("White Christmas" written by Irving Berlin, Jewish); 5-b (poinsettias, Mexican); 6-g (the X in Xmas is from the Greek letter *chi*, used to abbreviate Christ's name); 7-c (Christmas seals, Danish)
Pardon Our French 1. Spanish; 2. Dutch; 3. Yiddish; 4. Italian; 5. German
Good Idea (a) Iroquois
Nation Identification 1. (Kwai Chang) Caine; 2. Gretchen Kraus; 3. Jorge and Yortuk Festrunk; 4. Ricky Ricardo; 5. Arnold (Matsuo Takahashi); 6. Illya Kuryakin; 7. Topo Gigio; 8. Soon-Lee Klinger; 9. The Pigeon Sisters (Gwendolyn and Cecily); 10. Latka Gravas

7

133 ROUND AND ROUND

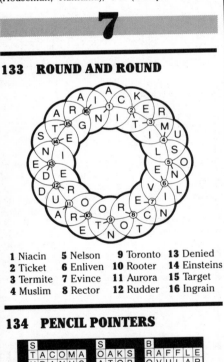

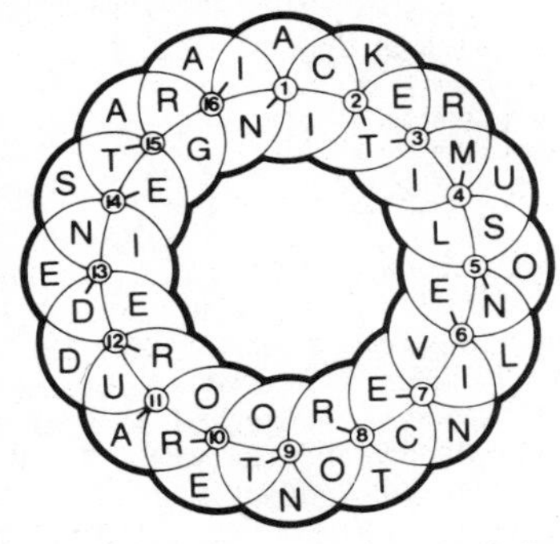

1 Niacin
2 Ticket
3 Termite
4 Muslim
5 Nelson
6 Enliven
7 Evince
8 Rector
9 Toronto
10 Rooter
11 Aurora
12 Rudder
13 Denied
14 Einsteins
15 Target
16 Ingrain

134 PENCIL POINTERS

135 SPELL-WEAVING

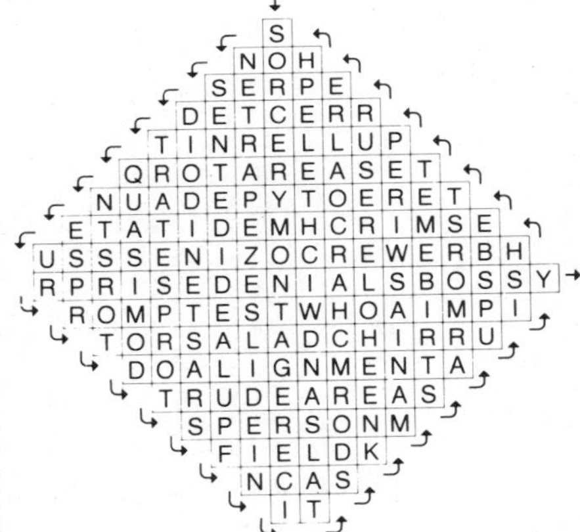

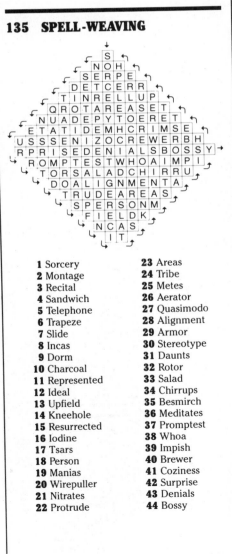

1 Sorcery
2 Montage
3 Recital
4 Sandwich
5 Telephone
6 Trapeze
7 Slide
8 Incas
9 Dorm
10 Charcoal
11 Represented
12 Ideal
13 Upfield
14 Kneehole
15 Resurrected
16 Iodine
17 Tsars
18 Person
19 Manias
20 Wirepuller
21 Nitrates
22 Protrude
23 Areas
24 Tribe
25 Metes
26 Aerator
27 Quasimodo
28 Alignment
29 Armor
30 Stereotype
31 Daunts
32 Rotor
33 Salad
34 Chirrups
35 Besmirch
36 Meditates
37 Promptest
38 Whoa
39 Impish
40 Brewer
41 Coziness
42 Surprise
43 Denials
44 Bossy

136 GOING PLACES

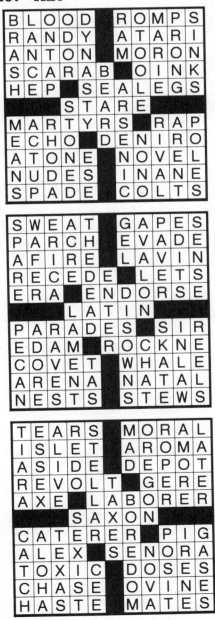

A	U	T	O	M	O	B	I	L	E			T	R	A	I	N
I						I				C	A	R				
R		R	A	C	E	C	A	R				U		U		H
P				A		Y						C	A	N	O	E
L			T	R	I	C	Y	C	L	E		K		I		L
A				R		L								C		I
N				I		E			S	U	B	W	A	Y		C
E		W		A			L		L			H		C		O
	H	A	N	G	G	L	I	D	E	R		E		L		P
		G		E			N		D			E		E		T
S		O					E			C		L				E
T	A	N	K		C	A	R	A	V	A	N					R
E										R		A			C	
A			B			S	C	O	O	T	E	R			O	
M			O				A					K	A	Y	A	K
E			A	U	T	O	B	U	S						C	
R	A	F	T							S	L	E	I	G	H	

137 TRIO

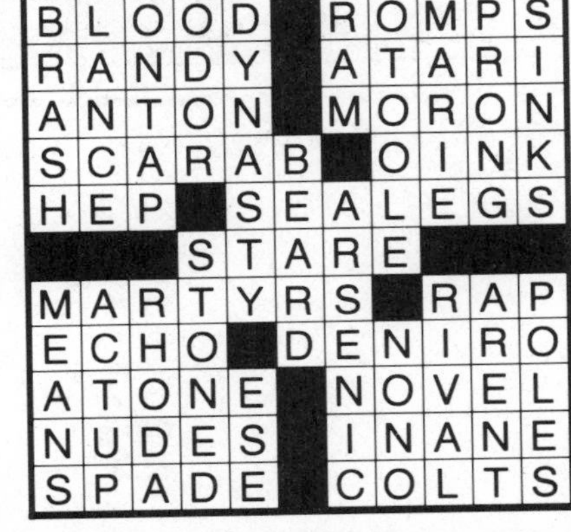

S	W	E	A	T		G	A	P	E	S
P	A	R	C	H		E	V	A	D	E
A	F	I	R	E		L	A	V	I	N
R	E	C	E	D	E		L	E	T	S
E	R	A		E	N	D	O	R	S	E
			L	A	T	I	N			
P	A	R	A	D	E	S		S	I	R
E	D	A	M		R	O	C	K	N	E
C	O	V	E	T		W	H	A	L	E
A	R	E	N	A		N	A	T	A	L
N	E	S	T	S		S	T	E	W	S

T	E	A	R	S		M	O	R	A	L
I	S	L	E	T		A	R	O	M	A
A	S	I	D	E		D	E	P	O	T
R	E	V	O	L	T		G	E	R	E
A	X	E		L	A	B	O	R	E	R
			S	A	X	O	N			
C	A	T	E	R	E	R		P	I	G
A	L	E	X		S	E	N	O	R	A
T	O	X	I	C		D	O	S	E	S
C	H	A	S	E		O	V	I	N	E
H	A	S	T	E		M	A	T	E	S

138 JUMBO CROSSWORD

MALCOLM ATBAT SCREAM
OCEANIA APEACH ALUMNI
STATUTE POLICESTATION
LIP SEWER LEONID LIX
EVER RELIED PRAN GENE
MEDES SYLVESTER VESTS
THAT FEAT MESON
ASPIRE WONTED SPIRALS
WARNERBROTHERS ICECAP
ALOUD OILS LEO RESCUE
RACE CASS SWABBED IRA
DAR CURT RHOMBUS ODER
SMASHED WEARIED EVENS
SHED CRACKED WREN
ROTOR THICKER HEARTHS
ARID HEATHER BARS PEU
BIN PERSEID DAVE CRAB
BEARER TIN TITO COOPT
INTEND ENGLISHCHANNEL
STEPPED SOOTHE ARTERY
EARED UPTO THOR
PENAL FIFTEENTH MODEM
AMAT PAVO DREARY LENA
NED COMERS SPEED TDS
DRILLSERGEANT AMOROUS
AGREES SEAWAY DENTURE
SESAME ERNST SNEERED

140 SQUARE ROUTES

1 Spread
2 Amuses
3 Terrapins
4 Stream
5 Sent
6 Escallop
7 Nation
8 Alarming
9 Glean
10 Early
11 Mash
12 Heart
13 Disperse
14 Pole
15 Sparse
16 Raiment
17 Pickets
18 Rise
19 Taste
20 Night
21 Sidearm
22 Unsoiled
23 Tsar
24 Idler
25 Seeing
26 Esprit
27 Gulp

144 BOOMERANGS

141 WRAPAROUNDS

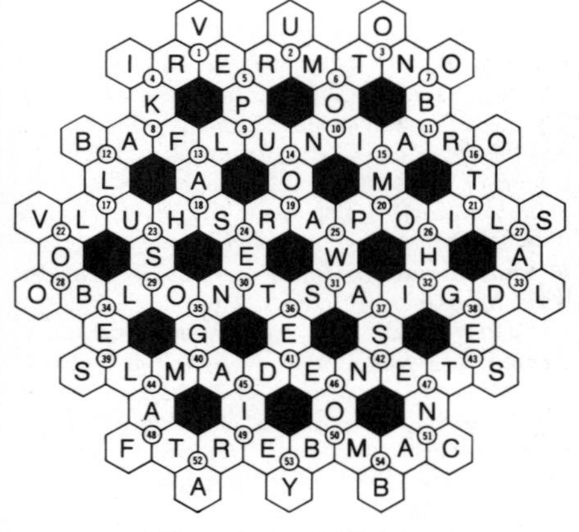

1 Verve
2 Murmur
3 Tonto
4 Kirk
5 Prep
6 Tomtom
7 Bonbon
8 Kafka
9 Pulp
10 Onion
11 Barb
12 Blab
13 Alfalfa
14 Noun
15 Miami
16 Trot
17 Lull
18 Hash
19 Roar
20 Pomp
21 Tilt
22 Volvo
23 Hush
24 Erse
25 Pawpaw
26 Ohio
27 Salsa
28 Boo-boo
29 Oslo
30 Entente
31 Saws
32 High
33 Alda
34 Elbe
35 Gong
36 Tsetse
37 Asia
38 Edged
39 Else
40 Magma
41 Deed
42 Sense
43 Test
44 Alma
45 Aida
46 Neon
47 Tent
48 Taft
49 Erie
50 Bomb
51 Cancan
52 Tartar
53 Bye-bye
54 Bamba

144 CROSS ANAGRAM

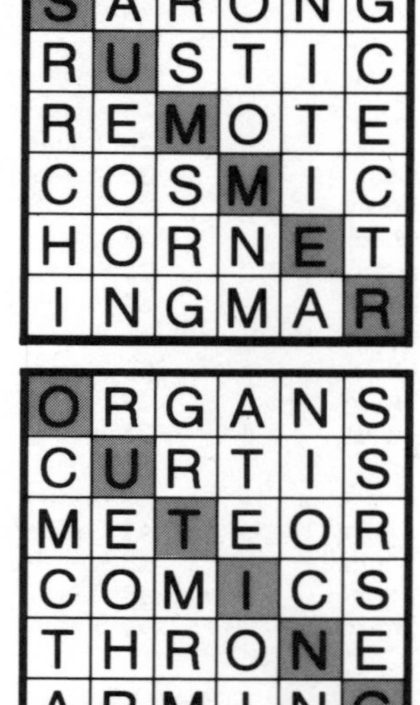

142 WORD GEOMETRY

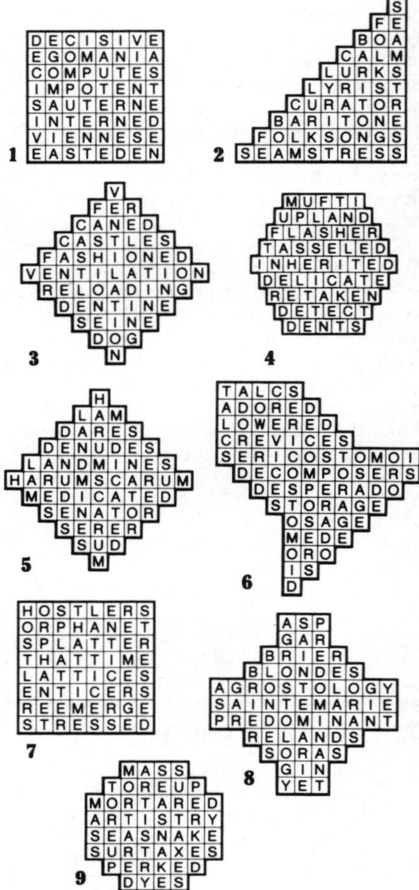

Puzzle Credits: 1. C. B. Stewart, *The Ardmore Puzzler,* July 1, 1902; 2. Scott Marley; 3. E. J. McIlvane, *The Eastern Enigma,* May 1913 (revised); 4. F. P. Morse, *The Ardmore Puzzler,* July 1, 1902 (revised); 5. Leonard Shapiro, *The Enigma,* September 1936 (revised); 6. V. E. Beckley, *The Eastern Enigma,* December 1917; 7. Frank Brandt, *Mystic Tree,* February 1898; 8. C. W. Ferguson, *The Eastern Enigma,* June 1911; 9. Mike Shenk. Many old clues have been changed. Thanks to Murray Pearce for his help with research.

145 MISSING LINKS

145 TO THE NINES

1. Dishwater
2. Bartender
3. Community
4. Vaporizes
5. Turntable
6. Shirttail
7. Phoniness
8. Afterglow

"Seize the day; put no trust in the morrow."
—Horace

146 CROSS COMICS

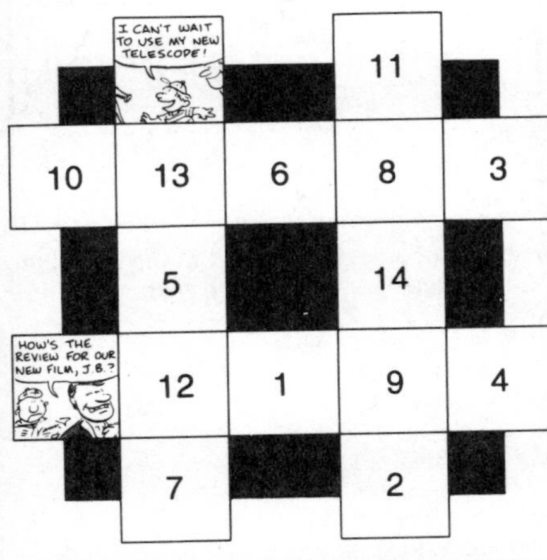

148 LEFT AND RIGHT

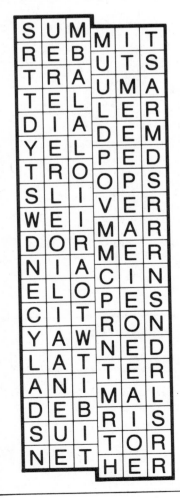

SUM	MIT
REB	UTS
TRA	UMA
TEL	LER
DIA	DEM
YEL	PED
TRO	OPS
SLI	VER
WEI	MAR
DOR	MER
NIA	CIN
ELO	PES
CIT	RON
YAW	NED
LAT	TER
ANI	MAL
DEB	RIS
SUI	TOR
NET	HER

149 SPLIT ENDS

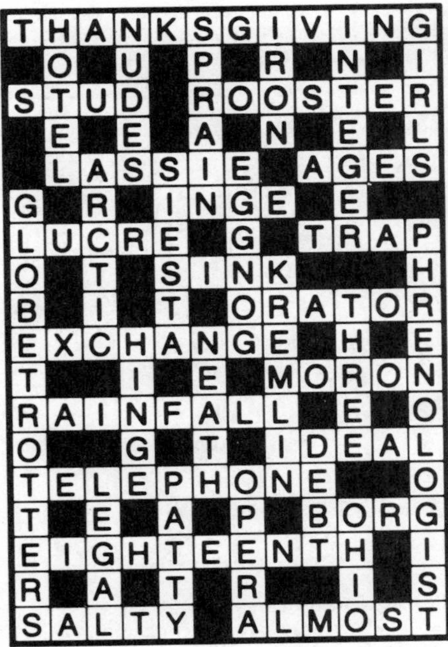

The clue parts for each answer are as follows: 9 = 6 + 3; 15 = 5 + 10; 26 = 14 + 12; 29 = 9 + 20; 32 = 31 + 1; 33 = 7 + 26; 43 = 28 + 15; 44 = 2 + 42; 46 = 16 + 30; 52 = 19 + 33; 58 = 13 + 45; 60 = 39 + 21; 61 = 23 + 38; 65 = 57 + 8; 68 = 36 + 32; 70 = 52 + 18; 71 = 67 + 4; 74 = 25 + 49; 75 = 40 + 35; 79 = 62 + 17; 83 = 56 + 27; 84 = 60 + 24; 85 = 44 + 41; 88 = 77 + 11; 96 = 22 + 74; 98 = 34 + 64; 99 = 70 + 29; 100 = 63 + 37; 102 = 54 + 48; 104 = 46 + 58; 108 = 55 + 53; 109 = 43 + 66; 115 = 65 + 50; 118 = 47 + 71; 120 = 69 + 51; 129 = 68 + 61; 132 = 59 + 73; 148 = 76 + 72; 153 = 78 + 75.

150 MARCHING BANDS

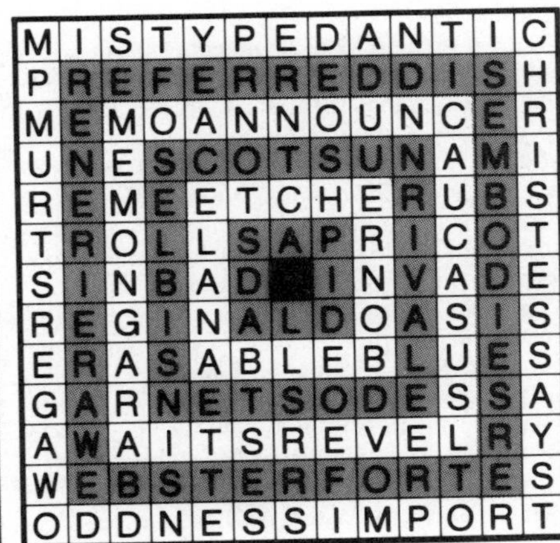

151 PATHFINDER

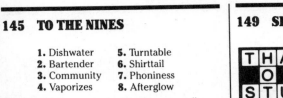

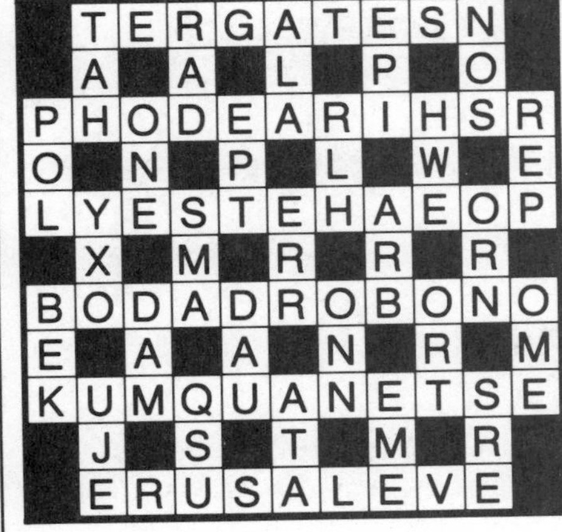

1S Radon
2W Greta
2E Gala
3S Adept
4N Petal
5N Onset
6S Polyester
7N Hate
8W Ship
9N Pearl Harbor
10N Whirl
10S Wear
11W Herr
12N Persons
13N Xylophone
14N Roper
15W Bonnets
16N Adobe
17N Adams
18N Monroe
19E Kumquat
20N Madam
21N Jukebox
21S Jerusalem
22N Squadron
22S Sure
23N Metronome
24S Revel
25E Satan
26E Verse

152 A TO Z

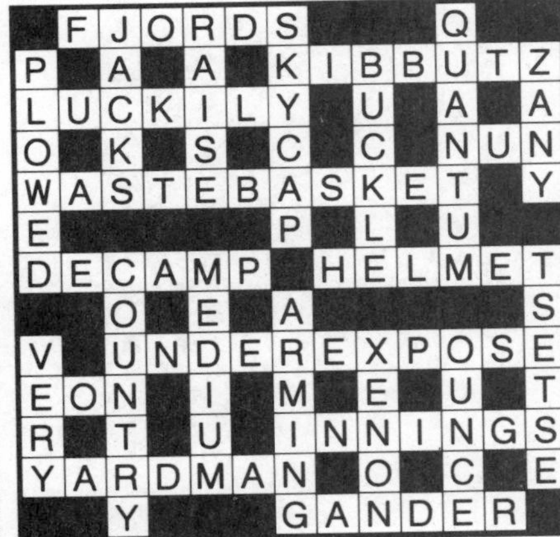

The initial letters and clue answers are as follows:

1 F, plowed
2 J, wastebasket
3 R, yardman
4 S, nun
5 Q, very
6 P, buckle
7 K, quantum
8 B, medium
9 Z, country
10 L, raise
11 N, innings
12 W, luckily
13 D, zany
14 C, helmet
15 M, gander
16 H, xenon
17 T, decamp
18 A, tsetse
19 V, fjords
20 U, ounce
21 X, jacks
22 O, skycap
23 E, arming
24 I, kibbutz
25 Y, eon
26 G, underexpose

8

153 MAGIC RINGS

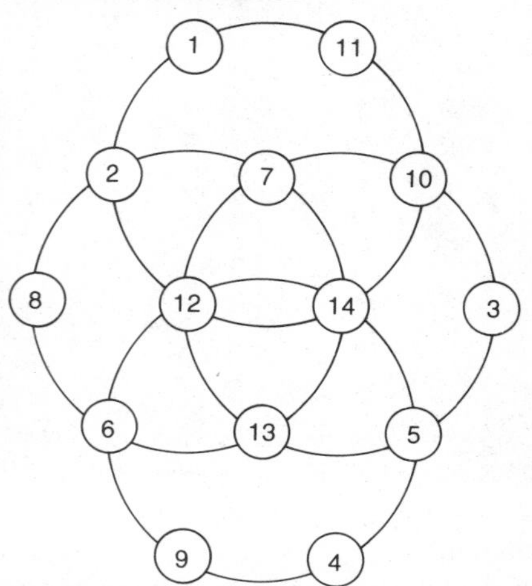

154 CARD ADDITION

There are two fundamentally different possibilities for the card values to make the addition correct:

KQQ = 422	QQK = 334
JKA = 149	JKA = 148
JAA = 199 or	JAA = 188
JKQ = 142	JKQ = 143
AJQ = 912	AJQ = 813

In either case, the leftover card must be a king.

155 FIGURE EIGHTS

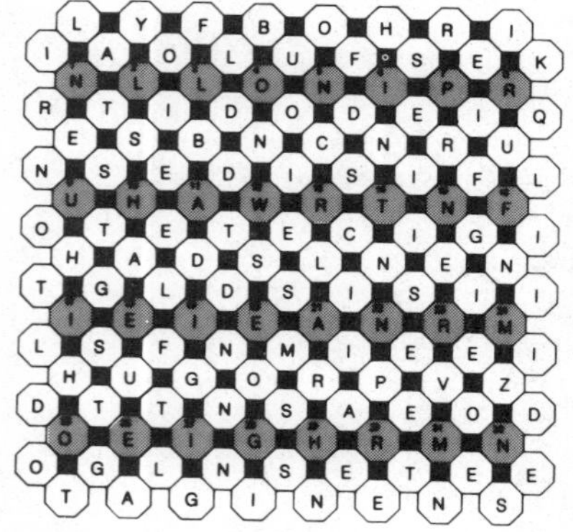

1 Internal
2 Loyalist
3 Billfold
4 Doubloon
5 Confound
6 Fiendish
7 Perspire
8 Quirkier
9 Nuthouse
10 Sheathes
11 Deadbeat
12 West Wind
13 Circlers
14 Instinct
15 Infringe
16 Fluffing
17 Lightish
18 Fuselage
19 Fiddling
20 Demoness
21 Air-mails
22 Ninepins
23 Reveries
24 Minimize
25 Dogtooth
26 Tutelage
27 Tingling
28 Singsong
29 Harshens
30 Repartee
31 Movement
32 End zones

156 BASEBALL LINEUP

1, Schmoe, c; 2, Kent, 2b; 3, Simmons, 3b; 4, Blow, 1b; 5, Schmidt, lf; 6, Kitt, cf; 7, Whitt, rf; 8, Roe, p; 9, Kowalski, ss.

157 MYSTERY THEME

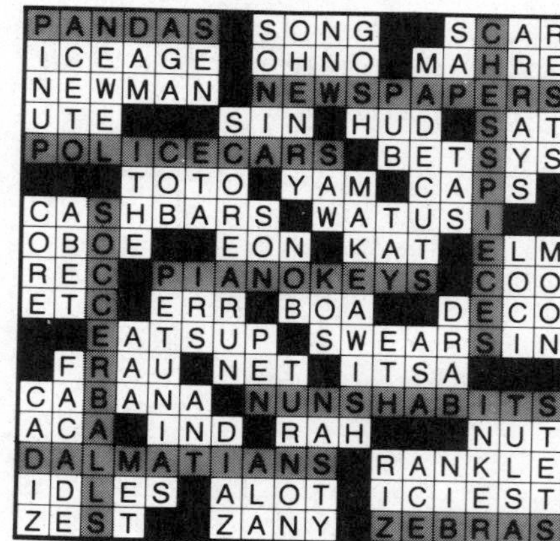

The nine shaded answers are all names of things that are *black and white.* Other black and white items include dominoes, tuxedos, football referee shirts, some televisions, and (of course) crossword puzzles.

158 HOW FAR TO ZEQUOP?

From signs 3 and 4, you know that Wimpster is six miles from two different towns. The only town this can be is F, which is six miles from both town A and town B. Since town F is Wimpster, signs 3 and 4 belong in towns A and B in some order.

If sign 3 went in town A and sign 4 went in town B, then Vogton would be five miles from A (and could only be town C) while Xendic would be three miles from B (and again could only be town C). Since C cannot be both Vogton and Xendic, signs 3 and 4 must belong the other way, with sign 3 in town B and sign 4 in town A.

Xendic is three miles from sign 4 (in town A) and can only be town D. Vogton is five miles from sign 3 (in town B) and can only be town G.

Sign 5 is six miles from Vogton (town G) and must be in town C. Yunjar is three miles from sign 5 (in town C) and must be town B.

Sign 6 is four miles from Yunjar (town B) and must be in town E. Zequop is four miles from sign 6 (in town E) and must be town A.

Sign 2 is three miles from Vogton (town G) and must be in town F. Ubania is seven miles from sign 2 (in town F) and must be town C. The remaining town, Tidville, must be E.

Sign 7 is one mile from Tidville and must be in town D. The remaining sign, sign 1, must be in town G.

Thus, the towns, matched with their locations and signs, are:

- Tidville, town E, sign 6
- Ubania, town C, sign 5
- Vogton, town G, sign 1
- Wimpster, town F, sign 2
- Xendic, town D, sign 7
- Yunjar, town B, sign 3
- Zequop, town A, sign 4

The missing distance to Zequop on sign 7 is 3 miles.

159 SPOONERISMS

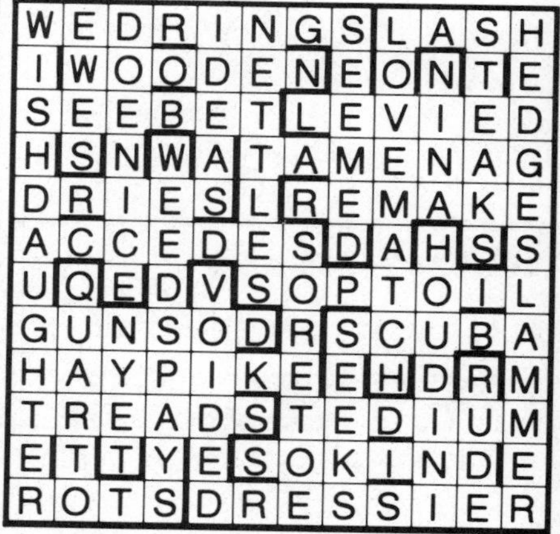

Where a spoonerism occurred in the definition, the unspoonerized phrase is given in italics.

ACROSS
1 Redwings (grid's new)
7 Lash (Hal's; *bind with cords*)
10 Wooden (woo + den; *built of teak*)
12 Beset (best + E)
13 Levied (led + I've)
15 Nametag (gateman)
16 Dries (rides; *gets sere*)
17 Remake (rake + me)
18 Accedes (axe seeds)
23 Topsoil (spot + oil)
24 Sun god (sung + do)
26 Scuba (S + Cuba)
27 Pay hike (key a hip)
29 Treads (t + reads; *patterns on a sole*)
30 Tedium (tide + um; *boring state*)
31 Co-signed (C + dingoes)
32 Rots (Roots – o; *turns bad*)
33 Dresser (Dreiser's)

DOWN
1 Dishwater (herds wait)
2 Ewes (yew's; *lady sheep*)
3 No dice (nod + ice)
4 Ideas (Ides + a)
5 Nettles (Lee's TNT)
6 Seemed (see + Dem.)
7 Love match (two meanings)
8 Steaks (s + Kate's; *T-bones*)
9 Sledgehammer (Merl's game he'd)
11 Nina (Ni + Na)
14 Speedways (say spewed)
19 Torso (toro + s)
20 Houdini (I hound + I; *magic tricks*)
21 Quarto (Q + at our; *page size*)
22 Voided (dove I'd)
25 Nyet (NYmphET)
26 Seeks (S's + eek!; *tries to gain*)
28 Rude (rue + D; *bad manners*)

163 PENTATHLON

Finishers are listed from first to last for each event and for total pentathlon points:
High Jump—Ken, Nick, Lee, Mike, Jay
Shot Put—Ken, Nick, Lee, Jay, Mike
Mile—Jay, Lee, Ken, Nick, Mike
Hurdles—Mike, Jay, Lee, Ken, Nick
Dash—Mike, Lee, Jay, Nick, Ken

Pentathlon—Lee (13), Ken (14), Jay (15), Mike (16), Nick (17)

160 WORD QUEST

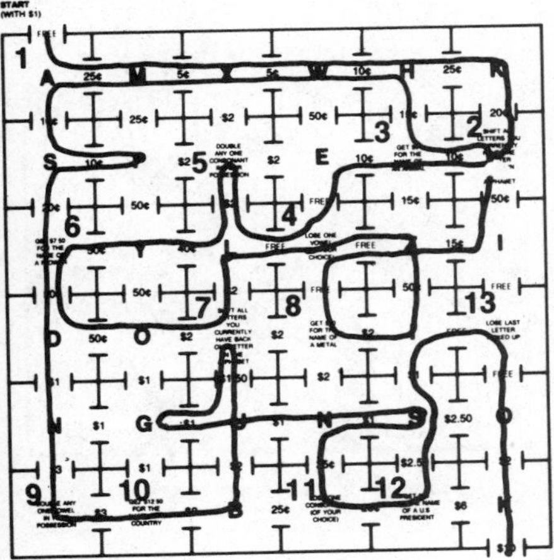

The correct route is shown above. Except in the first room, take all letters as soon as you find them.

The following actions are done in the numbered rooms (listed in the order they occur). The amount of money and any letters you have at each point are given in parentheses.

1. Don't take the A. ($1.00)
2. M-X-W-H-K becomes N-Y-X-I-L. (10¢; N-Y-X-I-L)
3. Get $5.00 for LYNX. ($5.00; I)
4. Lose the E. ($4.90; I)
5. Double the L. ($2.90; L-L-I)
6. Get $7.50 for LILY. ($7.50)
7. D-O becomes C-N. ($4.50; C-N)
4. No vowel to lose. ($2.50; C-N)
8. Get $10.00 for ZINC. ($10.00)
4. No vowel to lose. ($10.00)
2. I becomes J. ($9.35; J)
3. No action. ($9.25; J)
1. Take the A. ($8.65; J-A)
6. No action. ($8.15; J-A-S-P)
9. Double the A. ($3.65; J-A-A-S-P-N)
10. Get $12.50 for JAPAN. ($13.15; S)
7. S-B-U becomes R-A-T. ($7.65; R-A-T)
11. Lose the S. (90¢; R-A-T-G-N)
12. Get $15.00 for GRANT. ($15.65)
13. No letter to lose. ($12.15)
14. Escape with 15¢ and letters O-K left.

162 LOCKER ROOM MYSTERY

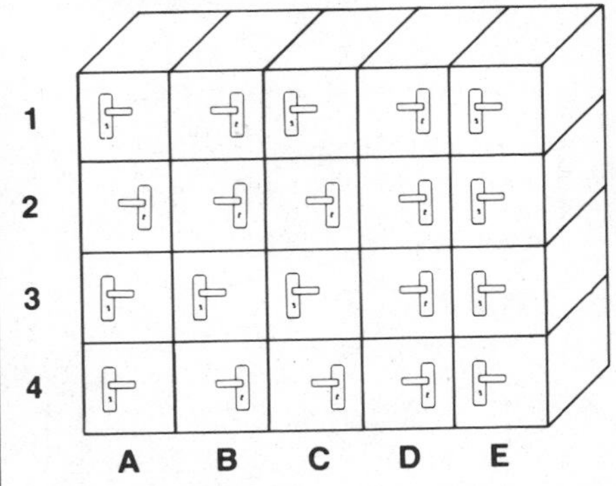

Each of the five columns has a different number of left-handed lockers, so every possible number from zero to four must be represented. Therefore, there are 10 (= 0 + 1 + 2 + 3 + 4) left-handed lockers, and the other 10 lockers must be right-handed.

One column, then, contains no left-handed lockers, while another contains *all* left-handed lockers. So each row contains at least one left-handed and one right-handed locker. Each of the four rows has a different number of right-handed lockers, so every possible number from one to four must be represented.

From the overhead view, columns A, B, C, and E each have at least one left-handed locker, so D must be the column with four right-handed lockers. Columns A, C, and E each have at least two left-handed lockers, so B is the column with just one. That one is B3, so B1, B2, and B4 are right-handed.

We know of two right-handed lockers in rows 1, 2, and 4, so row 3 must be the row with only one right-handed locker. A3, C3, and E3 must be left-handed.

From the overhead view of column C, C4 must be right-handed. Rows 2 and 4 now have at least three right-handed lockers, so row 1 must be the row with only two. A1, C1, and E1 must be left-handed.

From the overhead view of column A, A4 must be left-handed. Column A has three left-handed lockers, so column C cannot also have three. C2 must be right-handed.

Finally, column E must be the column of all left-handed lockers.

161 FULL HOUSE

165 CRYTPIC CROSSWODR

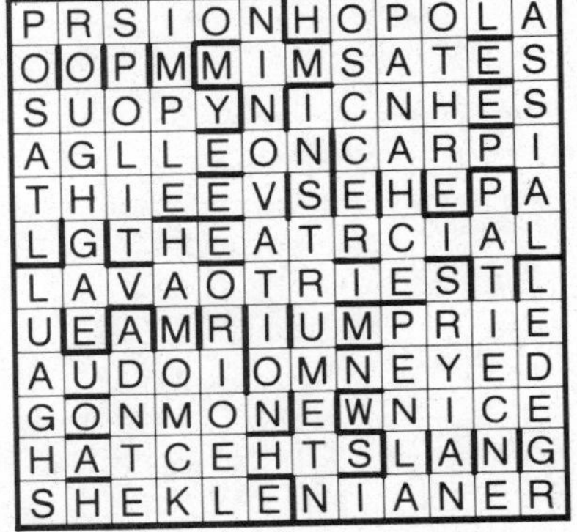

ACROSS
1 Prison (pr. + is + on)
6 Hoopla (Al + Pooh)
11 Mismates (M + Matisse)
12 Soupy (soy + up)
13 Inches (in + chess – s)
14 Galleon (gone + all)
15 Capri (c + Apr. 1)
16 Thieve (wealTH I EVEntually)
18 Theatrical (hit Lear act)
20 Lavatories (Ava loiters)
25 Umpire (um + p + ire)
27 Audio (Audi + O)
28 Moneyed (Mon + eyed)
29 Gnomon (acceptinG NO MONey)
30 Wince (c + wine)
31 Hatchets (t + hatches)
32 Shekel (she + K + el)
33 Inaner (in + an + ER)

DOWN
1 Postal (to pals)
2 Roughage (hag + rouge)
3 Spoilt (PO + silt)
4 Impel (IIMP ELbows)
5 Innovation (inn + ovation)
7 Soccer (socker)
8 Panache (pan + ache)
9 Other (the + or)
10 Assail (ass + ail)
13 Instrument (trust in men)
17 Patience (nice paté)
19 Hammock (ham + mock)
20 Laughs (lug has)
21 Oriole (or + I + olé)
22 Syrian (yarn is)
23 Ledger (led + Ger)
24 Dante (date + n)
26 Penal (pen + Al)

164 WORD GAMES

Missing Links
1. half
2. worldly
3. gang
4. tender
5. junk
6. bottom

Opposites
1. ablaze
2. feature
3. goodbyes
4. reward
5. fairway
6. rhymed

Ratios
1. quarter (two bits = 25¢)
2. weight (homophones of synonyms)
3. fine arts (GA in ED; FI near TS)
4. East Berlin (anagrams)
5. emphasized (synonyms of reversed words)
6. Hiawatha : Minnehaha

Common Factors
1. feet
2. jam
3. hook
4. doubles
5. foam
6. checkers

Lists
1. noon
2. love (tennis scores)
3. Austin (state capitals alphabetically)
4. glue (colors of spectrum with first letters changed)
5. quicksilver (synonyms of Mars, Earth, Venus, Mercury)
6. pluribus unum (A cappella, B movie, C-note, D-day)

The Verse
A slave of Queen Cleo named Mark
Found galley life lonesome and stark.
He jumped in the bay
But he froze right away
For her bight was much worse than her barque.

166 PUZZLE DECATHLON

The ten events may have seemed just as grueling as their Olympic counterparts. They *are* devilish—including a few diabolical traps set to catch all but the most careful solvers.

1. TEN TAKEAWAY

Only 5 is a winning choice. For example, if instead you choose 1 or 6, your opponent can choose 6 or 1, respectively, leaving two equal stacks (each containing three blocks). After that, your opponent can win by imitating you: However many blocks you take from one stack, your opponent will take the same number from the other stack.

If you choose 2 or 8 initially, your opponent wins by taking 8 or 2. A choice of 3 or 7 loses to 7 or 3 (since if you then take 6 or 8, your opponent can safely play 8 or 6). And, of course, 4 and 9 lose to 9 and 4.

After you choose 5, you'll win if you follow the same strategies outlined above. If your opponent responds 1, you choose 6, and vice versa; etc.

2. CRISSCROSS

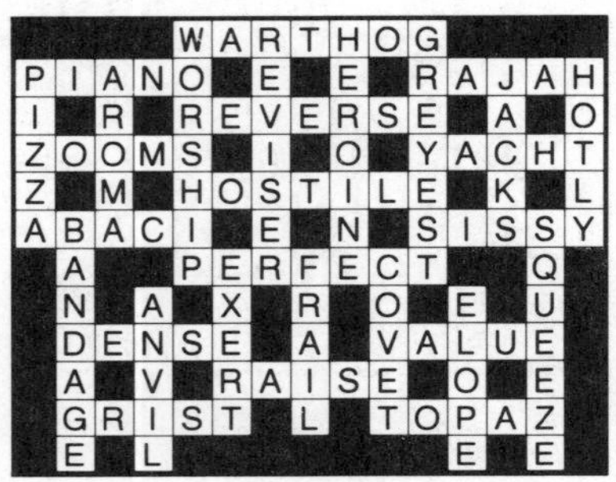

3. DOUBLE-CROSTIC

A. CRETANS
B. OFF THE CUFF
C. NEWSWEEK
D. THESE
E. EVALUATE
F. SPRIT
G. TROLL
H. WE RISE
I. IRONED
J. NODDY
K. NIGHT OWL
L. ECONOMIST
M. RIYADH

"To find the answer you seek, write consecutively and respace the following entries from the word list: D, A, H, F."

Following these instructions yielded the message THESE-CRETANS-WERISE-SPRIT, or THE SECRET ANSWER IS ESPRIT. (The acrostic—CONTEST WINNER—was extraneous.)

4. COMPLETE THIS SEQUENCE

The first syllables of the pictured words were homophones of consecutive letters of the alphabet: O (oboe), P (peanuts), Q (cucumbers), R (armadillo). The sequence was continued: S (eskimo), T (teapot), U (unicycle), and V (Vietnam).

5. COUNT THE TRIANGLES

The 82 triangles are of the following types:
24 upward-pointing, one unit wide
22 downward-pointing, one unit wide
13 upward-pointing, two units wide
9 downward-pointing, two units wide
6 upward-pointing, three units wide
6 downward-pointing, three units wide
1 downward-pointing, four units wide
1 upward-pointing, five units wide

6. WORD SEARCH

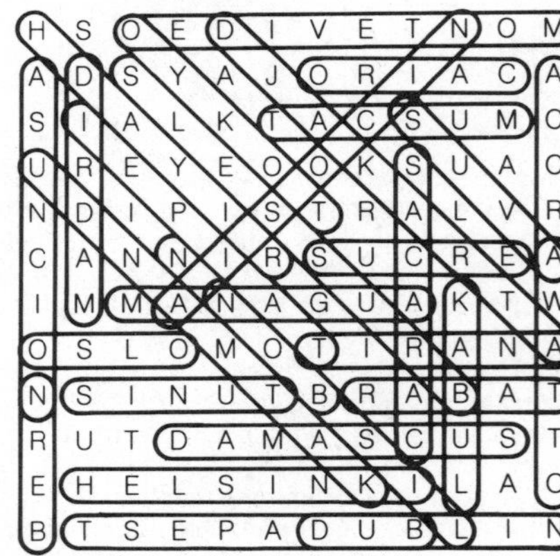

The 30 capitals in the grid are:

Accra	Dublin	Oslo
Asuncion	Helsinki	Ottawa
Bern	Kabul	Rabat
Bonn	Katmandu	Riyadh
Brussels	Lisbon	Sucre
Budapest	Madrid	Suva
Cairo	Managua	Taipei
Caracas	Montevideo	Tirana
Damascus	Muscat	Tokyo
Djakarta	Nicosia	Tunis

7. DIGITITIS

```
        43917
   23)1010101
       92
        90
        69
        211
        207
          40
          23
          171
          161
           10
```

8. CRYPTOGRAM

The cryptogram, when decoded, reads: What word meaning "beach" consists of a synonym for "broadcast" around "certain hairstyle"? This leads to the answer SEAFRONT (SENT around AFRO).

9. CROSSWORD

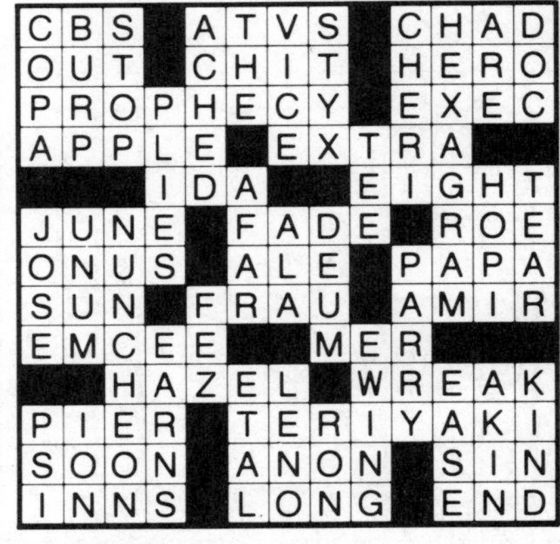

10. PINBALL MAZE

The best arrangement of the arithmetic signs, and the highest-scoring route, is shown here:

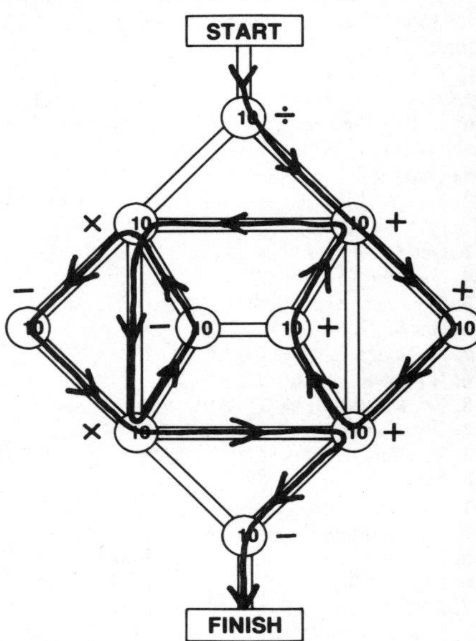

170 THE LAST ROUNDUP

The pieces are from the following games:
1. Inferior Decorator
2. Twisted Television
3. Sketchwords
4. Baseball Lineup
5. Egyptograms
6. Radio Activity
7. Out of This World
8. Knight Moves
9. Nine Psychic Guesses
10. When the Boomers Were Babies
11. Match Play
12. Family Pictures
13. How Far to Zequop?
14. Quote Boxes
15. Untrue Confessions
16. Alphabet Soup
17. Left and Right

Filling the blanks with the first letters of the games' titles gives this quote: "It's better to know some of the questions than all of the answers."

Acknowledgments

WORKMAN PUBLISHING

Publisher Peter Workman
Editors Suzanne Rafer, Carol McKeown
Assistant Editor Shannon Ryan
Production Wayne Kirn, Jacques Williams
Book Design Mark Freiman
Cover Design Charles Kreloff

GAMES MAGAZINE

Editor R. Wayne Schmittberger; *Senior Editor* Will Shortz; *Articles Editor* Curtis Slepian; *Associate Editor* Mike Shenk; *Games & Books Editor* Scott Marley; *Copy Editor* Karen Anderson; *Rights & Permissions Administrator* Peter Gordon; *Editorial Assistant* Caroline Surin; *Art Director* Barry Simon; *Assistant Art Director* Todd Betterley; *Designers* Peter Fahrni, Patti Nemoto; *Production Director* Barbara Smith Stark; *Advertising Production Manager* Elaine M. Callender; *Editorial Production Manager* Melanie Shandroff; *Promotion Production Manager* Robert Jimenez; *Typesetter* Marcie Bush Herkner, Dylan Kreuzer; *Contributing Editors* Matthew J. Costello, Emily Cox, Martin Gardner, Burt Hochberg, Henry Hook, Robert Leighton, Andy Meisler, Andrea Messina, Marvin Miller, Stanley Newman, Trip Payne, Henry Rathvon, Merl Reagle, Gloria Rosenthal, Sid Sackson, Ronnie Shushan, Mary Ellen Slate, Stephanie A. Spadaccini; *Contributing Artists and Photographers* Keith Bendis, Stan Fellerman, Keith Glasgow, R.J. Kaufman, Nick Koudis, Mark Mazut, Walter Wick, Don Wright

President and Publisher Jerry Calabrese; *Chief Financial Officer* Sam Ananian; *Associate Publisher/Group Marketing Director* Richard M. Fontana, Jr.; *Business Manager* Ben Wolman; *Marketing Director* Will Marks; *Controller* Marjorie S. Kottler; *Assistant to the Publisher* Linda Verdun; *Operations Coordinator* Victor Calabrese; *Accounting Coordinator* Linda Chapman; *Receptionists* Barbara Anderson, Tanya White; *Group Circulation Director* Trish Edelmann; *Circulation Director* Cathy Woll; *Promotion Manager* Bill Richards; *Circulation Managers* Diane Bigotte, Paula de Brito, Holly Penning; *Advertising Director* Paul J. Roberts; *Senior Sales Representatives* Renee Krumper, Deborah Mignucci; *Director, Direct Response Advertising* Joe Failla; *Gallery Sales Manager* Dirk Johnson; *Advertising Assistants* Yadira Feliciano, Greicy Montano; *Direct Response Sales* Elaine Sharpe

—October 1988

ART CREDITS

Page

3 *Introduction* Illustration by R. J. Kaufman.
15 *Family Pictures* Illustrations by Claudia Karabaic Sargent.
28 *The Beadless Abacus* Illustration by Jon Valk.
29 *Terror Incognitus* Illustration by Patricia Wynne.
37 *A Switch In Time* Illustration by Peter Fasolino.
41 *Signs of Life* Illustrations by Michael Witte.
51 *Stories from the Safari* Illustrations by Phil Scheuer.
54 *Untrue Confessions* Illustrations by Phil Scheuer.
65 *Riddle Maze* Art by Anna V. Walker. Photograph by Dean Powell.
70 *The Egg Hunt* Photograph by Allan Lieberman.
72 *Murder for Breakfast* Photography by Dan Nelken.
76 *Scenic Route* Illustrations by Sandra Forrest.
85 *Rebusiness* Illustrations by Plato Taleporos.
90 *Evolution* Illustration by Phil Scheuer.
92 *Limbericks* Illustrations by Rick Tulka.
95 *Alphabet Soup* Illustration by Greg Scott
98 *Word Golf* Illustration by Mary Beth Farrell.
101 *Dszqtionary* Illustrations by R. J. Kaufman.
102 *Added Attractions* Illustration by Monica Incisa.
110 *Twisted Television* Illustrations by R. J. Kaufman.
114 *Second Guessing* Illustration by Michael Witte.
116 *A Herculean Atlas Quiz* Illustration by Peter Eiwell.
130 *The Melting Pot Quiz* Illustration by Stephen Sweeny.
167 *Puzzle Decathlon: Complete This Sequence* Illustration by Claudia Karabaic Sargent.
191 *Acknowledgments* Illustration by R. J. Kaufman.